The Dressing Room

The Dressing Room

Backstage Lives and American Film

DESIRÉE J. GARCIA

Rutgers University Press
New Brunswick, Camden, and Newark, New Jersey
London and Oxford

Rutgers University Press is a department of Rutgers, The State University of New Jersey, one of the leading public research universities in the nation. By publishing worldwide, it furthers the University's mission of dedication to excellence in teaching, scholarship, research, and clinical care.

Library of Congress Cataloging-in-Publication Data

Names: Garcia, Desirée J., 1977– author.
Title: The dressing room : backstage lives and American film / Desirée J. Garcia.
Description: New Brunswick : Rutgers University Press, 2025. | Includes bibliographical references and index.
Identifiers: LCCN 2024016267 | ISBN 9781978819245 (paperback) | ISBN 9781978819252 (cloth) | ISBN 9781978819269 (epub) | ISBN 9781978819283 (pdf)
Subjects: LCSH: Dressing rooms (Performing arts) in motion pictures. | Motion pictures—United States—History. | LCGFT: Film criticism.
Classification: LCC PN1995.9.D676 G37 2025 | DDC 791.43/62579—dc23/eng/20240828
LC record available at https://lccn.loc.gov/2024016267

A British Cataloging-in-Publication record for this book is available from the British Library.

Copyright © 2025 by Desirée J. Garcia
All rights reserved

No part of this book may be reproduced or utilized in any form or by any means, electronic or mechanical, or by any information storage and retrieval system, without written permission from the publisher. Please contact Rutgers University Press, 106 Somerset Street, New Brunswick, NJ 08901. The only exception to this prohibition is "fair use" as defined by U.S. copyright law.

References to internet websites (URLs) were accurate at the time of writing. Neither the author nor Rutgers University Press is responsible for URLs that may have expired or changed since the manuscript was prepared.

∞ The paper used in this publication meets the requirements of the American National Standard for Information Sciences—Permanence of Paper for Printed Library Materials, ANSI Z39.48-1992.

rutgersuniversitypress.org

For Edith Aliza, my backstage baby

Contents

	Introduction: Show People	1
1	Maids	17
2	Sisters	42
3	Wives and Mothers	68
4	Leading Men	93
5	Masqueraders	120
	Epilogue: The Drama Is Real	146
	Acknowledgments	151
	Notes	153
	Bibliography	169
	Index	177

The Dressing Room

Introduction

●●●●●●●●●●●●●●●●●●●●

Show People

> There is magic in the theater, but it's not in the dressing room.
> —Harvey Fierstein, 2008

In his backstage dressing room, a broken-down, bloated Jake LaMotta (Robert De Niro) tells his reflection that he "could have been a contender." This final moment in Martin Scorsese's *Raging Bull* (1980) endures as one of the most memorable dressing room scenes in American cinema. The film charts the rise and fall of LaMotta in and out of the boxing ring, showing the deterioration of his career and personal relationships. For Scorsese, the dressing room scene provides a reckoning of sorts, a chance to access the boxer's innermost thoughts and to witness a rare moment of self-awareness before he performs his one-man show. LaMotta prepares backstage by delivering Terry Malloy's monologue from *On the Waterfront* (1954), a speech about missed opportunity and failure. He recites the words in front of the mirror, "Remember that night at the Garden, you came down to my dressing room and said, 'kid, this ain't your night.'" The squalid surroundings, which Scorsese reveals with close-ups of an exposed lightbulb, wire hangers, and dirty paint on the walls, visually convey how Malloy's words have personal relevance for the boxer; like Malloy, LaMotta was "an up and comer who is now a down and outer."

Many other directors have exploited the cinematic potential of the dressing room. Among the more well-known examples are Joseph L. Mankiewicz's staging of the first encounter between Eve and Margo in *All about Eve* (1950), Mervyn LeRoy's presentation of strippers singing "Ya Gotta Have a Gimmick" in *Gypsy*

Jake LaMotta quotes, "You could have been a contender." *Raging Bull*, copyright 1980 by United Artists.

(1962), and Spike Lee's framing of Blackface minstrels in *Bamboozled* (2000). Some dressing room scenes, such as the confrontation between Sarah Jane and her mother, Annie, in Douglas Sirk's *Imitation of Life* (1959), exist only in our imagination—a function of that film's strategic denial of the dressing room space to an interracial woman.

With this book, I set out to understand why dressing rooms have been such a long-standing and popular space for filmmakers to explore. Sometimes the space appears in films unexpectedly, such as in *Raging Bull*, a boxing film framed by dressing room scenes at the beginning and the end. In this instance, Scorsese draws on their rich representational qualities to prompt ruminations on the spectacle of one man's failed potential. But *Raging Bull* also demonstrates how the dressing room is a pliant space that easily moves across genres. As Scorsese depicts it, the dressing room belongs to both the boxing arena and the nightclub; it emphasizes the spectacular nature of fighting in an arena, and it frames LaMotta's one-man show as another battle he must win. The dressing room bridges the spaces of ring and stage, suggesting that LaMotta's survival hinges on a good performance in both. As the real LaMotta told a reporter in 1983, "All my life all I knew was how to hurt people to entertain 'em. . . . Now, instead of throwing punches, I'm throwing lines."[1] It is the performance of identity that dressing rooms foreground in literal and metaphorical ways.

The project of the dressing room is to construct the self, to imagine and realize the role to be played. This process plays out in dozens of backstage films from the beginnings of cinema to the present day. To understand why American film keeps returning us to the dressing room necessitates grappling with how identity is essential to American success, a cultural preoccupation that dates back to the rags-to-riches literature of the early nineteenth century. The McGuffey children's readers advocated the notion of self-help in which hard work results in upward mobility. And Horatio Alger, whose stories about Ragged Dick stirred the imaginations of young Americans in the 1860s, introduced the element of luck to tales about American opportunity.[2] The Warner Bros. musicals of the 1930s engaged these historical narratives by delivering the industrious but unknown chorus girl to stardom at film's end.[3] But backstage film extends well beyond the codes and conventions of the musical and has rehearsed the myth of American success in genres ranging from melodramas to mysteries, from stories about ballerinas to superheroes. Widening our lens to encompass the entirety of backstage film production exposes how the genre has been a primary vehicle with which Americans have sustained a belief in, and envisioned access to, the myth of social opportunity.

An analysis of the genre also exposes the falsity of the myth, especially regarding the proximity of people of color to this dominant cultural script. Writing about the enduring appeal of *Sparkle* (1976), critic Armond White observed in 1984 how the film's setting in the world of entertainment is a metaphor for Black experience.[4] A film about three Black sisters who try to make it as a singing group, *Sparkle* features multiple entertaining moments when the women perform onstage. But it is their backstage struggle that makes explicit the impact of race, class, and gender on their lives. In the dressing room, the sisters transform themselves into the types of women who will be successful. The adoption, as White points out, of certain socially sanctioned looks, behaviors, and ways of speech, and the jettisoning of others, is necessary for the Black performer. In this way, the dressing room is a cinematic space laden with meaning and consequence. The stakes are high in dressing room scenes because they rehearse larger questions about identity and its performance, negotiating who can succeed in this society and who cannot, and on what terms.

Some films have made the connection between dressing rooms and performance plain, such as when the white star and her Black maid stage a dressing room number at the Ziegfeld Follies in *Somebody Loves Me* (1952). In others, the performance is more figurative. *Applause* (1929) uses the dressing room couch as an expectant mother's "stage." And *All about Eve* (1950) divides the dressing room into stage and audience space as a duplicitous fan tells lies about her past. But ultimately, all dressing rooms have spectacular qualities, with their split and reflected sightlines of characters looking at themselves and one another, with their tools of transformation, and with the sense that time is fleeting; they draw us in with the promise that there is something important to see there.

Unlike other backstage realms, like the stage door or the wings, dressing rooms take on the character of their inhabitants. Because they spend so much time in the space, performers make the dressing room their own; it becomes an extension of their private and public selves. With a visual iconography that includes family photographs, congratulatory telegrams, trunks, and costumes, filmmakers have exploited the dressing room to convey an understanding about the occupant inside. The enclosed, quasi-private construction of the space allows for a dynamic interaction between performer and material location, where mirrors become an extension of the self and physical thresholds like doors, windows, and screens demarcate the difference between self and other. Time spent in the dressing room reveals how performers produce the space as an act of habitation, but also how the space produces performers.[5]

Cinematic dressing rooms offer moments of pause and consequence for their inhabitants, presenting opportunities for contemplation and reckoning, introspection and regret. Because of the unfettered contact they offer us, we are allowed an intimacy with their inhabitants, serving as witness to the self-reflections that happen inside. Our access to this otherwise hidden space satisfies our curiosity about who resides within. But unlike other commonplaces such as small towns, train stations, hotels, or apartments that recur in film because of their familiarity to audiences in real life, dressing rooms are exclusive spaces accessed only by a few.[6] The backstage realm is "practitioner space," as Gale McAuley has argued, and the dressing room is distinguished by being removed from sight.[7] Cinematic representations of the space satisfy our desire to see what is hidden from us in everyday life. American film has lifted the curtain on the dressing room dozens of times for audiences, thereby making familiar that which is strange.

But is it just the promise of seeing something hidden that drives our fascination? Writing about the musical specifically, a genre in which dressing rooms are common, Rick Altman suggests that "by pulling aside the backdrop or peeking into the wings we are able to satisfy our natural desire to look beyond, behind, and beneath."[8] This "natural desire" is a function of what Richard Dyer calls the "star phenomenon," which encourages this kind of prying behind the scenes, prompting us to question what a star is "really" like. As Dyer argues, "It is the insistent question of 'really' that draws us in."[9]

While our society's obsession with stars certainly drives the popularity of films in which the lives of celebrities are given fictional or documentary "behind the scenes" treatment, this explanation does not account for the persistent creation of dozens of films in which backstage access is a major structural and thematic feature. The "backstudio film" and the "stardom film" are enduring genres for examining the function and meaning of Hollywood stars and star-making, but there are numerous other films set in different performance contexts (theater, television, the musical stage) that do not necessarily take stardom as their central concern.[10] *All about Eve*, for example, is less about Margo's stardom and Eve's desire for it than the nature of female desire and competition. *Gypsy* shows the rise of burlesque artist Gypsy Rose Lee to stardom, but the dramatic conflict of the film stems from the relationship between a mother and her daughter. And while *Bamboozled* makes celebrities out of its Blackface minstrels, the film is more concerned with the destructive, lasting effects of an entertainment tradition born of American racism.

This is to say that while stars are certainly enticing, they are not the primary reason we insist on going backstage. Rather, what draws us in is our desire to know the people we find there and to understand how they are relevant to our lives. Show people, as dressing rooms reveal, both resemble and are different from ordinary folks. Itinerant troupers who constantly moved from one town to the next, without roots in family or place, show people (long used as a derogatory term) were considered untrustworthy for their questionable morality and ability to deceive. This distrust emerged in the nineteenth century, when changes in modern life produced geographical and social mobility like never before. Archetypes of this modern world, as Karen Halttunen has shown, were the "confidence man" and the "painted woman," men and women who used the confusion of identity to manipulate and advance their own social position.[11] Theater troupers were an extreme version of these archetypes, painting their faces and assuming different personas as they moved from place to place. Remnants of this prejudice appear in twentieth-century films about backstage life, especially in the 1930s when the Hollywood musical strove to satisfy our curiosity about performers and simultaneously vindicate them as good, upstanding Americans (see *Gold Diggers of 1933*, 1933, and *Babes in Arms*, 1939). The adage "born in a trunk" stems from the idea that show people are simultaneously fascinating and potentially frightening; they are associated with an object intended for travel and temporary habitation, they are set loose from social strictures, and they change their identity as the performance demands. The backstage scene gives us access to these strange and interesting characters, confirming or assuaging our anxieties about them in the process.

The men and women who inhabit cinematic dressing rooms pose a challenge to society by their choice to lead a life of performance, to aspire to the creation of art, to eschew the trappings of domesticity, and to transform their identity at will. Wives and mothers populate dressing rooms because the tension between public and private spheres is a constant for American women; backstage wives and mothers rehearse the drama of having to choose between home and work, a theme that has persisted in American film since the early twentieth century. We also find sisters in the dressing room, actual kin relations as well as collectives of women who tantalize us with their secret female activities but also rehearse what it means to be a woman in a society in which "good" and "bad" girl tropes leave little room for gender complexity. Leading men complicate the feminine features of the dressing room, specifically its objectifying function, and render it a space where male fragility and homosocial relationships can be explored. And forms of racial and gender cross-dressing harness the dressing room's potential for masquerade, providing a means for Black, Latino, and queer artists to thwart stable notions of the self and conjure new identities necessary for survival.

Social divisions often make their way into dressing rooms in consequential and disruptive ways. The Black maid is an archetype that persists for much of the twentieth century whose background orientation is essential to establishing the power dynamics of the dressing room. Without a voice or even a credit to her name in many of these films, the maid's spatial position becomes the justification for her permanent servitude. Focusing on this backstage space reveals her persistent and tenuous inhabitance.

Steeped in concerns about what these dressing room occupants represent, to themselves and to society, American films keep returning us to this space. Scenes featuring the dressing room, a private realm, reveal more than they conceal. Filmmakers use them to present fraught representations of wives and mothers, sisters, leading men, maids, and masqueraders that respond to, debate, and disassemble the social identities of American life. They provide scenes of self-reflection—often literally with the use of mirrors—satisfying our curiosity to be sure, but not about stars per se. Rather, these scenes fulfill our desire to reckon with the social actors we find there.

A Scene behind the Scenes

This book does not only focus on cinematic representations of dressing rooms. It contextualizes these cinematic incarnations with the historical creation and function of dressing rooms, as well as the material locations themselves. The earliest use of dressing rooms was a response to two critical, if somewhat threatening additions to the theater: women and masks. The Greek *skene* (tent or hut), whose creation is attributed to Aeschylus in the fifth century B.C., housed the actors, including women, as they transformed from one character to another.[12] Skenes sat near the orchestra and "across from the audience to provide 'offstage' space for actors to change costumes and masks and to furnish rapid and easy entrances to the acting arena."[13] Positioned directly behind the stage, the skene had a porous partition, in the form of a curtain or door, separating it from the site of performance. As Marvin Carlson describes, "The skene house provided a tangible sign for the hidden 'other' world of the actor, the place of appearance and disappearance, the realm of events not seen but whose effects conditioned the visible world of the stage."[14] Placed behind the stage, the skene quite literally formed the backdrop, rendering the backstage space integral to the performance itself.

As many theater scholars have noted, the word "theater" stems from the Greek *theatron*, meaning "a place for seeing."[15] Theater architecture evolved to capitalize on spectators' desire to see by creating a series of contact points that brought them ever closer to the actors. From the box office, spectators moved through the lobby, then to the auditorium, where the proscenium arch and the curtain provided an interior point of contact. Some privileged spectators, typically royalty and the wealthy, gained access to the private boxes that sat adjoining the stage. But the dressing room, of course, was the most exclusive and desired of these spaces. McAuley writes of how in the 1600s, French spectators were allowed to sit directly on the stage and visit the backstage realm at will, becoming a nuisance to the players and management in the process.[16]

In England, the "tiring room" was the place "where the players make them ready," but it too was a porous space. A "site of discovery," it was, like the skene, a space meant to be seen. The tiring room of the Renaissance theater (1558–1642) had the dual function of providing a space for the actors to dress and offering a separate point of entry for wealthy patrons. The introduction of women to the English stage during the Restoration (1660–1700), however, gave spectators, particularly men, new incentive to penetrate the backstage. As Tita Chico argues, the female body was put on display both onstage and backstage in this period, documented by Samuel Pepys's diary entries about his many tiring room visits; as she observes, spectators like Pepys were "simultaneously intrigued, pleased, and troubled" by these encounters with female intimacy, desiring access to their bodies but also feeling unsettled by actresses' use of costume and makeup to alter their appearance and deceive men.[17] Chico observes that Pepys's visits backstage demystified women, but his discoveries did not prevent him from returning again and again.[18] So while the dressing room's history reveals a dynamic of exclusion and access, its identity as a site of spectacle was heightened by the presence of women on the stage. A performance behind the performance, as Chico describes it, these early dressing rooms were a theater of their own.[19] Later dressing rooms of the nineteenth-century American stage inherited these associations, especially as popular entertainment forms like burlesque and musical comedy depended on phalanxes of women to populate the stage.

Since the beginnings of cinema in the late 1890s, filmmakers have played with this desire to see in the theater, providing views of the stage but also asserting the power of the camera to transport audiences directly behind the scenes. Whereas spectators in the theater are "involved in a vast range of different looks" at the stage and at one another, spectators of the cinema are under the control of the camera.[20] As I explore in a video essay about dressing rooms and cinematic interiority at the turn of the century, these early films make up for the loss of control by giving audiences unique access, beyond what any theater spectator can enjoy.[21] Some filmmakers were vaudeville performers who, nervous about the popularity of the new medium and its ability to replace live entertainment, integrated the movies into their acts. Artists like Adolph Zink created live entertainment-film hybrids that merged their onstage shows with filmed scenes behind the scenes in their dressing rooms. Others created films that take place entirely in dressing rooms, giving them titles that provocatively announce entry to the space (*A Dressing Room Scene*, 1897; *A Hot Time in the Dressing Room*, 1900; *Mr. Jack Is Caught in the Dressing Room*, 1904). A search of the Library of Congress and the American Film Institute catalogs reveals no fewer than thirty of these backstage films made between 1897 and 1910, an indication of the cultural salience of the space at cinema's beginnings.

To this day, however, the dynamics of access and denial constitute the form and thematics of backstage film, in which the mobile camera conjures a privileged spectator who can cross the barriers of the stage door, the proscenium arch, or the studio security gate with ease. While other genres, particularly melodrama, transport audiences into intimate realms like family homes and women's boudoirs, the backstage film makes a point of calling the spectator's attention to forms of access. Emboldened by the camera's mobility, a liberated spectator watches the performance along with the diegetic audience but also ventures into the space behind the stage to witness a performer in the state of becoming. The dressing rooms we think we know are a figment of our collective cultural imagination made possible by cinema's unbound potential.

From the beginning, filmmakers have understood the dressing room to be liminal, sitting at the intersections of space (between the stage and the world outside), identity (as a performer transforms in and out of character), and society (the incarnation and repetition of social types). As Aoife Monks has noted of the dressing room in painting, it is "quite literally a changing room."[22] The performer inside the space transforms his or her exterior, but these changes also have "interior effects," indicating that "the surface has repercussions for the soul, and that dressing rooms are places of transition from one psychological state to another."[23] Like in painting, films frame these changes inside the dressing room as display for an audience, presenting otherwise personal transformations as a performance of social significance.

It is this performative aspect of the dressing room that filmmakers have exploited, using the space's liminal qualities to give literal and metaphorical meaning to the transformations taking place inside. Makers of backstage films have used access and its denial to generate interest in the space, but also to convey the insecure status of its inhabitant. Partitions and thresholds such as screens, doors, and windows create layers of an interior world that can be easily penetrated. The porousness of dressing rooms has long been a concern in the world of entertainment, as confirmed by the many reports in *Variety* about dressing room thefts that take place while the inhabitant is performing on the stage. Complaints from actors to management prompted the widespread use of dressing room signage announcing that the theater owners are "not responsible for stolen goods." Other reports of "peeping toms," the topic of one early backstage film, *Peeping Tom in the Dressing Room* (1905), or of attacks on women and children suggest that despite its qualities of privacy, the dressing room is ultimately experienced as an insecure, potentially dangerous space.

Filmmakers frequently produce scenes in which partitions and thresholds are violated. *Peeping Tom in the Dressing Room* is one example of a dressing room's sanctity being compromised. Others include the tearing down of dressing screens (*In the Dressing Room*, 1903; *Mr. Jack Is Caught in the Dressing Room*, 1904), unwanted intrusions (*Glorifying the American Girl*, 1929; *Dance, Girl, Dance,*

1940), and sonic disturbances such as stage music, voices from another dressing room, or the knocking of a stagehand announcing the player has "five minutes" to performance (*Dance Girl Dance*, 1933; *Dance, Girl, Dance*, 1940; *Lady of Burlesque*, 1943; *Somebody Loves Me*, 1952), as well as incursions caused by technological devices (*Birdman*, 2014) and the camera itself (*Paris Is Burning*, 1990). In each case, violations of the privacy of the dressing room produce an interruption that temporarily halts the processes of self-reflection and self-transformation happening inside. Using the camera's mobility, filmmakers have shown us that we are complicit in these acts, calling attention to our own intrusive behavior, such as when director Mervyn LeRoy places us in the wardrobe of the women's dressing room in *Gold Diggers of 1933* or when a character closes the door on the camera before we can follow the performer inside (*When My Baby Smiles at Me*, 1948; *Opening Night*, 1977).

More subtly, however, backstage films expose dressing room insecurity through elements of the mise-en-scène. As Whitney Bolton, the drama critic for the *Morning Telegraph*, wrote in the 1950s, "Contrary to anything you may have seen in Hollywood's opulent movies, theatre dressing rooms are fairly dull and grim cubicles." He lists their equipment, "a chair or two, a metal shelf on which makeup is put, a probably streaked mirror above that in the wall and two electric lights, guarded from theft by wire mesh, beside the mirror," surmising wryly, "Some kennels are prettier."[24] While opulent dressing rooms abound in Hollywood film, especially at midcentury (*White Christmas*, 1954; *Imitation of Life*, 1959; *Gypsy*, 1962), their lavishness does not protect them from intrusions (Mama Rose barging into Gypsy's dressing room), nor does their décor guarantee a right to ownership over the space. As Bolton notes, the electric lights that adorn the vanity mirror are "guarded from theft by wire mesh." Miriam Young, author of *Mother Wore Tights*, recalls asking her mother in the dressing room about the "little wire cages," wondering if they exist to keep people from burning themselves or from stealing them. At the time, her mother lied that it was the former, hoping to preserve her daughter's innocence about more illicit forms of backstage behavior.[25] These wire cages appear in even the more opulent Hollywood dressing rooms; for example, we see them in the commodious men's dressing room in *White Christmas*. As visual markers of potential theft, the cages indicate a fundamental distrust between theater management and the performer. They also manifest, in visual form, the financial instability suffered by show people who must steal light bulbs because they cannot afford their own. Lefebvre's argument that space "is also a means of control, and hence of domination, of power," is useful for understanding the recurrence of this common dressing room object.[26] The cages protect private property and communicate, by their persistent presence, that the inhabitant should not make themselves too comfortable in the dressing room because it is ultimately not theirs.

Signage on dressing room walls also indicates non-ownership in backstage films. With directives like "No smoking," "No drinking allowed," "Keep cigarette butts and ashes off the floor," "Turn out the lights," "No credit will be given," and "Not responsible for valuables lost or stolen," the signs form a complex backdrop, governing the activities of the inhabitants inside. These too are vestiges of dressing room instability, wherein the performers are allowed to occupy but not lay claim to the space. Responding to real concerns about fire in the theater, the No Smoking signs are the most abundant in dressing room mise-en-scène. But they are also the signs that filmmakers like to flout most often, showing performers flagrantly lighting up cigars and cigarettes right below them (*Adolph Zink*, 1903; *Pretty Ladies*, 1925).

Dressing rooms are functional sites, necessary for the production of a show, but as McAuley notes, their functionality is related in no small part to "complex questions of self-esteem and morale."[27] The assignation and appointment of dressing rooms have been and remain today no small matter. As the *New York Herald Tribune* reported in 1934, "An actress' fame is measured by stairs she climbs," suggesting that the farther from the stage the dressing room, the less successful the performer.[28] In 1976, the actress Lonette McKee, fresh off her success in *Sparkle*, walked off the set of *The Greatest* (1977), a biopic about Muhammad Ali, because she was not given her own dressing room and refused to share one with other actors.[29] Today, McAuley notes that in the theater the "allocation of dressing rooms (who gets a private room, who must share with one or two others, who is in the communal room, who has the dressing rooms with convenient access to the stage, who has four flights of stairs to negotiate, who has the luxury of a private shower or bathroom) is clearly a very delicate matter and potentially a source of friction."[30] The ubiquitous symbol of the "star" on the door of the most privileged dressing room is a visual shorthand for communicating such social hierarchies and has been spoofed a number of times, including in the 1952 Warner Bros. cartoon *Show Biz Bugs*, in which an irate Daffy Duck is assigned a converted men's bathroom while the star dressing room goes to Bugs Bunny.

These insecurities strike at the heart of the player's sense of self and have resulted in performers' efforts to exert a modicum of control over the dressing room. Despite being shared and owned by someone else, dressing rooms are the most domestic space in the theater, a site of retreat and refuge for the performer. As Harvey Fierstein, whose long run in the revival of *Fiddler on the Roof* demanded that he spend much time in the theater, explained to the *New York Times*, "We are in our dressing rooms more than we are in our houses." Making the space feel like home was necessary given that "most dressing rooms are pretty horrifying," a fact that led him to insist, "There is magic in the theater, but it is not in the dressing room."[31] The elaborate décor for his own dressing room (which involved sewing his own curtains—"Doesn't everyone?") masked the harsher qualities of the space. Backstage films show these personal touches in even the barest of dressing rooms, indicating how the performers who inhabit them try to make themselves at home by draping clothing over the chairs and screens, tucking postcards and telegrams from well-wishers into the mirror's edges, and adorning their dressing table with framed photographs of loved ones. In some films, the characters use superstitions to control the space, as when Fanny Brice (Barbra Streisand) admonishes her maid for whistling in the dressing room (*Funny Lady*, 1975) or the male members of the jazz band forbid one of their own from bringing a woman inside (*Mo' Better Blues*, 1990). Fights over space abound in films where groups of women occupy the backstage, such as *A Scrap in the Dressing Room* (1904) and *Lady of Burlesque* (1943). And disobedient behavior—drinking, smoking, hiding animals and children in the space—reflects the ways that dressing room inhabitants attempt to make the space theirs, if only temporarily so.

Space and materiality define the dressing room as a place where performers' relationships to each other and to theater management are given expression, but the element of time also plays an important role. Whereas time seems to pause on the stage, especially in our understanding of how the backstage musical works—the narrative of the film takes a break while the performance is given and then resumes at the end—time is always hurtling forward in the dressing room.[32] Temporality is felt in the dressing room in ways similar to other generic spaces where there is a ticking clock that suggests a character is on the move from one place to another (such as in hotels, train stations, and airports).[33] The familiar knock on the door announcing "five minutes" or "places" is a constant reminder that time is passing. Temporarily inhabiting the space, performers must ready themselves to take the stage or enter the world outside. In this way, time is experienced as anxiety and pressure in the dressing room, where change must happen in order for the show to go on. A show hanging in the balance of a performer's readiness is a reference to the time when performers would not be paid if the show did not go on.[34] But the show in backstage film is always a metaphor; one's identity needs to be resolved if one is to function successfully in society. The dressing room is the temporally determined space where the performer must prepare for the role he or she will play onstage and in life. All the world might be a stage, but in backstage films, the world is a dressing room.

Dressing the Part

Dressing rooms set up expectations for the kind of narrative action we will encounter and the types of characters we will meet. A spatiotemporal trope, as scholars have argued regarding the apartment, the skyscraper, and the Black city, the dressing room structures and gives meaning to backstage plots.[35] Scenes in the dressing room are especially consequential in backstage film, a genre that is "spatially mobile," traversing across the well-known genres of musicals, melodramas, comedies, biopics, thrillers, superhero movies, ballet films, and jazz films.[36] They can take many forms, including backstage rooms, bungalows, tents, locker rooms, and even kitchens, suggesting the ways in which backstage films move easily across different kinds of performance settings. The "show" in backstage film takes place in large and small theaters, Hollywood backlots, television and radio studios, music and concert halls, nightclubs, strip joints, and traveling shows. The performances in these films are equally varied, encompassing legitimate drama, musical comedies, minstrel shows, vaudeville, burlesque, the circus, classical orchestras, opera, jazz, stand-up comedy, prize fighting, and one-person shows. And like Steven Cohan argues about the backstudio picture—a genre with which the backstage film overlaps—the longevity of the backstage film renders it more than a cycle, extending as it does from the earliest days of cinema through to the present day.[37] Over this span of time, the backstage film has ranged across a variety of modes, including documentary, big-budget features, filmed vaudeville performances and Hollywood adaptations of Broadway shows, independent cinema, and race films.

Only by looking across genres and modes do we see recurrent archetypes form, like the maid or the leading man, and their corresponding cultural significance take shape. Like Pamela Robertson Wojcik has argued about the apartment in film, the dressing room is "more than setting."[38] It is a space that gives characters the tools for self-definition, where intimate relationships are born and destroyed, where life decisions are made and consequences are reckoned with. A privileged site of display for film audiences, the dressing room stages a performance all its own.

Focusing on space as a determinant in genre study, I depart from Rick Altman's division of semantics and syntax. In his foundational book on the American film musical, Altman argues that identifying the "backstage musical" as such is limiting to our comprehensive understanding of the genre. It "has not served the musical well," he observes, to emphasize the backstage setting over considerations of plot and theme. Instead, he explains, a categorization according to syntax has the benefit of expanding the range of films that we study in relation to each other. Renaming what had heretofore been considered a "backstage" musical a "show" musical, Altman hopes to reorient our focus to the plot of making entertainment rather than the space where it happens. He argues, "The standard is not whether the film takes place backstage, but whether it is primarily concerned with putting on a show."[39]

Sharing Altman's desire to expand our critical lens to a more capacious group of films, I argue that space is essential, not just to the analysis of the musical but to the analysis of all genres in which the backstage figures prominently. As Wojcik observes, "it makes a difference" whether a musical is set in "rural America" or "backstage on Broadway."[40] So too, it matters that spatiotemporal tropes like the dressing room populate the backstage musical and, in all their guises, a variety of other genres as well. Many of these are concerned with putting on a show and include a parallel romantic subplot, as Altman identifies, but many do not; for example, the films that foreground the relationships between mothers and children (*Applause*, 1929; *Judy*, 2019), between women (*Dance, Girl, Dance*, 1940; *All about Eve*, 1950), and between performers and their craft (*Bamboozled*, 2000; *Birdman*, 2014). Space gives meaning and consequence to these relationships. As Henri Lefebvre has shown, space is "neither a mere 'frame,' after the fashion of the frame of a painting, nor a form or container" but rather "it is to lived experience what form itself is to the living organism, and just as intimately bound up with function and structure."[41] Dressing rooms are not neutral, in other words. Their spatial dynamics fundamentally shape backstage stories about who we are and the relationships we value.

Thematically, backstage films range across romance plots, stories about a performance team or collective, narratives about the fate of an entertainment form, and even tales of mystery and murder. Ultimately, however, backstage films hinge on the promise of mobility through transformation. The changes of identity that happen in the dressing room determine how far the performer can go professionally and, by extension, in society. A trope of the backstage film charts the rise of the performer from unknown to star with a parallel shift in the appearance of his or her dressing room. For example, as singer Ruth Etting, Doris Day's dressing room transforms from a squalid backroom at the beginning of her career to a luxurious chamber by film's end in *Love Me or Leave Me* (1955). But as we know from *Raging Bull* (1980), dressing rooms can also be symbolic of a performer's downfall. A spatial metaphor for the potential of its inhabitant, the dressing room is a manifestation of success or failure; it measures how well the performer has dressed the part. These representations correspond with the theater adage that "an actor has three stages in his career": when he is a beginner, "he is assigned a room on the third floor of a theater," with success he gets "the star dressing room," and if he "declines into character parts he starts to ascend the stairs again."[42]

As portentous as dressing rooms are, however, only certain kinds of people get access to them. Focusing our attention on the dressing rooms of backstage film reveals how exclusive they have been. It becomes apparent when looking back across a century of backstage film production that white inhabitants have been granted far more access to the space than people of color. From the nineteenth century to the present day, the genre has given white performers the chance to self-realize and seize the opportunity for transformation again and again. Black Americans, Latinos, and Asians, by contrast, make appearances in the genre in attenuated form. Black women inhabit the dressing room, but for much of the genre's history, only as maids. Asians appear infrequently, but when they do, they are dressers and valets. And Latinos' talents are well represented on the stages of backstage film, but they occupy the backstage dressing room only in productions made outside the mainstream. By the

1970s, opportunities increased somewhat for people of color in the dressing room, but not enough to produce lasting change. So, to the extent that the backstage film participates in the expansion of the idea that America is a place of opportunity, the genre has persistently restricted access to social mobility along racial lines.

Nevertheless, a diverse group of filmmakers have developed a cinematic language for expressing self-discovery, transformation, mobility, and consequence through dressing room scenes. Mirrors are central to these concerns, as they are able to refract the sightlines of the dressing room in myriad ways. The common sight of a performer sitting at her dressing table and gazing at her reflection materializes the implicit question of "Who am I?" while it simultaneously prompts the audience to ask, "Who are you?" As Gilles Deleuze has written, the mirror-image is inherently theatrical, able to produce multiple realities. He writes that the actual and the virtual "enter into a circuit which brings us constantly back from one to the other; they form one and the same 'scene' where the characters belong to the real and yet play a role."[43] The mirror functions as yet another "scene" in dressing room scenes, offering another visual layer to express the destabilization or expansion of the self. For stories about people of color and queer performers, these mirror shots have the power to expose and challenge social marginalization. Mirrors are able to split and multiply the self, producing masquerades of racial and queer identity.

The dressing room's cramped and enclosed features have also given filmmakers the chance to explore a range of female identities and experiences. As the most domestic space in the theater, and its most private, dressing rooms are typically depicted as a female domain. They are often shared by bevies of chorus girls whose frantic movements and cacophonous voices distinguish the space from the stage, which is the purview of the (male) director and choreographer. In other female dressing rooms, the space is pregnant with expectant mothers and children. Filmmakers use the sanctity of the dressing room to suggest a womb-like enclosure in which babies are born and cared for, delivering a spectacle of motherhood in the process. And in what I call "man in the mirror" shots, the tension between female performers and their husbands is given ominous, visual expression in films about backstage marital relations.

Finally, the spatial dimensions of the dressing room allow for explorations of social dynamics between female co-occupants of the space as well as groups of men. Placed in close proximity with one another, women look at other women, sizing one another up, desiring and loathing one another. Men also look at each other in the dressing room, in which confined space prompts opportunities for male spectacle and homosocial intimacy. But space gets its most profound expression as a determination of social dynamics in the many films that include a Black maid. She defines the background of the dressing room and clearly demarcates the racial hierarchies of the genre. Her presence is not without tension, however, as her movements to the middle and foreground force a reckoning with her social position, as we see in Jeni LeGon's films and in *Imitation of Life*.

Dressing room scenes shape our interpretation of the social actors we find there. Some of these figures, like the Black maid, are relatively short lived; she first appears in backstage films of the 1920s and persists, although less frequently so, through the midcentury when the civil rights movement and Black activism in Hollywood put a halt to her representation. Similarly, stories about female collectives such as sister acts were numerous in the first half of the twentieth century but dwindled in the second half. Among these, stories about female competition rather than female friendship predominated (*All about Eve*, 1950; *Black Swan*, 2010). And while on some level all backstage films are about masquerade, those films that truly embrace the radical potential of masquerade as a means of calling attention to inequities in society (*Paris Is Burning*, 1990) have been made with less frequency over the genre's history. More resilient have been stories about wives and mothers, including those women who choose to forgo romance and domesticity for a career, and the troubled leading man. In the twenty-first century, these social actors continue to capture our imaginations with their stories of regret, pain, and weakness, reminding us of society's boundaries and our limited ability to surpass them.

From maids to masqueraders, I center the intersectional dynamics of race, gender, and sexuality in the making of backstage film. The book begins with an examination of the maid, the social actor most overlooked and circumscribed within the genre. From there, it moves to analyses of those for whom the dressing room is a less restricted space, groups of white women, wives and husbands, mothers, and the male lead. In these chapters, I note the exceptional instances when performers of color embody dressing room archetypes, such as the sisters in *Sparkle*, the wife in *What's Love Got to Do with It* (1993), and the leader of a jazz band in *Mo' Better Blues* (1990). Finally, the last chapter foregrounds the relatively few but significant experiences of nonwhite and queer performers for whom the terms of entry to and exit from the dressing room prove necessary to social survival.

To be sure, dressing rooms are not restricted to American film. They have occupied the imaginations of filmmakers all over the world. I have chosen to focus on the American context as a means of exploring what dressing rooms have meant in a society in which the myths of individuality, opportunity, and success hold particular dominance. Looking at dressing rooms in American film produces a series of paradoxes about who we are as a society. What does it mean that white women most frequently occupy dressing rooms but are simultaneously censured for taking advantage of the transformative potential that the space represents? How have nonwhite and queer filmmakers engaged the backstage film's investment in restrictive social hierarchies? And why are male performers always in crisis about their role as leading men? Answering these questions necessitates placing films from different genres, modes, and time periods into conversation with one another, from contemporary films like *Joker* (2019) to well-known Hollywood classics like *Imitation of Life*, from documentaries like *Paris Is Burning* to backstage films made in the first decades of cinema. Through these discussions, we not only come to recognize the persistence of certain archetypes in American life, we also grapple with our fascination with, and fear of, who we really are as a society. In order to find out, we must venture behind the scenes, and into the dressing room.

1
Maids

••••••••••••••••••••

> Ina Claire's [dressing room] at the Guild Theatre was long and narrow, like a biscuit box, with just room behind her chair for the Negro maid to pass, if she pulled herself in. (All the maids, apparently, are Negro.)
> —*The Stage*, April 1934

"I didn't want to be a theater maid," explained Cleo Young to the *New York Herald Tribune* during an evening's performance of *Pal Joey* in 1941. Sitting in the dressing room of her employer, musical comedy actress Vivienne Segal, at the Ethel Barrymore Theater, Young explained to reporter Helen Ormsbee that she used to do "maid's work" for "Miss Viv" before working backstage. The expanded responsibilities required her to "make a list of all Miss Viv's costumes and the shoes, stockings and ornaments that went with them." Young, who had worked for Segal for nearly two decades, confessed, "Many's the time I was ready to walk out on her because she'd get mad and say things." She added, "Sometimes when she gets mad here in the dressing room I say: 'You better pull yourself together, Miss Viv. You've got to go out there and sing.' She goes, and when she comes back it's all over and forgotten."[1]

While Young's voice is filtered through the white female reporter, her interview is noteworthy for its foregrounding of a Black maid's perspective in the pages of a mainstream publication.[2] Often rendered invisible, their backstage labor being hidden from view, or characterized as willfully submissive to their employers, Black maids have been relegated literally and figuratively to the background of the majority of show business narratives. Young navigates her role carefully in the interview. Playing the part of the faithful servant, Young is critical, but also repeatedly insistent that "Miss Viv" is "lovely" and "kind." She also makes sure to communicate her own authority in the dressing room, admonishing her employer to control her emotions so that she can perform her best onstage. "Patience," Young tells Ormsbee, is the most important qualification for the job. Segal, who enters the dressing room while the interview is taking place, disagrees. Confessing that she wants to "hear all about" the interview in progress, she corrects Young by telling the reporter that "efficiency," not "patience," matters most in a maid.

The personal cost of such efficiency, however, comes through in Young's account: in addition to the trials of managing the outbursts of the star, Young details how she has had to separate from her family and from her church, the Abyssinian Baptist in Harlem, a place that she mentions with a mix of pride and regret. "I don't get to go there often these days, because we live out in Mount Kisco and drive to town for the show." Maid to "Miss Viv" at home and at the theater, Young's work extends across the domestic and professional spheres of her employer. After Segal leaves the dressing room for a dinner engagement, Young offers a last comment, "I didn't want to be a theater maid in the beginning, but now I love it."[3]

What are we to make of Young's qualifying statements? To be sure, the desire to safeguard her employment figures prominently in the interview, but she also reveals her careful navigation of Segal's moods, different spaces of work (the home and the theater), and her complex role as both the manager and servant of the dressing room. Ormsbee describes this delicate balance when she admits that Young is both a "psychologist and diplomat" when it comes to Segal. Young "mothers her, bosses her and humors her by turns, knowing which method to apply on which occasion."[4] Knowing when to speak up or remain silent, be willful or submissive, assert herself or recede into the background, Young, like backstage maids before and after her, had to know her place in the dressing room.

As a historical actor and a cultural symbol, the Black maid figures prominently in American film. While stories of maids abound in popular news accounts from the 1920s–1940s, it is their repeated incarnation in dozens of backstage films that legitimized and naturalized their subservient presence in the dressing rooms of American culture. Films with Black backstage maids originated in the 1920s, a moment that witnessed the simultaneous migration of Black women to the North in search of work, the rise in popularity of musical comedy on Broadway, and the increasing narrativization of backstage life in Hollywood. Appearing with marked consistency in the 1930s and 1940s, the maid's presence tapered off with the beginning of the civil rights movement and culminated in the mid-1970s, when altered racial representations and nostalgia for earlier, simpler times converged to produce some of the last, albeit revised, images of her. From *The*

Goose Woman (1925) to *Funny Lady* (1975), films have reflected the public's fascination with the maid, notable for her seeming ubiquity in the backstage world; as one contemporary observer noted of the backstage quarters belonging to actresses Ina Claire and Lillian Gish in 1934, "All the maids, apparently, are Negro," a phrase that captures how, as Gwen Bergner has observed, "US labor practices worked in tandem with discursive systems such as the movies to make the 'Black maid' ubiquitous and the modifier unnecessary."[5] As the title of this chapter indicates, to refer to the backstage maid in this twentieth-century moment was to infer a Black woman whose racialized and gendered body circulated between reality and representation.

But for much of the maid's history on film, her existence has served to call attention to the white women in the room. *Glorifying the American Girl* (1929) is a case in point. Aspiring showgirl Gloria Hughes (Mary Eaton) leaves her job as a department store song plugger for fame on the Ziegfeld stage. Gloria's pursuit of her dream, however, alienates her from her good friend, Barbara (Gloria Shea), and her boyfriend, Buddy (Edward Crandall), who ultimately find solace in each other's company. At the end of the film, while Gloria gets ready in the dressing room for her star turn in the Ziegfeld Follies, she receives a telegram from Buddy that announces his marriage to Barbara. She whimpers in front of her vanity mirror, receives a comforting embrace from her mother, then bravely marches to the stage for the final performance. Her maid (uncredited) solemnly carries the train of her dress behind her. The ambitious ingenue has gotten her wish, but at the price of love. Barbara, on the other hand, has found personal fulfillment in marriage.

The dressing room is the rare space in Hollywood film in which we see white and Black actresses sharing the screen, often intimately. In their scenes together, the women are alternately friends and foes, enjoying camaraderie or engaging in competition. No matter the nature of their relationship, however, these scenes are fundamentally about the power differential between white stars and their Black maids. Like the interview with Cleo Young at the start of this chapter, the backstage film reflects and reshapes behind-the-scenes social hierarchies, at times reaffirming the docility of the maids and at other times gesturing toward real-life tensions in such relationships. Whether silent or vocal, the maid begs attention because of her persistence in dressing room scenes. These are not incidental appearances. Rather, the maid's presence is vital to the intersecting negotiations of race and gender that persistently take place in these narratives.

Background

In *Close Harmony* (1929), an early sound-era film about romance behind the scenes of a vaudeville show, the star, Marjorie Merwin (Nancy Carroll), spends much time in her dressing room worrying about the show business career of her boyfriend (Charles "Buddy" Rogers). Her maid (uncredited) attends to her.

While no known print exists of the film, the script's scene headings convey critical information about the setting in which the action takes place and each character's role within it. While the maid occasionally has a line of dialogue, her most frequent appearance in the script is in the scene headings, which read, "(Maid b.g.)." Occupying the "b.g.," or "background," of these dressing room scenes, the maid both resides in and is associated with the anterior space of a room located behind the scenes. As such, "Maid b.g." reinforces the dressing room's interiority, but also creates a spatial demarcation of how race operates backstage, with the maid always positioned, noticeably, in the back.[6]

The backstage film's use of the Black maid echoes representations of Black supporting figures in other mediums. Referencing the practice of including Black servants in early modern portrait painting, Peter Erickson notes a dynamic in which the servant "is secondary but nevertheless 'portrayed,'" creating an awkwardness and a "built-in tension" within the text. Similarly, in his analysis of the Black (female) backup singer in popular music, John Corbett argues that her position in the background is as essential but ultimately nameless support. She "extends the potential" of the (male) lead by the mere presence of her raced and gendered body. Analogous to servants and backup singers who occupy an enclosed, "background" space, the maid's inferiority is signaled by her raced body, which then spotlights the protagonists' whiteness. And her emplacement in the dressing room renders the space one of "claustral" confinement that justifies the power relationships it encloses and makes visible.[7]

But while she extends the value of whiteness in the backstage film, the maid also constricts the potential of white femininity. She functions as a corrective to the female protagonist who has risen too quickly and achieved too much. Restricted to the background, the maid's mere presence is a critique of white womanhood. Press accounts in newspapers and trade magazines repeatedly emphasized the difficult and demanding personal qualities of female stars in musical comedy and implied their need for discipline. Likening them to high-strung "thoroughbreds," the *New York Herald Tribune* explained how the maid must be like a well-trained jockey who makes sure there are no burrs under the horse's saddle: "The rare voiced songbird of the stage who thrills an audience is a good deal like the thoroughbred.... Her maid can make her or mar her in a good many ways." As a result, the maid must create an atmosphere of "soothing tranquility" that will "appeal to the high-strung mistress the instant she enters." In anticipating her mistress's needs, the maid must be vigilant in preparing the dressing room: "Everything from a comb to a toilette bottle must be exactly placed. A dressing table light at the wrong angle casts a distorted shadow. Even a cracked picture on the wall or a fugitive scrap of paper on the rug may be an irritant. Shoes and stockings without imperfection, must be placed in exact order of requirement. If the lights suddenly blow out the maid should be able to place her skilled hand upon everything or anything with the unerring accuracy of one born blind." These tasks necessitate a combination of characteristics, the article continues, including docility, serenity, and a sense of humor, all qualities that the "colored maids" possess, rendering them "nearest to perfection." As the perfect example, the article references Marilyn Miller's maid, who is "affable and close mouthed and wise," winning attributes for dealing with the "volatile" star.[8]

Other accounts showcase how white women in popular theater use maids as a false sign of status. In an earlier article about how dressing rooms cause friction among female principals, the *New York Tribune* profiles a series of performers who describe their relationship to their dressing rooms. Suggesting that the women of the chorus are the most insecure about their position, the writer points out that she observed "a number of colored women in the wings." When she asked the star which one was "her maid," the star responded, "'Stars' can't afford to have maids; these belong to the chorus girls." So numerous were the maids for that production that they had to "flatten out against the wall most of the time, for there is not room for them in the crowded dressing rooms, but the chorus must have them to keep up the dignity of their position." Queried how the chorus girls pay for them, the star explained, "Ask Wall Street." In this case, maids were both symbols of status, thereby elevating the poor chorus girl's position in the theater, and payment for favors given to wealthy businessmen.[9]

Occasionally, accounts described how maids used their position as coveted status markers to their advantage. During a production in the Manhattan Theater in 1926, for example, two rival female stars insisted on having the same backstage comforts, with neither appearing more privileged than the other. When "Miss Seaton" noticed that "Miss Linden" had a "colored maid," she hired one as well. But recognizing that neither star was particularly smart or observant, "the two colored girls have an arrangement whereby one leaves for a few hours, the other serving the two mistresses meanwhile." With dressing rooms facing opposite one another, the maids were able to deceive their employers based on the fact that "neither of the singers is yet well enough acquainted with her 'maid' to distinguish one from the other." The article reinforces and confirms the idea that "colored maids" are prone to duplicity, but it simultaneously delivers a critique of their white employers as status-hungry and ambitious female stars who get what they deserve.[10]

Simultaneous cinematic depictions of the maid confirmed these assumptions about the nature of white women in the dressing room. In *The Goose Woman* (1925), theater star Hazel (Constance Bennett) has a Black maid, a sign of the performer's status and desire for luxury. We are therefore meant to suspect Hazel's sincerity when she professes her love for Gerald (Jack Pickford), a poor man who has little to offer. The maid often stands patiently in the background, ready to adorn her employer with a fur coat or string of pearls. Such dressing room scenes provide visual evidence that the white star is ill-suited for a life without material extravagances.

The maid has a stronger role to play in the subsequent year's feature, *The Marriage Clause* (1926) by Lois Weber. The rare backstage film directed by a woman, *The Marriage Clause* tells what would become a familiar story about a woman's ambition for a stage career and the costs to her personal life that it entails. While Weber tempers her critique of actress Sylvia (Billie Dove), she nevertheless explores how a life on the stage can lead women astray from their more natural roles as wives and mothers. In order to take the lead part, Sylvia must sign an agreement that she will not marry for the duration of her engagement in the show. This places significant strain on her relationship with her fiancé, Barry (Francis X. Bushman). The lovers become estranged and Barry goes away, leaving Sylvia with a broken heart. In the meantime, however, we see how Sylvia's rise produces an array of status markers, including stylish clothing, expensive jewelry, and a Black maid. Played by Carolynne Snowden, a frequent performer in Hollywood cabarets, the role of Sylvia's maid necessitates that she remain positioned in the claustral spaces of the backstage.[11] But Weber gives Snowden the most critical line for understanding Sylvia's newfound social position. Observing Sylvia's erratic behavior on the stage, she tells the porter standing next to her, "She sho' am a different actin' lady since they let Mr. Barry go." Snowden is both the symbol of Sylvia's status and its critic in this moment, marking Sylvia's rise in the theater as one that is ultimately too costly to be sustained.

But it is in the series of films about the Ziegfeld Follies that white women are most explicitly critiqued with the emplacement of a maid. Typically, these films are set at the turn of the century and against the backdrop of the Ziegfeld Follies, a popular entertainment form that exalted white femininity at precisely the moment that American racism and nativism were particularly virulent. Florenz Ziegfeld, the entertainment mogul and creator of the Follies, used his position to celebrate his "Ziegfeld girls" according to his own standards of beauty and female decorum.[12] Both exalted and contained, Ziegfeld girls were at once symbolic of female achievement and male discipline. In Hollywood, the Ziegfeld Follies appear as an entertainment form that gives the girl her big break (*Glorifying the American Girl*, 1929; *Easter Parade*, 1948; *Somebody Loves Me*, 1952; *Love Me or Leave Me*, 1955; *Funny Girl*, 1968; *Funny Lady*, 1975). The sudden appearance of a Black maid in her luxurious dressing room confirms the girl's success, to the detriment of her moral character and personal relationships. The dressing room literally contains the Black maid while it elevates whiteness, but it also justifies the constriction of women's empowerment and checks their mobility.

Dressing room scenes invoke the space's cultural representation as a site of female power. In Tita Chico's analysis of eighteenth-century satirical fiction, dressing rooms are spaces where sexual excess, theatrical dissembling, and feminine agency have free rein precisely because of the space's private and transformational qualities. They are at once the focus of male fascination and critique, preparing "the woman for public display as well as serving as sites of display in their own right."[13] Male intruders into the space justified their actions by demonstrating that female manipulation and expression required censure and control.

Ziegfeld was famous for his management of the female performers in his productions; as one *New York Herald Tribune* article commented, it was one "gift among many" that the producer possessed to create and maintain "harmony" in "star dressing rooms," even though "he rarely enters one."[14] Behind such social control, however, is the maid whose function is to manage the temperament of the stars so that they can appear at their best onstage. A secondary function of the maid, it is implied, is to monitor the dressing room, occupying the private space of women in ways that men, including Ziegfeld, cannot. The maid may be in the background in these films, but her spatial location allows her to critique the otherwise celebrated Ziegfeld star.

In a dressing room scene near the end of *Glorifying the American Girl*, the first film of the Ziegfeld cycle, Gloria's maid shakes her hand after a successful performance. The maid quickly recedes into the background until Gloria is ready to exit once again. Her static presence in the dressing room renders it a stable and safe place for Gloria to grapple with her newfound identity as star. Meanwhile, the maid's celebration of Gloria's stardom and attention to her dress make her a figure of support and comfort, as Corbett notes about the role of the backup singer. The maid stands and works while her mistress sits and contemplates her reflection. She occupies the anterior of the space while Gloria is at the forefront. The maid wears a drab smock while Gloria displays a bedizened gown. And her maid remains silent and nameless while Gloria has free expression and assumes an exalted identity. In this way, the maid provides visual evidence of her own fixedness while she marshals the transformative qualities of the dressing room to amplify her mistress's rising social position.[15]

Later films in this subgenre are more critical of the white women who ascend to Ziegfeld stardom. Ziegfeld headliners possess inherent character flaws in *Easter Parade*, *Somebody Loves Me*, *Love Me or Leave Me*, *Funny Girl*, and *Funny Lady*. Such flaws include flagrant ambition and the desire for fame and wealth at all costs. The maid appears in the white protagonist's dressing room to signal or confirm stardom. But these sequences also bring confirmation of the star's personal failings or, at the very least, reservations about the value of her achievement.

As the last two iterations of the Ziegfeld star and her Black maid, *Funny Girl* and *Funny Lady* are based on the life of the real Ziegfeld headliner Fanny Brice, played by Barbra Streisand. Set in the first few decades of the twentieth century, they chart Brice's rise out of the immigrant ghetto of the Lower East Side to Broadway. The emphasis on Brice's ethnic Jewish heritage notwithstanding, the films are in keeping with earlier narratives that follow a white woman's rise to fame on the Ziegfeld stage. And as in those other films, the maid figures in the dressing room space as a helpful and attentive servant. In this way, the films are consistent with past representations, which is remarkable given that they were produced after the civil rights movement. They are more in keeping with the earliest depictions of maids in film, emplacing her in the background without any adjoining critical commentary and therefore demonstrating the continued appeal and effectiveness of the maid as a cultural symbol for white female ambition and white female loss even in the 1960s and 1970s.

To be sure, both films justify such a representation by situating their plots in the early twentieth century, a moment that saw the real-life employment of Black women as domestics as well as the repeated representation of their role in Hollywood film. And unlike in earlier Ziegfeld films, the maids in these instances—Mittie Lawrence as Emma in *Funny Girl* and Royce Wallace as Adele in *Funny Lady*—are not silent; they have minimal dialogue, and in Lawrence's case, she does not wear a maid's uniform. As a nod to the times, Lawrence's Emma appears in a subdued, professional blouse and skirt with no allusion to those markers of servility, the white collar and headpiece. Another indication of changing times is Lawrence's casting in the role itself. Young and attractive, Lawrence was only twenty-seven years old at the time of *Funny Girl*'s release. Offscreen, as the *New York Amsterdam News* reported, she was a model of fashion, and the article pictures her in a slinky "head-to-toe body hugging crepe," under which the caption reads, "Black Is Beautiful." The paper also touted her role in *Funny Girl* but was just as quick to note the change in her persona from screen to real life. "After completing her filming schedule on the Hollywood set of the William Wyler-Ray Stark production of 'Funny Girl' a Columbia Pictures release, Miss Lawrence took time out to be photographed in a few of her favorite looks for evening."[16]

These shifts in representation notwithstanding, *Funny Girl* and *Funny Lady* ultimately use the dressing room maid as a visual symptom of Brice's unhappiness. As Pamela Robertson Wojcik has identified them, both films are a part of the musical variant "the Streisand musical," in which the struggle between romantic longing and female independence plays out on both narrative and formal levels. A consummate performer, Barbra Streisand's talent cannot be contained or restricted in these films, often manifesting in grandiose solos and anthems that reinforce her character's desire to be free. These are powerful, quasi-feminist moments in which Fanny Brice proves that she is a survivor.[17] Nevertheless, in the quieter, nonmusical moments of the dressing room, Fanny must reckon with her choices, fighting back the tears as Nick Arnstein (Omar Sharif) leaves her again and again. Both films make it clear that Fanny's choices (not the personal failings of her romantic partners) have led to the breakup of her relationships. Near the end of *Funny Girl*, Fanny sits at her dressing table while she explains to Florenz Ziegfeld (Walter Pidgeon), "I don't want to make the same mistakes so if it means giving up the theater, I hope you'll be a sport about it." And in *Funny Lady*, she tearfully explains to Nick, "I don't blame you for divorcing me. You got hit by this steam engine the papers call Fanny Brice." She confides, "I don't blame you for wanting to dig out." Later in the film, she loses a second opportunity for happiness with Billy Rose (James Caan), who tells her after they have divorced, "Being married to you was like being married to a parade." Implying that she placed her career above their marriage, he lists her entourage: there was "you, Nick, Adele, Bobby . . . and me." In each of these examples from *Funny Girl* and *Funny Lady*, it is Fanny's career that gets in the way of successful romantic relationships, reaffirming once again the irreconcilability of personal and professional happiness for a woman, a fundamental theme of the Ziegfeld backstage film.

Billy's inclusion of Adele in the list of people who won more of Fanny's attention is telling. Like the others, Adele is symbolic of Fanny's devotion to her career; Nick initially helped her to achieve social mobility; Bobby (Roddy McDowall), a performer himself, also supports her as a friend and confidant; and Adele sorts out her costumes, helps her to dress, and looks out for her physical well-being backstage. Including Adele in this cast of characters acknowledges her importance to the star (something that earlier films did not do) but also emphasizes the ways that Brice's career is dependent on the emotional and physical labor of a Black woman.

Being served by a maid signals the danger of having achieved too much in both films. In *Funny Girl*, Emma appears in Fanny's dressing room long after the latter becomes a Ziegfeld star. But her timing coincides with trouble in Fanny and Nick's marriage. In three separate dressing room sequences, Emma attends to Fanny when there is doubt about Nick's investment in the relationship. In keeping with the earliest of backstage films, Emma emerges from and recedes into background space as she performs her work. The film establishes her presence even while many of the shots in these scenes do not include her; but because she is intermittently visible, she hovers in offscreen space. In the final dressing room sequence, Emma enters the room only in reflection; the camera is positioned just behind Fanny, who sits at her dressing table. The film cuts to a medium shot of Emma asking if Fanny is all right and then cuts back to the dressing table, where we see Emma reflected in one of the side mirrors; she exits, again by way of the mirrored reflection, as Ziegfeld enters. This emphasis on reflection highlights Fanny's loneliness. Her interaction with Emma happens only through the refracted and cropped image of the reflection; the mirror becomes a barrier to interpersonal communication, thus leaving Fanny alone to deal with her failed marriage.

While Wyler uses Emma to distance Fanny from personal happiness, director Herbert Ross positions Adele to function more traditionally as a backstage maid. Despite being made seven years after *Funny Girl*, *Funny Lady*'s representation is atavistic, more akin to the earliest representations of the maid. Adele wears servile garb, a black dress with white cuffs and collar, and she remains in anterior space whenever Fanny is present. Her representation is also regressive for the way that it suggests, albeit subtly, that she takes advantage of her privileged position in the private space of the dressing room. Waiting for Fanny to return, Adele surreptitiously peeks at the card that came with a basket of roses sitting on the dressing table. Ross allows us to ponder this act for several

The maid (Mittie Lawrence) stands in the background. *Funny Girl*, copyright 1968 by Columbia Pictures.

seconds before Fanny disrupts it by running in for a costume change. In that time, however, we see Adele give a disapproving glance at the card, an action that a mirrored cabinet in the background reflects. The shot forces us, therefore, to see her indiscretion twice, in the foreground and in the background, doubling Adele's secret behavior in the dressing room.

Middle Ground

The depiction of maids in the background suggests the persistence of their value as a cultural symbol, of Black servility and of white female ambition, despite the larger sociocultural shifts that happen over the course of their representation in film. The maid's docility, regardless of the occasional moment of indiscretion, was lauded by the press in the 1920s, 1930s, and 1940s and confirmed by contemporary Hollywood films like those discussed earlier. But the archive also challenges this narrative while midcentury backstage films indicate cracks in the otherwise harmonious relationship between white mistress and Black maid.

Accounts of maids suing for unpaid labor and physical abuse appear in Black newspapers of the era. For example, in 1925, the *New York Amsterdam News* reported that Jennie Harrison, maid to "temperamental dancer" Evan Burrows Fontaine, "filed an affidavit in the Supreme Court demanding $2000 damages." The publication recounted how Harrison demanded her three weeks' pay, plus the money she had spent on newspapers for the dancer. Fontaine reacted by "threatening her with a revolver and hitting her in the head with a coat-hanger, cutting her left cheek, causing loss of blood."[18] The paper reported later that year that Carrie Sneed, maid to actress Imogene Wilson, claimed in court that Blackface comedian Frank Tinney had "treated her rough."[19] Such abuses prompted a group of maids to organize in 1926 as the Colored Ladies' Dressing

Association in New York. Hoping to "enlist the support of every colored maid in show business," the organizers pointed to the common practice that required maids to be a "combined maid, nurse, secretary and laundress." "They render first aid in case of sickness, they launder silk stockings and undies, they run errands, some write letters and also act as bodyguards and what not."[20] Often going without remuneration, these additional forms of exploitation on the job formed the crux of their grievances. The archive does not reveal whether the maids ultimately organized, but a high-profile case involving Tallulah Bankhead's maid some decades later, in which Evelyn Cronin alleged that the actress had forced her to pay for "marijuana cigarets and cocaine" with her own paychecks, suggests that their efforts were ultimately unsuccessful.[21] As these stories of exploitation and violence convey, maids were in a vulnerable position when it came to their own safety, and their remuneration was insufficient to justify the risks they took for their employers. In this way, backstage maids were just as susceptible to abuse as domestic maids, many of them, like Cleo Young, occupying positions at home and theater at once.[22]

Maintaining a fiction of Black docility, backstage films do not admit that such exploitation of maids occurred. Nevertheless, by midcentury, the image and behavior of the maid began to shift slightly. Advocacy and activism on the part of the NAACP highlighted the problems associated with typecasting Black actresses as maids. As Ralph Matthews of the Baltimore *Afro-American* reported, NAACP executive secretary Walter White met with Wendell Wilkie and "other distinguished citizens" in Los Angeles in 1942 in order to "draft a new race charter for race characterization on the screen, and to obtain pledges from the movie industry that the lot of both the colored actor and the portrayal of colored people on the screen would be greatly improved."[23] But while the organization found Hollywood moderately receptive, the Black actors including Hattie McDaniel and Lillian Randolph insisted that the revised characterizations limited rather than empowered them. Both actresses expressed incredulity that they were not consulted by the NAACP in its efforts. McDaniel, who had worked in the industry the longest, insisted that by setting an example of "exemplary conduct" on and off the screen, she was already doing the work of improving Black representation. She explained how she was now "given every courtesy," pointing to her own "portable dressing room, a stand-in, a hair-dresser, and other attendants" as hard-won gains.[24] Randolph also witnessed improvement without the NAACP's intervention, arguing that she used to have to "wear a bandanna" and darken her skin, whereas now she wears "the best of clothes" and gets as "much attention from the make-up men and hair-dressers as anybody." After the NAACP's convention, however, Randolph told how her role as a maid was rewritten for a white housekeeper: "The reason cited was that Walter White had given them to understand that colored people did not want colored people appearing as servants as the matter was controversial, they thought it best to delete the character all together."[25]

While these actors cite the unintended consequences of activism, they also communicate a perspective that forces an appreciation for their labor and their efforts to change the industry by personal example. McDaniel emphasizes how she employs "artistry" in her work, using dialect only when it suits the character ("An antebellum slave would talk in dialect but a modern house servant would not"[26]). Other actors of the time, both in theater and in Hollywood, echo this approach to cultural change: "People ask me don't I get tired of maid roles," stated Broadway actress Pauline Myers. "Sure I do, but I'm one of these working actresses.... Other roles are few and far between. As long as I don't, which I won't, play the fool cutting maid, I'll get along. No one as yet has accused me of disgracing the race."[27] Similarly, Louise Beavers, who, as the *New York Amsterdam News* related in 1935, had "appeared in more maid roles than any screen actress and has played maid to some of the most famous actresses in films," emphasized the work that it took to master the speech of the onscreen maid: "I couldn't even understand the language of the southern colored people when I started, but I kept studying, reading books and poems and finally mastered the dialect sufficiently to use in screen roles."[28]

The debate about how to change Hollywood and give Black actors the credit due to them occurred in the background of backstage film production at midcentury. Nevertheless, we can see traces of revised representations in the ways that maids occupy more of a middle-ground position in midcentury films. Neither entirely docile in the background nor foregrounded as leading characters in their own right, the maids in two postwar musicals, *Easter Parade* (1948) and *Somebody Loves Me* (1952), reside in a liminal physical and social space.

While the films subscribe to a logic of racial hierarchy, the maid, played by Jeni LeGon in both, challenges her position by resisting, undermining, and competing with her mistress. These are brief moments of insubordination that, once uttered, are quickly suppressed. Their silencing, both narratively and musically, is part of the censuring and containment of Black and white women as the price of both of their transgressions. As Susan Courtney writes about miscegenation films, the "temporary transgression of one register of difference is negotiated or stabilized through the reassertion of another" in backstage musicals as well."[29] In these films, the Black maid's misbehavior challenges the authority of her white mistress. The mistress in turn corrects her servant but is ultimately disciplined by male patriarchy and the convention of heteronormative coupling. The backstage musical's fascination with women who eschew domestic life in favor of their careers had particular resonance in the postwar era, when the pressure to domesticate both men and women was acute amid Cold War anxieties of social (and national) dissolution. In the dressing room we witness white and Black women stepping out of bounds and needing to be disciplined in both public and private ways.

As the maid, LeGon serves Nadine (Ann Miller) in *Easter Parade* and Blossom Seeley (Betty Hutton) in *Somebody Loves Me*. An exceptional tap dancer and singer, LeGon was the daughter of Black migrants to Chicago and danced in all-Black revues before going to Hollywood and eventually earning a long-term contract with MGM, the first Black woman to do so. The contract proved to be limiting, however. In an interview conducted later in life, she tells the story of being denied a role in *Broadway Melody of 1936* (1935) because she was "upstaging" Eleanor Powell's dancing. Similarly, while she has prominent billing in the cast of *Easter Parade*, LeGon's one song-and-dance number was cut from the final print of the film, a further indication that producers feared she might have upstaged Ann Miller, Judy Garland, and Fred Astaire, the stars of the film.[30] As Miriam J. Petty argues, notions of "upstaging" and "stealing the show" were frequently applied to Black American singers and dancers in 1930s Hollywood as a means of circumscribing and devaluing Black performance.[31] LeGon's story certainly fits this model. Frustrated by her relegation to minor roles, she ultimately left the United States for a teaching career in Canada. Her move shows the effect of Hollywood's racial politics on the lives of Black performers. Nevertheless, it would be a mistake to dismiss LeGon's maids as just stereotype if we are to understand how the backstage film functions. LeGon's characters serve the critical function of checking female vanity in the dressing room. And they highlight her talents while exposing the cinematic mechanisms that keep her in check.

In *Easter Parade*, LeGon plays Essie, Nadine's duplicitous maid. Nadine is a Ziegfeld star who spurns her longtime partner, Don Hewes (Fred Astaire), in order to pursue a solo career. We quickly come to understand Nadine as a deeply flawed character. While she is beautiful and talented, she is cold, materialistic, and shallow. She orders Essie to spy on Don's show. Essie lies and delivers the message that the show is a flop, gratifying Nadine. Essie returns to Nadine's dressing room and is joined by Johnny (Peter Lawford), friend to both Nadine and Don. Having just returned from watching Don's show, Johnny looks slyly at Essie, who is busying herself with Nadine's costumes, and says, "Well, Essie, I see you got here before me."

The frame's composition in the scene reveals a spatial geography that signals Nadine's lack of character and Essie's duplicity. The mirror plays a particularly important role in the power dynamics of the room. The scene shows Nadine sitting at her dressing table gazing at Johnny's reflection. Johnny is positioned off-screen, as is Essie, whose hand and profile occasionally enter the frame from screen left. As Julian Hanich has argued, these are "complex mirror shots" in which we see offscreen characters only through their reflections, actively alerting the viewer to the possibilities and meanings of offscreen space as a result. In this instance, the two offscreen characters, Essie and Johnny, are bearers of the true narrative, that Don's show was a success. Nadine's two-faced nature is communicated by the two versions of her that we see, the disingenuous one seen in her reflected look of sympathy, and her real self seated (between the camera and the mirror) at the table. The placement of Johnny's reflection between the two views of Nadine emphasizes the visual split between her true and false personas.

The maid (Jeni LeGon) hovers in offscreen space. *Easter Parade*, copyright 1948 by Metro-Goldwyn-Mayer.

Johnny's spatial location allows him to occupy a position of power from which he can deliver judgment on Nadine inside the mirror shot and share in Essie's lie outside it. In this way, he provides the requisite male oversight in this otherwise female space. Essie, who does not have a reflected subjectivity, remains in the offscreen shadows, an indication of her inferior social position and treachery.³²

While Essie steps out of bounds, the film ultimately justifies her transgressions because of Nadine's cold, careerist ambition. It is telling that just before Nadine's dressing room scene, we see Hannah (Judy Garland), Don's new dancing partner, in her own dressing room on the night of her big debut. The space is well appointed and organized in similar fashion to Nadine's, with the dressing table at the far right of the frame. The glaring difference, however, is that an elderly white maid attends to Hannah's dressing needs. The white maid might be a symbol of Hannah's relative lack of experience and her status as an unknown performer. But edited against shots of Nadine's private backstage realm, Hannah's dressing room scene exposes Nadine's status-hungry ambitions. The Black maid appears as a sign of extravagance while the white maid is a testament to Hannah's more virtuous and kind nature. The back-to-back dressing room scenes also suggest the potential for Hannah to be the rare female star who can achieve both professional success and personal happiness, provided that she has the right temperament.

Though Nadine's self-image suffers as a result of Essie's betrayal, *Easter Parade* maintains the racial status quo with its musical sequences. Just before Essie's visit to Hannah and Don's show, Nadine performs the Irving Berlin song "Shaking the Blues Away." Emulating Black dance movements ("Do like the voodoos do, list'ning to a voodoo melody, they shake their bodies so, to and fro"), Nadine embodies the Black performer, asserting her own dominance in the process.[33] And immediately after Nadine learns of Essie's deception, she goes onstage to perform "The Girl on the Magazine Cover," a Berlin ballad that celebrates white femininity ("She is fairer than all the queens"). So while Nadine's brand of femininity gets checked from below by her Black maid, her superiority as a white woman is ultimately upheld by the performance numbers in the film. *Easter Parade* engages in an interplay of racialized and gendered identity formations that temporarily unsettle but ultimately restore one another according to social norms.

In LeGon's subsequent film *Somebody Loves Me*, the dressing room and the Black maid are the subject of a musical performance. LeGon plays a critical role in a medley of songs sung as part of the star turn of Blossom Seeley (Betty Hutton) on the Ziegfeld stage. The number begins with a dressing room scene wherein Blossom and Delilah (LeGon) prepare for the show. The curtain closes as Blossom steps forward to sing a duet with her costar. The curtain opens again and she returns to the dressing room, changes costume, and exits once more to sing the final song. While Hutton moves between backstage space and onstage space throughout the performance number, LeGon is physically and musically segregated to the dressing room behind the curtain. The song that they sing together has no title and is not included in the credits for the film, effectively erasing LeGon's presence from the soundtrack. Nevertheless, the sequence lends LeGon's character a subjectivity that few Black maids are given and showcases LeGon's talents directly in counterpoint to Hutton's.

As a site of performance, the dressing room's power relationships and tensions move from private to public realms and from interiority to spectacle. Blossom performs as herself. It is her story of stardom and privilege that the number celebrates. As the first curtain rises, we see Blossom standing with her back to the theater audience, wearing a pink bustier bodysuit and gold high heels, admiring herself in a large mirror studded with lights in the center of the stage. The setting is hyperfeminine, decorated with flowers and draperies in pastel colors of white and pink and an elaborate crystal chandelier overhead. There is a tufted table below the mirror that holds the symbols of female vanity, including a hand mirror, brush, and powder puff. Draperies enclose the space and conceal the closets full of costumes.

Blossom calls for Delilah, whose entrance from one of the closets is punctuated by a change in the orchestration to a burlesque-style trilling of horns. Delilah wears a white lace apron and cap and a short black dress, the uniform of the maid and a symbol of her servility. But the two women share in the project of the dressing room, to prepare the star for her performance. They stand together in the center of the stage, bobbing in time. Delilah sings,

> Heard ya callin', heard ya callin', Miss Blossom
> Ain't this dressin' room a pretty sight?
> Watcha need, watcha wearin', Miss Blossom?
> Do ya want a dress that's comfy or tight?

Like a backup singer, Delilah's function is to soothe and amplify the lead performer. When Blossom returns to the dressing room later in the medley, Delilah gratifies her employer's ego, saying, "That was really something special, Miss Blossom. Betcha Mr. Ziegfeld had a smile." The sequence performs the reliance of white women on Black ones in order to effectively dress the part of the star.

Spatially, the archetype of the white female star traverses both narrative and performance and the Black maid remains in enclosed space. While she and Blossom occasionally perform the same movements, Delilah is always positioned a step behind Blossom, reinforcing Blossom's superior social position. Her anterior location becomes all the more apparent when the spotlight turns on and the curtain closes on Delilah, an action that is repeated twice in the medley; as our view of the dressing room closes, so does Delilah's access to the space of performance outside. Blossom moves outside the dressing room to sing two duets as different characters, an elegant lounge singer in "Rose Room" and a sexy jazz singer in "Way Down Yonder in New Orleans," while Delilah remains fixed in place and identity.

Delilah defies this fixity in subversive ways. Before hanging Blossom's pink boa in the closet, she quickly tries it on, shimmying with it while Blossom's back is turned. This brief indiscretion warrants a look of rebuke and the order to hurry with the next costume. Delilah hands her the new dress and belts the line, "And you've got every other singer beat, by a long, long mile." Singing "long, long," Delilah improvises and elongates the words so as to showcase the low and high registers of her voice. The lyrics she sings fulfill her role as support to Blossom, but the manner in which she sings them poses a provocative challenge. Delilah finishes her impromptu solo, looking pleased with herself and smiling at the camera. Blossom responds with an angry expression and a quick "thanks" before she exits the dressing room once more. At this point, the curtain never reopens to reveal Delilah. Instead, the end of the number is marked by Blossom and her male costar taking bows in front of the audience.

While Delilah's subordinate status is firmly established, spatially and formally, she uses these same techniques of cinematic language to break free from her constraints, if only for a moment. As in *Easter Parade*, LeGon's character in *Somebody Loves Me* performs the stereotype of the insubordinate Black servant. She wears Blossom's boa and co-opts a line in the song in order to showcase her own vocal prowess. But these moments of Black transgression are liberatory.

The white star (Betty Hutton) and her Black maid (Jeni LeGon) perform a dressing room scene. *Somebody Loves Me*, copyright 1952 by Paramount Studios. From the author's personal collection.

LeGon's characters are transgressive, constantly threatening to overturn the balanced system of power in the dressing room. Delilah claims the spotlight and reveals that her own talents match, and potentially exceed, those of her mistress. She exposes the power differential in the dressing room as a construction, like the dressing room number itself, and one that can be easily challenged. For a brief moment, Delilah claims the dressing room as a space of potential for herself.

Ultimately, however, the film contains both Black and white women's transgressions with the musical numbers that appear adjacent to the dressing room sequence. The song that immediately follows Delilah's misbehavior is one in which Blossom stages an act of racial appropriation. She sings of the "Creole babies" whose "flashing eyes softly whispering tender sighs" provide comfort and enjoyment "way down yonder." The number confirms her white dominance and perpetuates the fiction of the docile Black body, a myth that Delilah has just proved to be false. In the second instance, Blossom embodies the Black performer by wearing Blackface and singing a medley of "Mr. Banjo Man" and "Dixie Dreams," two songs that situate the "antebellum idyll" (as opposed to the modern city) as the rightful home for Black people.[34] Again, Delilah's very sophisticated performance in the dressing room provides a corrective to this belief, rendering the film's multiple representations of Blackness discontinuous.

Like earlier backstage films in which Black maids appear, the film is invested in using gender to re-establish the boundaries of race. These, however, also use heteronormative systems of control to discipline gender. While Blossom contains Delilah's transgressions, it is Blossom's love interest and eventual husband, Benny Fields (Ralph Meeker), who disciplines her. The timing of the dressing room number, which exalts but, with the use of Delilah, also qualifies Blossom's stardom and talent, is significant. It occurs just after she has met Benny and already attempted to control him by offering him an inferior part in her show. The number confirms Blossom's identity as star inasmuch as it relegates Benny to the role of secondary player. They marry, but Benny gets tired of being "Mr. Seeley." He divorces Blossom and strikes out on his own. It is not until Blossom decides to give up her own career in support of his that the film allows the couple to reunite. As she tells the audience upon making the decision, "I've got the billing I've always wanted, Mrs. Benny Fields." In the end, she performs the role of wife, erasing her professional identity as star in the process.

Foreground

LeGon's relatively transgressive roles in these musicals stand apart from the maid's conventional docility in the backstage narrative and place her in the liminal, middle-ground position of being neither silenced nor given full expression. *Imitation of Life* (1959), released only seven years after LeGon upstaged Hutton in *Somebody Loves Me* and over a decade before the maid's last appearance in *Funny Lady*, does more than any other backstage narrative to foreground the maid as a person and as a social being. Played by Juanita Moore, Annie is maid to Miss Lora (Lana Turner), a striving single mother whose dream is to become an actress. The film follows the pattern of a backstage film as it charts Lora's rise to fame after a series of struggles and setbacks. Also in keeping with the trajectory of the white protagonist in such films, Lora ultimately realizes success but quickly questions its value, acknowledging that "something is missing."

The scholarship on *Imitation of Life* has focused on the film's relationship to genre. Most prominently, scholars have analyzed *Imitation of Life* as a melodrama for its emphasis on the relationships between mothers and daughters and its orientation in domestic space.[35] Second to this interpretation is the analysis of *Imitation of Life* as a social problem film for its overt treatment of race and gender in midcentury American society.[36] And more recently, Gwen Bergner has argued for its consideration as a "melodrama-noir hybrid" for the ways that Douglas Sirk portrays the character of Sarah Jane, Annie's light-skinned Black daughter, as a femme fatale.[37] Building on this generic fascination with the film, and understanding that, as Jackie Byars has observed, "no single approach can account for the complexity and ambiguity of this film," I suggest that reading *Imitation of Life* against the long history of backstage narratives yields new insights about the role of the maid as well as the relationship between race and mobility more broadly in American film.[38]

While Lora's identity as an actress has received much attention in the scholarly literature, primarily for its narrative departure from the earlier 1934 production, Sirk's version places the film and its director in conversation with backstage stories and their attendant themes of mobility, belonging, and success in American life. As this book demonstrates, while filmmakers have positioned women most often at the center of these films, they have also used the backstage realm to convey and complicate what female success means, both to the woman herself and to society as a whole. By 1959, the trope of the working mother on the stage was well established (see chapter 3); but while the majority of these narratives were sympathetic toward women's struggle and ultimately reaffirm woman's place in marriage and the home, *Imitation of Life* goes furthest to reprimand its actress protagonist and to leave the outcome of her actions unsettled. As Byars has argued, for Sirk, a "woman choosing to work outside the home poses threat enough, but choosing acting as a career damns her more quickly than anything else."[39] And as Lucy Fischer has explored in an essay on Sirk's earlier backstage melodrama, *All I Desire* (1953), the director associates actresses with "excess" and "sexual exhibitionism" and portrays them as "an enemy of marriage, and an emasculator of men."[40] But while Sirk delivers a critique of Lora, as an actress who shirks her maternal role and forgoes marital happiness, he is also providing a critical assessment of the type of entertainment that Lora performs, the commercial theater of Broadway. In an interview with Michael Stern, Sirk described Lora as a "lousy actress" who "got to where she was by luck, or bullshit, or what-do-I-know, by dumb audiences."[41] Lora is doubly condemned as a result: she is not only an actress but an actress in a form of entertainment that serves and is shaped by a mindless public.

It is perhaps more accurate to think of *Imitation of Life* as an "anti-backstage film," in which the codes and conventions of the genre are presented and then subverted or turned inside out so as to prevent any legitimation of popular entertainment or belief in its representation of American opportunity. Sirk uses the backstage space self-reflexively as a comment on backstage film conventions, extending the application of the theme of "imitation" that is the film's title. Suggesting how Sirk's backstage setting instantly unsettles our relationship to the entertainment being provided, Charles Affron asks, "Can we be lost in the illusion if we witness it from backstage?"[42] In this case, the illusion is not the quality of Lora's acting—indeed, Sirk denies us any views of Lora's performances—but the ideology of the backstage narrative itself.

Central to the critique of the backstage is the falsity of relationships that it relies on. The maid is the symbol of all that the white female protagonist strives for—status, luxury, and support as she climbs to the top of the entertainment profession. In this way too Sirk delivers what we expect to see in a backstage film. As soon as Lora gets her break on Broadway, Annie appears as her backstage maid, joining a long line of real-life and cinematic examples of maids who follow their mistresses from home to stage. The *New York Amsterdam News* reported that Ethel Walker, maid to Hollywood actress Betty Compson, "ha[d] charge of the home, laundry, meals" and "accompanie[d] Miss Compson to the studio to take charge of her bungalow dressing rooms."[43] And we see the maid appear in both domestic and professional spaces in numerous films, including *The Marriage Clause* (1926), *Bombshell* (1933), *I'm No Angel* (1933), and *Easter Parade* (1948). Annie follows this trajectory once Lora achieves fame on the stage, denoted tritely in a conventional montage. The images of marquees and clapping audiences dissolve into one another on the screen and move us through time, conveyed by the years that successively flash on the screen. The montage soon reveals Annie backstage, clapping for Lora from the wings, with the image of the Music Box marquee and the year 1949 superimposed on her body. In this shot, Annie wears a maid's uniform, a drab gray dress with white lace collar, her body visually linked with Broadway and the passage of time; in this sequence, we learn how Lora has become a star and Annie has become the backstage maid who is both the reason for and the product of her mistress's success.

After the acclaim that the montage suggests, we see what the backstage film would have us expect: Lora has risen so far that she deserves a Black maid in her dressing room. Annie has become a status symbol and the caretaker of her mistress.[44] The continuity script for the film emphasizes Annie's anterior location, describing her actions while Lora and her producer exchange lines: "Annie is seen in the background, hanging up clothes."[45] The familiarity of Annie's presence and her behaviors aligns with Sirk's intent for the role, which was to portray the "typical Negro, a servant" who depended on her white mistress.[46] In Juanita Moore, producer Herbert Ross believed he had located such a typical figure, telling the press that the actress's "sincerity, warmth and natural qualities won the role."[47]

But as Sirk lays the foundation of the familiar, he just as soon disrupts it. The script emphasizes repeatedly how "Annie is seen" in the wings and in the background of the dressing room, drawing our attention to her location. Making her

Annie (Juanita Moore) moves to the foreground. *Imitation of Life*, copyright 1959 by Universal Pictures.

physical positionality in backstage space explicit, Sirk forces us to reckon with her social position as well. Annie's presence is overt, nearly taking over the frame in certain instances and distancing us from Lora. The script repeatedly directs Annie to move from background to foreground, sometimes standing or crossing in front of Lora. The result is an eclipse effect: Annie momentarily overwhelms Lora in the frame, her body in shadow but dominant compared with Lora's well-lit, relatively diminished figure. The dressing room scene opens with such a framing as Annie's figure crosses in front of the camera to reveal Lora seated at her dressing table. The second framing occurs near the end of the scene. Annie again moves into the foreground, her back to the camera and in nearly complete shadow as Lora faces her and exclaims, "Oh, Annie, what would I do without you!" Placing Annie between the audience and Lora creates a tension, a physical barrier between the audience and the characters we are trying to understand. Because we are not permitted to see Annie's reaction to Lora, the statement never receives a response and we are left to wonder what Annie really thinks.

Annie's moments in the foreground are juxtaposed to her mirrored reflections in the scene. Sirk moves Annie into and out of Lora's dressing table mirror. While Annie never looks at herself in the mirror, a privileged action for self-introspection, she repeatedly looks at Lora in the mirror. And Lora often returns the look. But these moments in which the white and Black women gaze at each other are mediated through the reflection, never direct. Sirk uses the lights of the dressing table to direct our gaze to the mirror at the right of the frame, rather than the shadowed profilmic space in which the characters are positioned. As a result, we encounter the women's relationship as a projection of their real selves, a performance of maid and mistress. Annie's presence in the mirror is far more substantial than that of any other maid in backstage film, and it signals the extent to which her subjectivity as a person and as the representative of a marginalized group constitutes the thematics of the film. As this dressing room scene reveals, the film is less concerned with assessing Lora's professional talent and personal choices and more invested in troubling the relationship between Lora and the Black woman she takes for granted. As Annie later tells Lora, who has expressed dismay that her maid has a wider social life beyond the home, "Miss Lora, you never asked."

To further complicate the backstage narrative, Sirk includes a second dressing room scene in which Annie does not appear. Lora has risen even further on Broadway. Her dressing room is opulent with upholstered furniture, plush carpet, and gilt décor. She stands in the room after a performance, bedecked in a white, sequined party gown, receiving dozens of visitors. A maid stands in the background closet hanging up clothing; it is not Annie but a white woman. Upending the convention, Sirk removes Annie from the dressing room just as Lora achieves the apex of her career. But Annie's absence does not imply that her mistress is no longer privileged and status hungry; the decoration of the dressing room prevents that interpretation. Nor does it imply that Annie no longer functions as a maid, since the subsequent shot is of Annie wearing her maid's dress while she works in Lora's kitchen. What this scene does signal is another example of Lora's falseness when it comes to her understanding of Annie. The dressing room scene follows a curtain call in which Lora and an interracial cast of actors take their bows. Playing a "social worker" in this new play, Lora has departed from her more frivolous roles in order to do something "important." While we are not given details about the performance—again, we do not actually see any part of it—we are made to understand by the suggestion of its importance and its cast that the play is about race relations. As the camera cuts to shots of the applauding audience, we see Black patrons mixed with white ones in the theater, a suggestion that this play is doing the work of fighting segregation. To employ Annie in her dressing room would undercut Lora's efforts to portray herself as the socially aware person she strives to be. But lest we believe that Lora has turned an enlightened corner, Sirk emphasizes how Annie has receded into the background once again, a space where we see her but Lora's adoring public does not. In this way, the sequence from curtain call to dressing room to kitchen reveals Lora's imitation of a social conscience.

Imitation of Life goes to great lengths to show the problem of Annie, and more specifically the problem of Annie and Lora, moving Annie from the background to the foreground and back again. But it does not go so far as to give the Black woman her own dressing room and the attendant experiences of self-realization and upward mobility that the space promises. This is where the missed opportunity of Sarah Jane (Susan Kohner), Annie's daughter, comes in. For while we never see Lora's performances, no doubt a comment on her "lousy acting," but do enter (twice) into her dressing rooms, we see Sarah Jane's performances on two different stages, but neither sequence provides a corresponding, and expected, dressing room scene. After her first performance at Harry's Club, Sarah Jane stands in the wings, where Annie confronts her. And the second performance, at the Moulin Rouge, a glitzy nightclub with a large cast of showgirls, is followed not by a dressing room scene but rather by a scene in a motel room where Sarah Jane changes out of her costume and meets Annie for the last time.

The absence of Sarah Jane's dressing rooms is another of Sirk's revisions of backstage film conventions. So odd is the omission that at least one scholar has mistakenly remembered dressing room scenes where they do not exist in the film.[48] But the very expectation that Sarah Jane should have a dressing room underscores the significance of its absence. As a light-skinned Black woman, Sarah Jane's race is intimately bound with her expression of sexuality. Her performances are erotic spectacles during which she attempts to achieve admiration as a white woman from white patrons. With Sarah Jane, Sirk engages what Sandy Flitterman-Lewis has referred to as the "sexualization of the radical 'otherness' of the black woman."[49] Because the logic of the film understands Sarah Jane as Black, albeit light skinned, she embodies racialized notions of Black women's, and especially the mulatto's, "natural" sexuality. Her performances, then, are not the result of labor and hard work but rather the organic expression of an already sexual being.

Kohner's identity as the daughter of Jewish talent manager Paul Kohner and Mexican actress Lupita Tovar led contemporary observers to see affinity between the actress and the character she played. Hedda Hopper referred to Kohner's "exotic appeal," with "burning slant eyes inherited from her Latin mother, and a sensuous smoldering quality which makes her ideal for off beat characters." In this case, "off beat" refers to "otherness," as Hopper explained that Kohner repeatedly played non-Anglo characters: "She has played an Italian girl twice, half Indian with Richard Widmark, the resentful mulatto in 'Imitation of Life,' and a young Judean girl and boy in 'The Big Fisherman.'"[50] Kohner's real-life distance from whiteness informed her role as Sarah Jane in ways that allowed contemporary observers to make a causal connection between being nonwhite and possessing "earthy," sexual qualities. Sarah Jane has no need for a dressing room because she has no need for transformation; she is always and already the person she projects on the stage.

Denying her the dressing room, however, also signals that Sarah Jane is doomed to failure. Not only is she refused the tools of transformation that the space furnishes, she must also forgo the opportunity for mobility and success that the transformation of the self conveys to the backstage film's audience. Whereas dressing room scenes would lend Sarah Jane moments of self-realization, personal makeover, the opportunity to experience female collectivity, and perhaps even the opportunity to challenge the notion that being Black condemns her to a life of tragedy, Sarah Jane's non–dressing room scenes seal her unhappy fate. These scenes with Annie in the wings of Harry's Club and the motel near the Moulin

Rouge do exactly what Sarah Jane does not want: they expose and restrict her as a Black woman once more.

Considering how *Imitation of Life* intersects with and alters the backstage film demonstrates the ways that it uses the convention of the maid in order to complicate understandings of race and gender, and of Black servility and white female stardom, a relationship that the genre has repeatedly naturalized. Moving Annie to the foreground, Sirk shifts the semantics of the genre from one invested in white women's opportunities in American life to the largely unseen and unheard labor of the Black women who enable it. Looking closely at the dressing rooms that appear and do not appear in the film signals how Sirk viewed the maid as a subject in her own right and the relationship with the white mistress to be a problematic one. But with the lack of dressing rooms for Sarah Jane, Sirk also rejects the opportunity to give the Black woman access to the forms of social mobility that the backstage narrative offers. *Imitation of Life* remains the only backstage film in which the maid moves figuratively and physically to the foreground of the story, but with Annie's death and her daughter's lack of mobility, it ultimately restricts the potential for where Black women can go.

In July 2000, Juanita Moore told a *Los Angeles Times* reporter about the time she toured Harlem upon *Imitation of Life*'s release. She recalled with pride how the Apollo Theater's marquee read: "'Imitation of Life' Starring Juanita Moore." Moore remembered her initial reaction to the rare moment that she received star billing over her costar Lana Turner: "I thought Lana would have a fit if she saw that."[51] The interview eerily replicates the onscreen relationship between Annie and Lora, in which the former assumes the subordinate position to her mistress but has the occasional moment when she eclipses the star. *Imitation of Life* ends on one of these moments of eclipse, with a massive, spectacular funeral for Annie, who is finally able to take center stage, a scene that the *Daily Boston Globe* called "ridiculously incomprehensible" and "farcical for a modest housekeeper."[52] As discussed here, more subtle but significant moments of eclipse occur in Lora's dressing room. It is in that space that Annie's person literally and figuratively moves to the foreground of the space and the film narrative. But as the attitude of the *Globe* reporter suggests, the foreground is not logically appropriate for the maid. She belongs permanently in the background, silent and knowing her place.

The backstage film is a genre that allows for the exploration of women working in the public sphere, as it charts the rise of aspiring performers and explores the private lives of stars. Of all backstage spaces, the dressing room is where the cinematic audience understands what is at stake for these women. As an enclosed, quasi-domestic space that protects the woman from the public sphere but also readies her to occupy it, the dressing room is a critical site of female character development. The Black maid is crucial in this project, for she renders the dressing room a site of comfort and support for the white star, highlighting the transformational and liberatory qualities of whiteness with her own lack of social mobility and spatial fixity. The Black maid also serves as a corrective for the female lead, checking the elevated status that comes with stardom. Her earliest representation as a symbol of extravagance extended from real life to the screen, culminating in the subversion of LeGon's postwar characters and Moore's portrayal of the most fully realized backstage maid character in Hollywood cinema. In this way, the backstage film reveals the inherent tensions in a genre that seeks to both celebrate female achievement and curtail it. Maids are essential to this process. They render the dressing room an ideologically meaningful space for racial hierarchies and women's relationship to social mobility. Moving within and around this space for much of the twentieth century, the maids of backstage film ask us to reckon with our need for their presence and our refusal to see them.

The ubiquity of white female characters in backstage film is one reason that their backstage maids have so rarely moved to the foreground of our consciousness. White women populate the genre more than any other demographic, but their social position is no more secure for their dominance. It is the performance of a precarious white female identity to which I turn next.

2

Sisters

• •

> Sisters, sisters
> There were never such devoted sisters
> Never had to have a chaperone, no sir
> I'm here to keep my eye on her
> —*White Christmas* (1954)

The December 9, 1944, issue of the *New Yorker* features a dressing room scene on its cover, one of six times it would do so over the course of the twentieth century.[1] Of these, five of the illustrations showcase women.[2] To be sure, women have long been associated with the dressing room, and the dressing room with women. On the December 9 cover, the *New Yorker* fills the page with them. The image has a diagonal orientation in which blond chorus girls, wearing only a pair of black shorts and a brassiere, populate the cover from extreme foreground on the left to extreme background on the right. These women extend seemingly into infinity as they intently lean forward at an elongated dressing table to apply their lipstick. Staring at their reflections in the mirror, the women's faces are blank except for their bright red mouths. The occupants intently make themselves look exactly the same as the woman who sits on either side.

What strikes one about the image, in addition to its display of endless femininity, is its multiplication of white womanhood. Beyond sharing their wardrobe, their hair color, and their lipstick, these women share the benefit of white skin. It is not surprising that dressing rooms should be represented this way in 1944. While musical comedies, that genre of popular theater that relied on chorus girls en masse, occasionally featured nonwhite performers (*Show Boat* in

1927 and *Carmen Jones* in 1943 are cases in point), female spectacle on the stage relied on the conflation of beauty, sex appeal, and whiteness.[3] We see these qualities at work in the *New Yorker* cover, but there is an unsettling quality to the image as well. As the women's bodies lean forward to gaze at their featureless faces, they emit a sense of nervousness regarding their efforts to transform into an ideal. That this action extends diagonally into infinity suggests how these white women's attempts to self-distinguish are futile given that they are surrounded by replicas of themselves. This particular brand of white womanhood is marked by the expectation of transformation and mobility represented by the dressing room space, but also the sense that time is fleeting and their position is precarious. The *New Yorker* cover illustrates qualities of white womanhood that are made plain by representations of dressing rooms in popular culture broadly, and in film specifically. It echoes the ways that filmmakers use dressing rooms to demonstrate how social opportunity is tenuous, governed by time and threatened by female competition, but also a privilege granted to those with white skin.

Backstage films and dressing room scenes are where we consistently see assemblages of women sharing intimate space in this way. The dressing room's association with interiority and transformation signals the dynamic processes of public and private identity-making that are most often ascribed to women precisely because of social anxieties regarding woman's place, and especially the single woman's place, in society.[4] Women in dressing rooms are simultaneously desired objects aspiring to a feminine ideal and desiring subjects in search of self-distinction. It is this tension that the dressing room draws out, presenting a performance of female identity-making enacted by different kinds of women working in close proximity to one another. But this is where the *New Yorker* illustration and cinema diverge; films have long used the dressing room to rehearse the differences among women, the young and the old, the highbrow and the lowbrow, the experienced and the novice, the sexually liberated and the inhibited, the worthy and the unworthy. Similar to the "divided self" that Lucy Fischer identifies in 1940s melodramas, dressing room assemblages of women represent "a rupture in the social conception of woman."[5] The sheer variability of female types that appear in dressing rooms from the 1920s through the twenty-first century suggests cinema's recurring obsession with understanding the complexity of female identity. These sister acts are a performance in and of themselves; they tease difference out of the display of female multiples through themes of solidarity and competition.

This chapter explores groups of women as a central dressing room trope in backstage films. It ranges across early cinema, backstage musicals, melodramas, comedies, mysteries, and thrillers to chart how women come to know themselves and each other through the unique spatial and temporal dimensions of the dressing room. These scenes foreground women as spectacle by providing a performance of identity formation behind the stage. What is on display is not their talent but rather their tenuous social position, at the heart of which are anxieties about race and gender.

Girl Clusters

In his 1963 essay on the relationship between popular entertainment and capitalist production, Siegfried Kracauer uses the example of the Tiller Girls, a British dancing troupe known for the precision of their dance formations, to reflect on the loss of individuality and humanity. He opines, "They are no longer girls, but indissoluble girl clusters whose movements are demonstrations of mathematics.... The regularity of their patterns is cheered by the masses, themselves arranged by the stands in tier upon ordered tier."[6] These "girl clusters" were to be found everywhere in American popular theater of the early twentieth century. They manifested in the rise of musical comedy and the Ziegfeld Follies in particular. As Susan Glenn has documented, such women were dehumanized in their stage performances, associated with modern inventions like taxicabs and airplanes, luxury goods to be consumed like cigarettes and jewels, or domesticated animals like chickens and ponies.[7] Choreographers George Lederer, Ned Wayburn, and Busby Berkeley made a science out of categorizing and disciplining women's bodies on the stage, turning them into mass symbols of male mastery and control.[8]

In 1920s and 1930s Hollywood, backstage films, and especially the popular cycle of backstage musicals, featured clusters of women on the stage, using the sheer number of female bodies on the screen as a selling point. The ads for *42nd Street* (1933) promised the "200 loveliest girls alive assembled in one cast"; posters for *The Broadway Melody* (1929) emphasized that "all" would be talking, singing, and dancing; and graphics for these and other backstage musicals displayed women in multiples, wearing the same costumes, or in a *mise en abyme* construction wherein women appear as a series of repeating and diminishing reflected images. Busby Berkeley's spectacular choreography for these films, as Martin Rubin has shown, situates women and their body parts as interchangeable objects to be placed in an ever-shifting array of geometric forms and objects. Rubin argues that despite their cinematic innovations and association with modernity, the Berkeley numbers, and backstage musicals generally, hark back to earlier stage traditions that emphasize aggregation, conjuring feelings of "abundance, variety, and wonder," as opposed to the modern forms of "unity, continuity, and consistency." Governed by these two modes, the backstage musical "remains in a state of unresolved suspension between spectacle and narrative," he writes, with the stage numbers largely occupying the former and the backstage plots occupying the latter.[9]

Understanding the genre as being structured by such a rigid spatial division, however, misses an opportunity to appreciate the ways that girl clusters as spectacle are a fundamental component of the backstage realm as well.[10] As "backstage" stories, these films narrativize the women of the stage in order to satisfy our curiosity about who they are, why they do what they do, and how they interact with each other in private. Dressing room scenes at once propel the plot forward and stage their own performance of femininity.

These backstage spectacles exist in direct contrast with stage numbers. Whereas women on the stage are choreographed into rational and orderly formations, women in dressing rooms are irrational and disorderly. Away from the prying eyes of male control, they can be their true selves, emotional, messy, and unruly. If the stage is a place where women are disciplined, the dressing room is where they go to be free. If the stage is where organized movements synchronize with carefully crafted stage scenery and props, the dressing room is where groups of women vie for personal space amid a chaotic mise-en-scène of costumes, hat boxes, and toiletries. And if the stage is where time is structured to allow for a smooth-running show, the dressing room is where time is frenzied, a metaphor for chaotic womanhood that always threatens to derail the success of the performance. While backstage signage abounds to regulate female behavior, from "No Smoking" and "No Drinking" signs to admonishments about valuables and costumes, most films from this era make a point to demonstrate how women disregard and flout such directives.[11] In the silent backstage drama *Pretty Ladies* (1925), for example, one chorus girl deliberately lights up a cigarette under a dressing room No Smoking sign. Another keeps a small dog next to her toiletries, while a third hides a baby in a box under her shared dressing table. These acts of female subversion balance the loss of power that occurs on the stage, restore women's humanity, and allow opportunities for female relationships away from masculine control.

To be sure, however, the satisfaction of male pleasure remains a foundational component of how dressing room scenes are conceived, structured, and filmed. As places wrought with titillating potential, dressing rooms have long been associated with female sexuality, voyeurism, and male pleasure, extending back to the introduction of women to the stage. As Rosamond Gilder documents, gentlemen's penetration of female dressing rooms, then referred to as "tiring rooms," was a common practice in Restoration theaters.[12] The feminine nature of the space, however, rendered it both exciting and something to be feared. In her study of the dressing room in eighteenth- and nineteenth-century English literature, Tita Chico emphasizes how dressing rooms were spaces that contained the tools for feminine dissembling; in dressing rooms, women had access to forms of dress, hair, and makeup that could lure and deceive men.[13] It was women's dressing as well as their undressing that drew men to the dressing room and signaled the need for male intervention.

Early American cinema revealed a fascination with dressing rooms as a setting for any number of scenarios involving female performers. In films like *From Showgirl to Burlesque Queen* (1903), the woman teases the (male) viewer by dipping behind a dressing screen just as she is about to remove all her garments, enticing him to keep watching as she reemerges in a burlesque costume. These striptease acts of the dressing room played out in real life as well. One notice in *Variety* reported that five chorus girls "were fined for displaying themselves in a nude condition before an open dressing room window" in a theater in Washington. The paper notes that the women were "careless" and had to pay a fine as punishment, but it is just as likely that the women enjoyed staging a show backstage as well.[14]

Most dressing room films of this era, however, show the space as one of unruly sisterhood into which men are drawn. The popular figure of "Mr. Jack" is a case in point. In at least two films, *Mr. Jack in the Dressing Room* (1904) and *Mr. Jack Is Caught in the Dressing Room* (1904), a portly older man enters a dressing room occupied by three chorus women. The women make a fool of the interloper by dressing him in women's clothes in the former and dousing him with soapy water in the latter. Both films were created on the same set and with the same cast, offering variations on dressing room activities while foregrounding dressing rooms as a space where women repeatedly threaten male dominance. The visual clutter of the space, with toiletries spread across the shared table in the background and costumes and clothing casually slung over chairs, is women's weapon against male intruders who are seeking to catch a glimpse of their private, collective world. In later dressing room films, mirrors serve as instruments of self-introspection, but in these early iterations, they reflect and amplify the chaos within, providing alternate views of men in women's clothing and female collusion.[15]

Casting female collectives as deviant and subversive was a frequent strategy of early Hollywood backstage musicals as well. The chaotic female dressing room appears again and again in films of this era. The unruliness of the space, and the women within, lends itself to deviant behaviors like smoking, nudity, and sexual perversion. In *The Broadway Melody* (1929), for example, we enter the chorus dressing room with a long shot in which women at dressing tables flank either side of the frame, with hanging costumes bifurcating the space. Stockings, clothing, and electrical cords hang from the rafters as dozens of girls excitedly chatter, monitored by a large, mannish matron dressed severely in dark clothes; her physical presentation is in stark contrast to the naked femininity that surrounds her. Into this confusion enters the effeminate costume designer, whom "the nearly nude girls seem to regard ... as one of themselves [rather] than as a man," the script describes.[16] As the women rush out of the room to make their cue, the matron takes pleasure in repeatedly spanking them as they leave. Gender and sexuality slip in this scene, registering the extent to which contemporary audiences associated Broadway with homosexuality, but also the ways that the dressing room is a site where homosexual identities can be given private expression.[17]

It was also in this period of backstage film production that directors teased audiences with access to the dressing room. As in the examples from the first decade of the twentieth century, many films from this era position the camera inside the space, asserting the privilege of the film spectator. By contrast, director Alan Crosland emphasizes how the camera is a peeping tom in *On with the Show* (1929) by placing it in front of a physical barrier that then gets removed. In this case, he locates the camera inside a wardrobe so that our view of the dressing room is initially blocked by dozens of hanging costumes. After a few seconds, a chorus girl pushes the costumes to the side and her nearly naked body fills the frame before she steps aside to be replaced by her fellow chorus members in various states of dress, each of whom removes one of the costumes from the foreground of the frame. As they do so, the audience gets a fuller glimpse of the dressing room, where women scramble to dress and quickly exit the space. The film's language treats this dressing room scene as a show within the show. Not only are we made aware that we are watching a scene unfold, perhaps surreptitiously given the camera's position, but the film makes a formal association between the raising of the proscenium curtain, which precedes the wardrobe shot, and the parting of the dressing room costumes. As the show begins for a theater full of patrons, the film cuts to a performance of a different sort and one that is the privilege of a select cinema audience.

The peeping camera reemerges four years later in a dressing room in *Gold Diggers of 1933*. Director Mervyn LeRoy places the camera behind the women's costumes, large cylindrical discs of sheer fabric that, when lined up together, obscure our view of the space. We learn later that the costumes are a part of choreographer Busby Berkeley's "Shadow Waltz" number, in which dozens of women, looking exactly like, play violins atop a series of curvaceous staircases. The symmetry and elegance of the number, however, play in contrast to the dressing room scene that it follows, which is one of visual clutter and confusion. As the film progresses to the "Shadow Waltz" number, we see how once again, disorderly women are disciplined into orderly formations and movements. This happens on an auditory level as well as a visual one. The film effectively silences what had been a cacophony of competing women's voices, frequently referred to in the dialogue script as a "confusion of girls' voices," in the dressing room into the melodious harmonies of a female chorus who echo Dick Powell's refrains.[18]

The male voyeurism that the peeping camera embodies, however, ultimately grants access to a space that is governed by a female collective. In the dressing room, we see women interacting with women. In *On with the Show* and *Gold Diggers of 1933*, we get only a brief glimpse of this dynamic, but in other examples from the first few decades of film production, we see a more sustained focus on and fascination with women's collectivity. In one of the earliest Edison films, *Larks behind the Scene* (1899), a chorus dressing room is the setting for female frivolity. Three women sit in the room in a state of transient dress with their shirtwaists open as they talk to one another. They appear to be drinking, as a few empty bottles are scattered around the floor. Another woman enters, picks up a bottle, and holds it high above her head. Two of the women stand, gather their skirts, and try to reach it by kicking their legs into the air. They laugh with one another as they do so, engaging in a mirthful activity of good-natured female competition. This early instance of female collectivity was referenced again and again in early cinema by the Mr. Jack films and others, like *The Gerry Society's Mistake* (1903), *Love and Jealousy behind the Scenes* (1904), *The Messenger Boy and the Ballet Girl* (1905), and *The Sleepy Soubrette* (1905), in which women help and enjoy one another's company in the dressing room.

Female mentorship, in which older women educate and prepare younger ones for the stage profession, is a common theme in dressing rooms as well. In this way, dressing rooms help to define these women's unique social position as single female workers. As Monica Stufft has documented in her study of chorus girl collectives, the everyday practices of chorus women, including the backstage rituals of applying makeup and adhering to codes of conduct, "shaped chorus girl communities" into a "shared chorus girl identity." In the dressing room, younger performers learned the tools of the trade, but also how to exert "territorial behavior en masse," protecting their space from unwanted intruders, applying social pressure to norms for sharing makeup and personal property, navigating relations with male suitors, and ultimately creating a kinship structure away from home.[19]

We see sisterly acts of mentorship in a film like *Love and Jealousy behind the Scenes*, in which older chorus members help the new ones get dressed in costume. But this mentorship could also take the form of initiation, as when chorus women tease a younger member for her modest pretentions by toppling the dressing screen where she is hiding from a male visitor in *In the Dressing Room* (1903). As a later *Esquire* article that promised to reveal "what chorus girls talk about" described, a younger member of the dressing room was "shocked" to find that the girls were "sneaking smokes, although smoking was strictly forbidden in dressing-rooms to anybody but the stars." "One or two tippled from whiskey bottles they had hidden in their lock-up make-up boxes," the witness went on. "They seemed to be the older girls." When one of the women told a "smoke-room story," the sort that only occurred in homosocial male domains, further shocking the ingenue, another chorus girl took pity on her, confiding that the women were merely initiating her into the ways of the space. The younger girl reflected to the *Esquire* author, "I found out that their usual conversation wasn't as tough as they made it that first night—for my benefit. But there was always an undercurrent of the underworld about those dressing-rooms."[20] The naïve chorus girl who enters a dressing room full of "sadder but wiser" women is a theme that would continue well into the twenty-first century and was a central plot device for characterizing the costs and consequences of the pursuit of stardom. From classical Hollywood backstage films like *Floradora Girl* (1930), *Ziegfeld Girl* (1941), and *Lady of Burlesque* (1943) to much later iterations of the plot device like *Showgirls* (1995) and *Burlesque* (2010), female mentorship and initiation offer filmmakers the opportunity to explore a range of female identities and to engage in an exploration of how those identities correspond to contemporary expectations of private female behavior and public expressions of their need for work and desire for a career.

The Color Line

Clusters of women in the dressing room have allowed directors of backstage films to represent an array of female types and to delineate the pleasures and perils of women on the stage. The films portray these women's social position as employed workers to be unstable, which is a common plot device in moments of economic downturn such as the Great Depression (*Gold Diggers of 1933*) and the 2008 recession (*Burlesque*). More generally, however, the genre emphasizes the insecurities women face as a result of competition with other women and the limited number of resources and opportunities available to them. As films like *Ziegfeld Girl* make clear, only some women can succeed at improving their station in life, while others will fail. In the first dressing room scene, populated by the new crop of Ziegfeld girls, the women sit at attention as the manager gives them instructions for their first performance. A prominent "No Drinking Allowed" sign hangs in the background over the girls' heads, a foreshadowing of the problem alcoholism will become for one of them. The manager's speech outlines the ways in which the women are on the threshold of potential success or failure. "Some of you," he explains, "are going to wind up with your names up in electric lights." He continues, "Some of you are going to wind up with a husband and kids." The manager takes a pause before he warns, "And some of you are going to wind up, well, not so good." The film rests in close-up on the faces of the three main characters as he speaks these words, Susan (Judy Garland), Sheila (Lana Turner), and Sandra (Hedy Lamarr). The manager's speech causes a momentary pause in action in the dressing room, during which he communicates that the women stand on a precipice, a thematic and visual theme in this film about the Ziegfeld Follies, an entertainment tradition renowned for its placement of beautiful women on vertical, potentially dangerous pedestals. As the film later shows, some of these women will successfully sit atop the pedestal and others will fall off.

Ziegfeld Girl delineates the paths that three women will take, which consist of a set of very limited options—stardom, marriage, or death—against the backdrop of an entertainment tradition that values and venerates female whiteness. Linda Mizejewski has documented the many ways in which Ziegfeld presented his Follies performers as "100% American," a response to xenophobic reactions to the immigration waves of the early twentieth century as well as to the increasing popularity of African American chorus girls on Broadway.[21] With glowing white skin and white costumes, the Follies women descended white staircases to strains of songs that celebrated their white beauty. Such a scene unfolds after the dressing room speech just described. The women's jitters and frantic activities to dress backstage are wiped away with the raising of the curtain for the "Dream" number, in which Frank Merton (Tony Martin) croons to dozens of elegant and shimmering bodies as they slowly glide around the stage. But as the previous scene just revealed to us, these women have been carefully selected, taught, and shaped to embody an ideal. Frank Merton indicates as much in the song: "You stepped out of a dream, you are too wonderful, to be what you seem." The film has just showed us, however, that the women did not step out of a dream; they stepped out of a dressing room.

Dressing room scenes such as this one present the constructed nature of a white feminine ideal. But not all women, *Ziegfeld Girl* communicates, are up to the task. In this way, such films use race and racialized performance as a leveling force that reasserts white female privilege at the same time that it distinguishes between good white women and bad. The "Minnie from Trinidad" number is an example of such a process. Judy Garland's character Susan is the featured performer in the number, wearing "dusky belle" makeup along with her fellow Ziegfeld girls.[22] The tropical locale and costumes immediately distinguish the number from others in the show, as its subject is not white female beauty but a Trinidadian woman. Eye rolling, shoulder shimmying, and other excessive bodily gestures allow the women to be more physically expressive in this number. Cultural appropriation takes the place of Black performance in order to allow for the enjoyment of Black culture while maintaining the racial status quo, a process that is marked by both "love and theft," as Eric Lott has identified.[23] But this number is a plot device as well. It is the number that at once confirms Susan's star status, restores Sandra to her husband (who is credited for writing the hit number), and witnesses Sheila fall from her pedestal. "Minnie from Trinidad" therefore marks a turning point in the film in which racial appropriation separates the worthy from the unworthy.[24] Sequences in which white dominance is restored through the appropriation of Black bodies and culture mitigate any threats to established racial hierarchies. Such musical sequences in which racial appropriation enables, confirms, or restores white stardom also constitute critical narrative moments in *Babes in Arms* (1939), *Holiday Inn* (1942), *Easter Parade* (1948), *Somebody Loves Me* (1952), and *Love Me or Leave Me* (1955).[25]

As a space weighted with transformational potential and upward mobility, dressing rooms are rarely populated by Black artists.[26] For much of the twentieth century, backstage films denied Black performers access to the opportunities that the backstage space offered. But as I showed earlier, dressing rooms are critical to affirming racial hierarchies because of the social precarities experienced by the groups of white women within them. This dynamic plays out in the distribution reports for backstage films released by the Production Code Administration. Always requesting caution regarding the modesty of women's costumes, they make special note of dressing room scenes as being potentially problematic. In some cases, these fears manifested as overt concerns, such as when the censorship board in Trinidad rejected *The Broadway Melody* because of the "number of women" appearing "half dressed." "If shown," the board warned, "it would place the white woman in a degrading viewpoint before the large East Indian and Negro audiences," which "must be avoided at all costs."[27] Dressing room sequences made white women's bodies the site of both erotic pleasure and racial insecurity.

Two backstage films, *Fox Movietone Follies* (1929), an early sound-era musical revue, and *Lady of Burlesque* (1943), a "backstage mystery," use the dressing room's physical thresholds to stage corrective racial encounters for its chorus women. In these films, doorways, corridors, screens, and windows become the physical symbols of separation between the white and nonwhite peoples of the backstage world. In each, the liminality of the female dressing room is a prominent thematic and visual device for suggesting and overcoming white female precarity.

Fox Movietone Follies is one of a number of films released by the studios in 1929 intended to capitalize on the popularity of sound. Like *The Broadway Melody*, *Glorifying the American Girl*, *On with the Show*, and many others, *Fox Movietone Follies* uses the appeal of musical performance and curiosity about backstage life to craft a narrative about putting on a Broadway show that is in peril. The management is indebted to creditors and everything hinges on the success of opening night. Feelings of precarity and uncertainty abound with the unemployment of dozens of women seemingly imminent. These feelings are exacerbated by the arrival of George, a wealthy Virginian, who dislikes the fact that his girlfriend, Lila, is a chorus girl. In the process of trying to get her fired, George purchases interest in the show and spends the opening night bumbling the show's backstage preparations. The show does indeed go on, but not without significant confusion along the way.

As the reviews for the film point out, however, the standout performance of the film is by actor Lincoln Perry (aka "Stepin Fetchit"), who plays Swifty, a Black southerner who has migrated North to the big city and now works backstage at the theater. Performing the comic act of the lazy and shiftless Black man, Lincoln Perry perfected his Stepin Fetchit persona as a servant who "fetches" things for white characters but does so on his own time or not at all. That character is intact in *Fox Movietone Follies*, but with a distinct twist.[28] While the film reveals Swifty as having come from a plantation, he circulates exclusively in urban space. Unlike in *Hearts in Dixie*, Perry's earlier film released just before *Fox Movietone Follies* in 1929, in the later film the actor plays a character who is not fixed in a timeless, rural past but in the modern present. Swifty is not a member of the cast but is able to transform himself into a performer when the need arises. Contemporary reviewers attributed much of the film's comedy to Perry's performative acumen, describing how he is "the real hit and the sole comedy element in the picture" and asserting that he "runs away with all the honors that there are for laughs."[29] To comedic effect, Swifty embodies the South and the North, the field hand and the star performer, by conjuring the binary spaces of the rural plantation and the urban city at will. He is a migrant who performs the shifts in identity that characterize modern life.[30] In this way, *Fox Movietone Follies* is the rare film to admit to the mass migrations out of the South in preceding decades.[31] But while his migration grants him mobility, in this case between backstage and onstage, he must still observe racial boundaries. A liminal figure himself, he occupies the threshold spaces of the dressing room.

Swifty's constant presence outside the dressing rooms of the theater ensures the maintenance of the color line backstage and ameliorates the chorus girls' precarious existence. He delivers flowers and gifts to the chorus women across the doorway, confirming his lower social position as a Black servant while elevating the impression of white women's desirability. When the creditors come to collect the ballet slippers, Swifty uses the backstage corridors to confuse and dodge them, thus allowing the women to perform.[32]

Beyond being a servant who fetches and delivers, however, Swifty is a critical part of the conversations that happen regarding how the show will go on. These occur twice at the dressing room doorway between George and Lila. The first involves a missing costume for one of the leading women, another sign of female precarity in the show. Looking for a quick fix, George mistakes a young Black man who is part of a "colored troup" of entertainers to be a servant and orders him to exit the theater and retrieve the missing costume. When the entertainer responds, "But, I'm on next," George responds, "Don't waste time—her number goes on in a couple of minutes!" In his ignorance, George cannot fathom that Black people might be professional entertainers, not servants, a comment on his unfamiliarity with racial dynamics in the North. Furthermore, his privileging of the woman's number over the "colored troup" act reinforces the higher value given to white performances over Black ones. When George's blunder produces a crisis onstage, the manager asks Swifty to step in for the missing performer. Swifty quickly reveals that not only is he familiar with the number, but he is the one who originally wrote it.

The second scene in which Swifty saves the show takes place again in the dressing room corridor. Lila must change into the star's costume because the leading lady has unexpectedly quit. In order to buy time with the audience, Lila and George instruct Swifty to go onstage and do the dance he used to do "at the plantation." Swifty obliges and transforms himself into a performer once more. He sings a song that references both his character and his real-life persona:

Start steppin', Stepin Fetchit
Turn around, stop and catch it
Now and then if you miss it
Start again, Stepin Fetchit.

This self-reflexive moment performs Swifty's/Perry's liminality. He exists in the thresholds of backstage space, ready to wield either his southern or northern selves, as servant or star, as needed.

The dressing room window draws a color line of a different sort in *Lady of Burlesque*. Originally titled "The G-String Murder Case," after the novel by striptease artist and author Gypsy Rose Lee, the film is a backstage drama about a series of murders that occur in the dressing room of a burlesque theater. Starring Barbara Stanwyck as burlesque star Dixie Daisy, the film foregrounds the dynamics between the many dancers who share a dressing room placed precariously at the top of the stairs in the back of the theater. The film opens by emphasizing the multiplicity of women in the show with a montage credit sequence in which a series of dissolves provide close-ups of dressing tables, each lined with cage-enclosed vanity lights and populated with different configurations of makeup, jewelry, and other belongings. "Girls, that's what the public wants," the manager explains to a box office attendant after we see a shot of the marquee advertising, "Girls Girls Girls." A dozen of these girls share a dressing room, arranged at two rows of tables that line the perimeter of the space. The women commiserate about the difficulties of their work, from managing the audience to working the leaky toilet in the dressing room bathroom. It is an easily penetrated space, as demonstrated by the shared vent between the women's and men's dressing rooms, through which the two genders communicate and listen in on one another; as one dancer describes, "This place has as much privacy as a hot dog stand." The porousness of the room foreshadows the danger that they are all in. As Dixie discovers over the course of the film, someone in the theater wants to kill them. The murderer strikes soon, strangling a dancer in the dressing room bathroom with her own G-string.

Predation is an ongoing theme in the film that reaches its climax with a series of murders, but it is complicated as well by another dressing room threshold, the window that leads to the world outside. Early in the film, a dancer is livid at observing a group of Chinese men, cooks and waiters who are sitting on the stoop outside a restaurant kitchen window across the street. Positioned at eyeline level with the dressing room, the men appear to be peeping into the women's space. Enraged, the dancer throws a glass bottle through the window and exclaims, "Someone had to teach them that a lady's entitled to some privacy." The camera takes us through the window and outside to reveal a waiter clutching at his bruised head as his friends crowd around him. Dixie reprimands the dancer, explaining that they had a right to "their porch" and that it was probably hot in that kitchen. Revealing that the men are not predatory at all but rather in need of some fresh air, Dixie exits the dressing room through the window and crosses over to the Chinese restaurant. She places ice on the injured man's head, secures the promise that they will continue to provide the dancers food at no charge, offers tickets to the burlesque show, and restores peace between the two spaces. As a parting gift, the men give her a box of ginseng root that will make her "live a long time."

The sequence is unique for its representation of Asian characters in backstage film. Rarely do Asians appear in this genre except for as the occasional

Burlesque performers spot a Chinese waiter (uncredited) outside their dressing room window. *Lady of Burlesque*, copyright 1943 by United Artists.

manservant to a male star (see, for example, Peter Chong in *Easter Parade*, 1948). Typically, such a character has few speaking lines and miniscule narrative development in the film. *Lady of Burlesque*, by contrast, represents Chinese men in their own space as workers rather than servants. Casting them as predatory initially, per the burlesque dancer's point of view, the film then corrects and reverses that interpretation to reveal them as safe and even helpful to the women.

The prospect of men peeping into the dressing room has always been a subversive, predatory act. As Joseph I. Breen warned in the film's Production Code file, "We assume, of course, that all the various dressing room scenes, in which the girls are changing their clothes, will be handled without any unacceptable exposure." But this same letter also warned the filmmakers, "With regard to the portrayal of these Chinese, we suggest you get proper technical advice, to make certain that there is nothing in your finished picture that might cause you difficulty with your export license."[33] Casting the peeping men as racialized Others peering into a space where white women undress is extraordinary given the contemporary laws prohibiting miscegenation that were still in place in the 1940s. Perhaps for this reason, the filmmakers followed Breen's advice and requested input from Earl H. Leaf, then a correspondent for the Office of Strategic Services (later the CIA), who had worked as a journalist in China during the 1930s. Leaf suggested to producers that Gypsy Rose Lee's original text be followed in filming the sequence. He wrote, "In the scene where the Chinese waiters are cooling off on the porch overlooking the dressing room, it is hoped you will avoid making the Chinese appear offensively peeping or staring into the girls' dressing room." He affirms that Lee's explanation that the men were merely getting "a breath of fresh air from their hot kitchen" is "quite satisfactory." Citing the need for a correction of the representation usually allotted Chinese waiters in Hollywood film, Leaf suggests, "This one could be different," and observes that "treating them with some dignity would be a real goodwill gesture."[34] While Leaf's warning that the powers of ginseng root are more a superstition than a widely held belief in China ultimately went unheeded in the final picture, Lee's original sympathetic portrayal of Chinese men remained.

The marriage of white women's precarity and potential Chinese predation is a spectral bogeyman in the film that is quickly dispelled. The sequence emphasizes the porousness of the dressing room and the white women's vulnerability within. Significantly, it is Dixie who crosses the threshold to make amends; she ventures into a space that is both male and Other and uses her feminine wiles to rectify the grievance done to them at the hands of a white woman. But while the potential of Chinese men's surreptitious desire for white women is disavowed, it is ultimately redirected toward the more acceptable context of the audience–burlesque performer relationship. In the end, it is Dixie who defines the terms by which the men look at white women's bodies, reinscribing the color line vis-à-vis female performance, all the while protecting the intimate space of the dressing room.

Gender Trouble

Gender trouble pervades the dressing room as well, driven by the scarcity of professional opportunities and the resulting competition between women. The dressing room has been a site where women encounter one another under these desperate circumstances. The line between female friendship and female competition gets blurred in the space, aided by the liminal objects that converge inside and outside, such as reflective surfaces, doors, and screens. Reaching across these thresholds, women search for their true selves ("Who am I?"), but this process is always contingent on exploring the identities of other women first ("Who are you?").

This dynamic, in which women define themselves by who they are not, reflects the ways the genre has been complicit in disseminating male understandings of female identity and relationships. Indeed, there are very few backstage films directed by women; one of the most prominent, *Dance, Girl, Dance* (1940), is discussed here.[35] But despite these exceptions, the backstage and the dressing room largely have been conjured by the male imagination. Perhaps for this reason, films about female friendships are relatively few compared with the male "buddy" film. And stories about female relationships tend to skew toward dynamics of conflict and competition.[36]

Such contradictory interpretations were present at the beginnings of cinema. In *A Scrap in the Dressing Room* (1904), two chorus women, one dressed in white and the other in black, fight each other for the duration of the film. They tear each other's costumes and tug at each other's hair, falling over each other on the floor in the center of the shot while two other women look on in distress. The mirrors behind them reflect the fight from alternate angles, providing the film audience with two views of the action while magnifying it. One woman runs out the door to the right of the screen and reenters with a man who pulls the fighting women apart and admonishes them with pointed finger and raised fist. Chagrined, the women sit down at their respective dressing table stations and the man exits the frame. *A Scrap in the Dressing Room* plays on the assumption that women performers are querulous and prone to violence if left unattended.

In a film made one month earlier, however, the same production company, American Mutoscope and Biograph, used the same dressing room set, four female performers, and costumes in *The Gerry Society's Mistake* (1903). In that film, the women are not competitors but rather advocates for one another. When the male representatives of the Gerry Society, the organization that enforced child labor laws in New York City, mistake one of the chorus women for a child (she is dressed in the costume of a young girl), they come to her dressing room to expose her.[37] Her fellow performers rush to her aid, gesturing that the men are in error. One of the women opens a trunk at the foreground of the frame and pulls out a wedding ring. When the younger woman puts it on her finger, the men realize that she is indeed an adult and shamefully exit the room while being shoved and laughed at by the chorus women. That these two interpretations of the female dressing room could emerge from the same production company and occur in the same profilmic space signals the extent to which portrayals of group female behavior were varied and complex. While both films could be interpreted as examples of manipulative and deviant female behavior, the latter also opens up possibilities for female collective action and solidarity in the face of male authority. This embedded potential for multiple readings of sister acts in the dressing room accounts for the range of representations that exist.[38]

Dressing room fights make explicit the precarious world that women occupy as performers in popular entertainment. But dressing rooms also reveal the proximities between women, their shared social position that allows for moments of observation and reflection on female identity. These sister acts produce a performance of self-discovery through the discovery of another, delineating and sometimes blurring the differences between women for the film's audience, and ultimately rendering the dressing room as a site of female discovery for the characters within and the audience without. Films in which actual "sister acts" appear, such as *The Broadway Melody*, *The Hard Way* (1943), *The Dolly Sisters* (1945), and *White Christmas* (1954), expose the differences between two sisters that lead them toward different socially prescribed paths for women (career vs. romance). Here, I am interested in those films in which the dressing room is a performance space for female relations, both kinship and non-kinship, that walk the line between female treachery and sabotage, on one hand, and fascination and desire, on the other.

An early scene in *All about Eve* (1950), Joseph L. Mankiewicz's film about female treachery in the theater, brings the dynamics of identity discovery and transformation to the foreground. Soon after the opening sequence, in which a successful Eve, played by Anne Baxter, receives an Actress of the Year award, the film uses flashback and voiceover in order to explain the turn of events that led to her big night. The flashback transports us to the evening after a star performance by Margo (Bette Davis). Assisted by Karen (Celeste Holm), Margo's best friend and wife of the playwright Lloyd Richards (Hugh Marlowe), Eve gains access to Margo's backstage dressing room. Margo and her assistant Birdie (Thelma Ritter) are at first annoyed that Karen would do such a thing, bringing in those "autograph fiends," "little beasts that run around in packs like coyotes." But Karen insists that Eve is different and persuades Margo to let her in. During the subsequent sequence, Eve explains how she came to be Margo's biggest fan, gaining the sympathy and acceptance of all in the room.

Despite Margo's star status, her dressing room is a drab space. It has dingy wallpaper, worn furnishings, and wire hangers. Exposed pipes line the walls, which are dimly illuminated by encaged sconces. Untidiness and clutter mark the space as one that is both frequently used and carelessly tended. It is a casual and intimate room that forces the inhabitants into close proximity, signaling their longtime connection to one another.

Eve enters the space as an outsider. She is a stark contrast to Margo, who, despite wearing a robe and smearing cold cream on her face, still manages to convey her star quality. As Karen tells her, "You're talented, famous, wealthy, people waiting around night after night just to see you, even in the wind and the rain." By contrast, Eve is "the mousy one, with the trench coat and the funny hat." While Margo has everything a successful woman could desire, Eve has nothing. Margo represents all that Eve desires for herself. It is in this dressing room sequence that Eve moves from an outsider, standing and then sitting awkwardly against the wall, to an insider, gaining acceptance by Margo and her friends and earning entry into Margo's intimate space. Ultimately, Eve's fascination with Margo is revealed as a treacherous plot to replace Margo completely.

The dressing room's drab presentation serves as a backdrop for Eve's seduction of Margo. But the film sets up the space as a place of performance, an alternate stage where the "real and the unreal," as Eve says in her story, converge. It is a place for making and unmaking identities, first indicated by Margo's face slathered in cold cream. Despite her state of undress, Margo is still giving a performance in the dressing room. When Karen first enters, the camera is positioned to the right of the room and tracks backward to Margo's dressing table, following Karen's movement into the space and resting at a point to the right of the table to capture Margo doing an imitation of an interviewer she recently met. Lloyd, Karen, and Birdie are arranged in the middle and background of the frame as her audience. She theatrically grandstands once again in the later speech about "autograph fiends." Once she has finished, the film cuts to Lloyd in medium close-up giving applause.

These two sequences establish the dressing room as a space for putting on a show. The star turn of the evening, however, is delivered not by Margo but by Eve. The act of looking, identified by Jackie Stacey as being a critical part of the film's "construction and reproduction of feminine identities," is central to Eve's monologue.[39] But the film does not emphasize Eve, the fan, looking at Margo; rather, it emphasizes Margo, who watches Eve. Foreshadowing the ultimate replacement that will take place later in the film, Margo becomes the fan and Eve the star.

The film's formal language accomplishes this in a variety of ways. The scene is framed in long shot, allowing for Eve's entire body to be centered in the background. The camera sits behind the figures of Birdie, Margo, Karen, and Lloyd, who form an audience in rapt attention as Eve tells her story. The sconce positioned directly above Eve's head becomes a spotlight for the unfolding performance. While she tells how she married and lost a husband in the war, the film abruptly introduces a mournful musical score with string instruments that add emotional weight to her tale and end in a fade-out as soon as she is finished. The film also uses frequent point-of-view cuts to shots of Margo and the others, a common device in the performance sequences of backstage musicals to reveal the affirmation of the diegetic audience. These cuts to close-ups of Eve's audience similarly communicate to the audience that her story is effective. As she reaches the end, the film cuts again to Margo, who has been brought to tears and reaches for a tissue to blow her nose. Referencing the melodramatic nature of what they have just witnessed, Birdie quips, "What a story! Everything but the bloodhounds snapping at her rear end."

Later, the film will reveal Eve's monologue to be a fabrication. Her self-presentation as a lonely, poor, and starstruck girl is a construction for the purposes of gaining entry into Margo's life. The performative space of the dressing room sets the stage for Eve's presentation of an entertaining story as well as the kind of "make believe" that she admits to being seduced by. The space's transformational potential allows for the two women to merge and change places while calling female identity into question.

The destructive qualities of female fascination are even more pronounced in two films that place female competition at the forefront, *Dance, Girl, Dance* (1940) and *Black Swan* (2010). While the differences between them are immediately apparent—the former was directed by a woman in the midst of the studio system in the 1940s and the latter directed by an independent, male director in the twenty-first century—their similarities are striking. The primary protagonist is a "nice girl," virginal and with aspirations to be the best ballerina she can be, while the secondary protagonist is treacherous and sexually promiscuous and treats dance as a means to an end. It is the struggle between the two women, and especially the good girl's transformation into a different kind of woman as a result of that struggle, that lends the films their central point of drama.

As I explore in the video essay "Intimate Thresholds" (2022), both films also feature extensive scenes of violence in which the women brutally attack each other as a result of their proximity in the dressing room; their competition over resources, space, and men; and their ultimate conflation into one, more fully realized woman.[40] In *Dance, Girl, Dance*, Dorothy Arzner establishes the precarity of the female dancers when the police raid the nightclub where they perform, throwing the women into a state of unemployment. They struggle to find work in New York, but to no avail until Bubbles (Lucille Ball) gets a job in a burlesque house. She needs a stooge for her act, someone who will play the "straight" woman to her striptease, and she offers it to her fellow dancer Judy (Maureen O'Hara), who personifies the "good girl" type that Bubbles is looking for. The film is in many ways an exercise in delineating the differences between women. Whereas Judy is chaste and thoughtful, Bubbles is promiscuous and rash. Whereas Judy dances ballet as a spiritual calling, Bubbles bumps and grinds for financial gain. And whereas Judy's dancing is highbrow and bores the audience, Bubbles's is lowbrow and excites them. This discrepancy and the ultimate humiliation of Judy as the stooge drove one *Variety* reviewer to comment that the film "unfolds more like a tragedy" than a musical comedy.[41]

Judy and Bubbles share a dressing room at the burlesque theater. This tight and enclosed space is the site where the two women prepare for their respective, divergent acts. Like the theater in which it sits, the dressing room is run down, with discolored walls and paint-chipped furniture. A screen stands in the background, allowing the women some measure of privacy when they change costumes, but the room is so porous given its proximity to the stage that the male managers enter and exit at will and the music and applause from the night's performance spill in.

Arzner draws out the significance of the two spaces, the stage and the dressing room, and their relationship to each other in a scene after Judy's first performance in the burlesque house. She performs the ballet number straight, to the boos and hisses of the audience. Coming offstage, she learns that she has infuriated the audience with her performance, making them hungry for Bubbles's more erotically satisfying act. Dejected, Judy makes her way back to the dressing room just as Bubbles passes her to take the stage. What follows is a crosscutting sequence between stage and dressing room, revealing in tandem the two women's simultaneous actions in each. First, the film rests on a shot of the closed stage curtains, through which Bubbles bursts to thunderous applause and poses awhile to lap it up. The film then cuts to another entrance, Judy hurriedly opening and closing the dressing room door behind her. She too stands at this threshold a moment, taking in what has just happened to her on the stage. The music and the applause provide a sonic bridge across the two spaces, present in more muted fashion in the dressing room but clearly establishing a continuity between both realms. After cutting back to Bubbles as she moves from curtain front to the middle of the stage, the film presents another parallel shot of Judy moving to a chair where she sits, tearfully glances at herself in the mirror, and then dejectedly rests her head on the table. Here the film cuts once again back to Bubbles, who is strutting on the catwalk, and we see a shot of the largely male audience smiling and clapping as she does so. Bubbles then launches into her number, "The Jitter Bug Bite," a song that explores the differences between women who are "ladies" and those who want to have fun.

Crosscutting sequences are rare in dressing room scenes. Typically, they are self-contained and enclosed moments in backstage film, privileging the dynamics within rather than the spaces outside. In Arzner's film, however, it is precisely the dynamic between outside and inside that she wishes to emphasize. As the more outgoing and popular of the two women, Bubbles's space is the stage, a site of public spectacle and female objectification. Judy's introspective and shy demeanor finds her better suited to the interior world of the dressing room, where the only person looking at her is herself. Both women enter their respective spaces through a threshold, blurring the line between inside and outside. Arzner uses these thresholds to demonstrate how there is both a difference and a continuity between the processes of looking and being looked at. It also matters, she suggests, who is doing the looking. These are gendered processes, as many feminist scholars have asserted about women's cinema generally; they involve women "looking back at ourselves" as the creators of film, as spectators of film, and as characters within film.[42] In this moment, the spectator is given multiple examples of women and their relationship to looking. On the stage, we see Bubbles looking at her burlesque audience and being looked at by them. And in the dressing room, we witness Judy looking at herself in the mirror as well as witnessing the act of looking at herself. Such mirror shots transform the woman into spectacle, echoing the dynamics of the stage but also capturing the process of being both subject and object at once. These shots hold spectacularization and self-reflection in balance. With this sequence, Arzner manages to spatially delineate the difference between the two women and, through framing and crosscutting, establish their shared social position as women.

Most attention to *Dance, Girl, Dance* has emphasized the importance of Judy's later monologue in which she talks back to the burlesque audience, an overt challenge to patriarchy, as Donna R. Casella has described.[43] Indeed, the moment is arresting for the ways that it reverses the hierarchy between male/subject and woman/object in the backstage musical and Hollywood cinema more broadly. But the earlier dressing room sequence also draws and disrupts these divisions. Judy is at once empowered by the camera to look at herself in the mirror, look at herself looking, and react to what she sees. By framing these shots with Bubbles's more traditional display of female spectacle on the stage, Arzner creates a dressing room scene that establishes a tense correlation between the onstage and backstage spaces. Visually and sonically penetrated by Bubbles's striptease act, Judy is entrapped and must violently free herself if necessary. Judy does just that immediately after her monologue in front of the audience. After receiving a slap by Bubbles, Judy attacks her, their writhing bodies spilling out onto the stage for all to see. The fight is lengthy and vicious, an addition by Arzner to the script and one that prompted some censors to demand it be cut. The sequence has received little attention from scholars, who prefer to focus on the previous scene of female empowerment between Judy and her audience. But the fight sequence is crucial to Judy's liberation from her earlier entrapment. In night court, she joyfully exclaims, "I wanted to kill her," and attributes her newfound sense of peace to allowing her temper to "boil over." Thus unencumbered, Judy finds the courage to pursue her love of ballet. The "tragedy" to which the *Variety* reviewer refers is short lived; Judy emerges from the cloistered depths of the burlesque theater as a new woman.

Only alluded to in *Dance, Girl, Dance*, murder becomes a reality in Darren Aronofsky's *Black Swan*. In the film, two dancers, Nina (Natalie Portman) and Lily (Mila Kunis), vie for the star turn in the New York City Ballet's production of *Swan Lake*. Here, too, tension builds in the semiprivate, interior space of the dressing room. As in *Dance, Girl, Dance*, the dressing room is a space of encounter where the two women meet and observe each other. Aronofsky uses the space, with its multitudes of women and reflective surfaces, as well as the conformist norms of female presentation in ballet, to amplify and refract the image of woman. Along with the other dancers, Nina covets the lead part, a revised role that casts the same dancer as both the white and black swans, requiring that the same woman embody the qualities of light and dark, good and evil. In the dressing room, the dancers are discussing how the senior dancer is too old to play the part, introducing an element of instability into their world, just as Lily, the newcomer, enters the space.

Nina immediately focuses her gaze on her; we sense in her look the mixed feelings of curiosity and fascination that will later transform into desire and fear. The film's prismatic mirror shots amplify Nina's complex encounter with Lily. As in *Dance, Girl, Dance*, the act of looking is privileged as multivalent. Shot after shot in this dressing room sequence fragments, crops, and displaces the image of women who occupy the space. Large mirrors line the walls opposite one another, in front of which the dancers sit, preparing themselves for the day's rehearsal. These mirrors simultaneously reflect the women in front of them, the women who sit at the opposite wall, and the reflection of the opposite mirror's reflection. Further refracting the image, smaller, round vanity mirrors sit in front of each dancer, capturing and multiplying the women's faces even more. In one medium shot of Nina, we see the back of her head in the foreground of the frame,

The many reflections of the women's dressing room. *Black Swan*, copyright 2010 by Searchlight Pictures.

a partial reflection of her face in the vanity mirror, a full reflection of her head and shoulders in the large mirror in front of her, the opposite mirror's reflection of her back, and a vanity mirror close-up reflection of the dancer she is talking to. The dynamics between self, as multidirectionally presented, and other are brought to the foreground with the use of such a dense and reflective mise-en-scène. Splicing the image into so many layers projects a sense of unease as the women talk about the end of their fellow ballerina's career.

Lily enters the space and immediately disrupts it. Aronofsky momentarily gives the audience a break from such complex visual compositions with a medium shot of Lily standing in the room's doorway. In a shot-reverse-shot pattern, Lily locks eyes with Nina and Nina corresponds. Quickly, however, Aronofsky returns to the use of mirrors to emphasize Lily's outsider status. A long shot of the dressing room reveals Nina and the other dancers looking untrustingly at Lila, whose full body is now reflected in a standing mirror in the center of the shot. The mirror's frame creates a border around Lily's figure, allowing her to occupy and remain separate from the space simultaneously. As Lily walks into the room and claims a place at the table, Aronofsky places both women in a complex mirror shot in which the profilmic figures of the women are off camera but their reflections are captured in Nina's vanity mirror.[44] We see Nina's fascination and desire given formal expression by her reflection and the shift of the camera's focus. Lily's face first appears clearly in the mirror but turns blurry when the camera racks focus to the face of Nina, who is watching her. These moments in which the film formally transfers the look from one woman to the other foregrounds female desire, which becomes explicitly erotic over the course of the film and ultimately produces the conflation of two women into one.[45]

Unlike in *Dance, Girl, Dance*, where the main protagonist finds freedom and a fuller sense of self as a result of her conflict with another woman, in *Black Swan* Nina's conflict leads to her demise. Nina's naïveté and confusion about erotic desire, for both the ballet's male director (Vincent Cassel) and Lily, combined with an overly protective mother (Barbara Hershey), prompts a psychological breakdown. During the opening performance of the "white swan" segment of the ballet, Nina imagines that Lily sits at her dressing table plotting to steal the star role. As Lily turns from the dressing table to look at Nina, asking, "How about I dance the black swan for you?" she transforms into Nina on an edit. The film splits Nina into two women, the white and the black, the good and the bad. The white swan shoves the black swan into a mirror and shatters it. The black swan retaliates by choking the white swan while yelling "My turn!" repeatedly. The white swan picks up a jagged shard of mirror, an object of desire turned weapon, and plunges it into the black swan's abdomen. Once she does so, the black swan transforms back into Lily, spits blood from her mouth, and dies. Terrified by what she has done, Nina cries as an attendant knocks on the door with a message that she must take the stage: "Black Swan places in five." This convention of dressing room scenes, in which the advancement of time is made apparent, draws attention to the female chaos within. Pressured by time, Nina drags Lily's body into the dressing room's bathroom and dresses for the black swan part. Later, Nina will realize that the abdomen she cut was not Lily's but her own. After dancing as both the white and the black swans, she collapses onstage and dies before the entire company.

This violent scene in the dressing room is an extreme iteration of female desire, competition, and destruction. At first a point of fascination, Lily becomes a site of danger, sabotaging Nina both professionally and psychologically. Like Bubbles in *Dance, Girl, Dance*, Lily's sensuality and confidence are both qualities that Nina lacks but aspires to. In the process of transforming herself, which we witness through the mirrored transference of looks and bodies in the film, Nina only finds misery. She is not empowered but harmed by this process. Arzner's and Aronofsky's interpretations of female relationships diverge critically here. Where Arzner saw complex female relationships as ultimately liberating and a catalyst for maturity, Aronofsky interprets them as delimiting and ultimately deadly. Nina's aspiration to find herself through another woman, *Black Swan* suggests, is a dangerous and self-sabotaging act. In other words, a woman cannot be the white swan and the black swan at once.

Violence of a different sort hovers over *Sparkle* (1976), the first backstage drama to feature a group of Black women. This story about three women struggling to make it in show business would be repeated later by the Broadway show *Dreamgirls* in 1982 and film versions of both *Dreamgirls* and *Sparkle* in 2006 and 2012, respectively. The original *Sparkle*, however, was the first to radically reimagine the backstage realm as a Black female space. To be sure, instances of Black cinematic performance were many by the 1970s. But backstage dramas, in which Black performers are given narrative consequence, were still few and far between. To the extent that the backstage film offers a vision of self-distinction and social mobility, Hollywood reserved the genre for stories of whiteness. By the 1970s, given the success of the Blaxploitation film and the lucrative Black market that it exposed, new possibilities for genre revision emerged, including the backstage film. Like Blaxploitation films, Black films about performance had strong ties to the music business, like *Lady Sings the Blues* (1972), produced by Motown founder Berry Gordy, and *Sparkle*, which featured an original score by Curtis Mayfield. Releasing the musical soundtrack, which showcased the vocals of Aretha Franklin, simultaneously with the film, *Sparkle*'s producers sought to capture both Black and white audiences with crossover, multimedia appeal.

While *Lady Sings the Blues* features the story of one Black female performer (Diana Ross as Billie Holiday), *Sparkle* offers multiple examples of Black womanhood. Three sisters, the eldest of whom is called Sister (Lonette McKee), strive to be a singing sensation in the Harlem of 1958. "A collage of many Black groups" that existed at the time, as producer Howard Rosenman describes it, Sister and the Sisters is made up of three women whose kinship binds them together despite their differences. Each one has a different trajectory: Sparkle (Irene Cara) yearns for musical stardom, Delores (Dwan Smith) seeks an education and racial justice, and Sister wants a life of luxury and fun. As in preceding stories that present groups of three women (such as *Ziegfeld Girl*), the women's values lead to success or failure. Sister's desire for wealth and a good time is her ruin. She becomes addicted to cocaine and dies of an overdose, while Sparkle ascends to stardom at Carnegie Hall and Delores leaves the sister act to pursue her studies.

While the narrative convention of using three women to display women's social options is formulaic, *Sparkle*'s characterizations are set against and shaped by contemporary Black, working-class life. As the tagline for the film suggests, this is a story that takes these women "from ghetto to superstars." The language of Black Power pervades the film, with its message embodied by Delores, who bristles at her mother's job as a maid for a white family. "We don't have to be slaves to the white establishment anymore," Delores tells her mother as she leaves the apartment in search of a better future. Their "ghetto" existence, Delores insists, is a function of racism, a form of precarity that *Sparkle* introduces into the backstage genre. In creating Sister and the Sisters, the women attempt to break out of these socioeconomic constraints. Unlike backstage films in which the women compete against one another, *Sparkle* presents a sister act that bands together in order to escape an insecure existence and to claim social mobility for themselves.

The dressing room scenes serve a critical function. Not only do they provide audiences with a deeper understanding of the women's sisterly bond, but the dressing room is also where the precarity of Black womanhood gets performed. There are three such sequences in the film. In the first of these, which takes place when the group is about to perform for the first time, the women help one another to get dressed and calm their nerves. The second and third dressing room scenes, however, reveal their increasingly perilous status. In the second, Sister enters wearing a broad-brimmed hat. The room is dimly lit and the hat obscures her face until she sits at the table and removes it, revealing her reflection to her sisters and the film audience. One side of Sister's face is black and blue, the result of a beating at the hands of her wealthy boyfriend, Satin (Tony King). The sisters are horrified. When Sister blames the injury on an "accident," Delores blames her for "runnin' around with that low-life." Sister responds by ordering Delores out of the dressing room. "It's my dressing room, too," Delores responds, but the older sister gets her way, casting Delores out and thereby fracturing their sisterhood in the process.

The shadows of the dressing room are more pronounced in a subsequent scene when Sister sits at the table alone. The camera is positioned behind her, which we can only see when Sister lights a cigarette, the flame illuminating her hand for a brief moment. When Delores enters, the light from outside materializes Sister's reflection, a lone figure surrounded by darkness. The dressing room's atmosphere is foreboding as the dim light reveals secrets hiding inside, the bruises on Sister's face. As the pressbook advertises, "'Sparkle' suggests a girl who's good to look at," but in these dressing room reflections, the film reveals a damaged view of female beauty, the consequence of male abuse.[46] Sister relies on the tools of the dressing room, including heavy stage makeup, to hide her face and largely succeeds for the purposes of the performance, a space where the outside does not intrude. But she also introduces her use of cocaine in the dressing room as another means of dealing with the beatings. She tearfully explains to Sparkle, "Baby, your sister can't fly on one wing," as she begs for more drugs. These are sequences in which an element of dread pervades the processes of getting dressed and undressed, preparing themselves for their moment of opportunity. The darkness of the space, its shadows and disturbing visuals, is symbolic of Sister's grim fate.

Sparkle's representation of Black womanhood and female kinship relations is set amid threatening external forces. Satin's depiction of a misogynistic and violent Black man has its likeness in numerous Blaxploitation heroes of the 1960s and 1970s. Indeed, Tony King played iconic roles in the Blaxploitation classics *Shaft* (1971), *Super Spook* (1974), and others. From his first appearance onscreen, dressed and behaving like an underworld kingpin, he is recognizable as a specific type of Black masculinity. But like the women in the film, Satin is only one of an array of Black male characters. Philip Michael Thomas stars as Stix, a composer in love with Sparkle who helps her career. And Dorian Harewood plays Levi, a friend of the sisters who gets caught up in Satin's crime ring. Taken together, they represent "the brothers who built them up and brought them down," as the film's poster describes their relationship to the sisters. In the end, *Sparkle* presents sisters who face precarity on multiple fronts, including their economic marginality as a working-class family, their Blackness in a racist society, and their gendered dependence on and vulnerability to men.

When placed into conversation with a vast array of backstage films in which sisters appear, *Sparkle* emerges as both an exception and a corrective. The presence of Black women in the dressing room immediately makes explicit the

The sisters grapple with evidence of physical abuse. *Sparkle*, copyright 1976 by Warner Bros.

pervasive whiteness of the dressing room in the genre up to that point and, to some extent, still. But by bringing the intersectional dynamics of race, class, and gender into the backstage space, it also allows for a more explicit engagement with the function of show business, the entertainment industry, and performance broadly in Black life. Writing about the state of Black film in the mid-1980s, film critic Armond White observes that *Sparkle* "uses McKee and show business as metaphors for the plight of minority existence in racist institutions, with very handy parallels to the movie business and to the costuming, mannerisms, and idioms black performers adopt to both succeed and fulfill their artistic and emotional needs." Whereas all backstage films comment on social position and mobility to an extent, *Sparkle* does so overtly through its narrative and formal explorations of marginality. Insisting on the genre's ability to achieve "full dimensionality" for the Black performer, White continues, *Sparkle* makes "the showbix genre as viable as it is ironic."[47]

Writing eight years after the film's initial release, White declares *Sparkle* to be the "first black cult movie," citing its playing with "unusual frequency in neighborhood playhouses and inner-city theaters across the country." He describes how the crowd for a screening at the Henry Street Settlement produced triple the usual attendance. The audience's fervor was comparable, he observes, to that for another film about women's relationships: "The crowd anticipated the dialogue and sang the lyrics as fanatically as audiences at the Regency act along with *All About Eve*."[48] While he intends to delineate the difference between the two films and their respective, racially defined audiences, he perhaps unwittingly links two films in which women's options in society, performance, and the backstage realm converge. Like *All about Eve*, *Sparkle* presents different kinds of women in backstage space who interact with a range of emotions, including jealousy, desire, and love. The dressing room reveals these relations in a private space to which only the film's audience gets access. Whether we find ourselves crossing the entryway with one of the characters, as we do in *All about Eve*, or we already occupy a space inside, as in *Sparkle*, these backstage films call attention to the audience's privileged position. Because of the intimacy we share with these women, we become invested in their relationship. As Jackie Stacey has written of female friendship films, they offer "pleasures for the female spectator, who is invited to look or gaze with one female character at another, in an interchange of feminine fascinations."[49] The dressing room is a site where such fascinations take place between the women in the film, as well as between the films' audience and the women on the screen.

Films in which sisters appear conjure an array of meanings beyond the objectification of women on the stage. Backstage we witness groups of women, in pairs, triples, and multiples, who, taken together, complicate the definition of femininity. While they often present "types" of womanhood, such as the good girl and the bad, they also indicate a range of options for women in a society where they occupy a marginalized position. Acknowledging, reacting to, and resisting that precarity renders the backstage film a cultural text that rehearses solutions to women's contemporary social position. While they have promised titillation, a function of the dressing room in Western culture more generally, cinematic dressing rooms have also been a productive cultural space for deciphering what it will take for women to succeed. Women compete with, advocate for, and assist one another in the dressing room, identifying internal and external threats to their social rise. Race and gender have been central to how sister acts secure their position. In the first half of the century, women's assertion of white privilege shaped the dressing room as a site that drew the color line across its doorways and windows, while across the extent of backstage film production, explorations of gender, different types of femininity, and the self-definition of one woman against another demarcated dressing room kinships and conflicts. As Eve recounts in her fictitious story, the dressing room is a place for the "real and the unreal," a realm for women to reflect and shape who they are, but also to imagine what they could be.

But what happens when these same performing women become wives and mothers? How has American cinema expressed the pressures of home and domestic life for women on the stage? And what happens to marital bonds when wives and husbands work together as professional entertainers? In chapter 3, I explore how dressing room scenes shift the focus from relations between women to relations between women and their children, and women and their husbands. In these films, dressing rooms function simultaneously as domestic and work spaces for the performing woman, where the social expectations for wives and mothers come into conflict with their dreams for a career.

3

Wives and Mothers

• •

> Jane Powell collapsed on the stage of Loew's State . . . and had to be carried to her dressing room. Miss Powell, whose 12-week-old baby was here with her part of the vaude engagement, looked weary when she arrived in Cleveland.
> —*Variety*, October 31, 1951

A pivotal scene at the beginning of Sam Mendes's melodrama *Revolutionary Road* (2008) takes place in a backstage dressing room. April (Kate Winslet) sits at her dressing table after a lackluster performance in a community theater production. She is unhappy with her efforts but hopes for some praise from her husband, Frank (Leonardo DiCaprio), nonetheless. As she looks at him reticently through the mirror, Frank confirms her worst fears, saying, "Guess it wasn't a triumph or anything, was it?" Tearfully, she stares back at her reflection. Like all mirrored surfaces, the one in *Revolutionary Road* holds actual and reflected material objects in the same space; bright vanity lights highlight April's virtual image in the middle, the posters of performances past fill the background, and photographs of her children and husband are tucked into the mirror's wooden frame. The shot effectively conveys entrapment; April is physically caught between her desire for a career as an actress and her reality, her identity as a suburban mother and wife. The dressing room sequence precipitates the conflict between husband and wife that eventually leads to April's death. Pregnant with a third child, April realizes that she will never be able to lead the interesting life

Wife and mother April (Kate Winslet) comes to terms with her failed attempt to become an actress. *Revolutionary Road*, copyright 2008 by Dreamworks Pictures.

that she envisioned for herself. She attempts to perform her own abortion and dies from the loss of blood.

Revolutionary Road echoes the themes of a film made one hundred years earlier, D. W. Griffith's *Behind the Scenes* (1908). As in the later film, a mother (Florence Lawrence) feels caught between the stage and her private life. Her child is ill, but the young mother is late for her job as a chorus girl, a position that pays for her meagre surroundings. Leaving her daughter with her grandmother, she rushes to the theater. In the dressing room, she frets as she puts on her costume and makeup. Whereas Mendes uses a close-up of April's reflection in the mirror to convey the conflict between stage and home, Griffith uses parallel editing to transport the audience between the two spaces. While the mother prepares for her performance, the film cuts to a scene at her apartment, where the doctor stands over the child and shakes his head in despair. This psychologically motivated editing style communicates the stakes of performance and the pathos of the mother's plight to the film audience. The mother returns home as quickly as she can, but it is too late. "The scene that follows," as the *Biograph Bulletin* describes, "positively defies description, and we can only say that it is unquestionably the most powerful shown in motion pictures."[1]

As these two examples convey, wives and mothers have been a central focus of stories about backstage life for well over a century. With few exceptions, American cinema has insisted that the traditionally female roles of wife and mother are irreconcilable with a performance career. The latter necessitates physical labor, frequent travel, long hours, and perhaps most prohibitively, the devotion of oneself to the audience; in *Torch Song* (1953), musical star Jenny Stewart (Joan Crawford) tells her producer she "fell in love" not with a man but with "the audience." Taking a woman's attentions away from her husband and children, a stage career threatens families, a harmonious home life, the division between private and public spheres, and ultimately, such films argue, the woman's own happiness.

Wives and mothers are present at the beginning of backstage film in the early twentieth century and they are still with us today, most frequently in melodramas like *Revolutionary Road* and in biopics about real female performers such as Tina Turner in *What's Love Got to Do with It* (1993), Gloria Grahame in *Film Stars Don't Die in Liverpool* (2017), and Judy Garland in *Judy* (2019). Female stars are a source of dramatic entertainment for they are both beautiful and tragic, full of potential and doomed to suffer. And as the epigraph that begins this chapter evokes, the woman collapsing in her dressing room has persistently been a real and imagined focus of American culture, seemingly confirming society's fears that motherhood and stage careers cannot mix, and if a mother tries, she will pay for it.

The wife and mother in backstage film, and the biopic in particular, tap into a fascination with the female performer, one that is very close to what Richard Dyer calls the "star phenomenon." These films give audiences a literal and figurative view of the backstage, where the star can be found in her "real" state, where they can find answers to the question of "Who is she really?" Using Eve Arnold's 1959 photograph of Joan Crawford as a case study, and as the frontispiece of his book, Dyer points to the ways in which the three versions of Crawford we see in the image (two reflections produced by two different mirrors and a back view of the actress in the foreground) prompt the viewer to ask which is the real one, a comment on our culture's simultaneous construction of stardom and its desire to demystify it.[2]

But while Dyer focuses on the composition of the photograph, it is also Crawford's location in space that informs this multilayered reading. The dressing table, with its mirrored surfaces and its opportunities for looking, produces this complex image of the star. Arnold exploits the sightlines of the dressing table—Crawford looking at herself, the reflected image of Crawford looking at herself, and the viewer looking at all three versions of Crawford that appear—to hold the woman as actress and image, subject and object, in tension. Dressing rooms are spaces for these multiple visions of the working woman to emerge, as we see in two other photographs that Arnold shot of Crawford that same year. In one, Crawford sits at her dressing room table on the set of *The Best of Everything* (1959)—a film that itself troubles women's entrance into the public sphere. Crawford has her head in her hands, doubly reflected in the dressing table mirror and the round vanity mirror, as she studies the script. A second image in the same dressing room shows Crawford smiling at the camera and flanked by her twin daughters, who kiss her on the cheek. Taken together, the two photographs show a woman at work and a woman as mother; Crawford appears to have balanced career and family harmoniously. But as we know from her daughter Cristina's later memoir *Mommie Dearest* (1978) and the eponymous biopic (1981) that allowed us even more intimate access to Crawford's life "behind the scenes," the narrative projected by the dressing room photographs is far from the truth.

Dressing rooms are critical to the construction of female star narratives. They provide the requisite spatial interiority and opportunities for self-reflection for stars to express their vulnerabilities. In backstage films that feature women, dressing rooms function as domestic space in the theater; they replicate the gendered associations of the private sphere in American life, including women's social positions as wives and mothers. As in film noir, backstage films typically use home as a "structuring absence"; placed in the world of entertainment and the public-facing structure of the theater, backstage films depict a spatial and temporal world that is often chaotic as opposed to stable, pressured instead of relaxed, and prone to disruption rather than self-sustaining.[3] Dressing rooms, the most private of spaces in the theater, are also filled with signs of disruption and transience, from the trunks and suitcases to the protective cages over the vanity lights to the No Smoking signs on the walls. And yet, when wives and mothers occupy dressing rooms, the spaces become quasi-domestic, producing a "temporary, modified domesticity" that allows for the identities of wives and mothers to be produced.[4] They become a space for pregnancy and children or for children to be taken away. They become a site where wives work with their husbands, but also where marriages become strained and dissolve. And dressing rooms are where we find aging women, whose long-ago choices to reject marriage and family have left them alone and full of regret. Stage mothers, absent mothers, working wives, and aging stars fill the dressing rooms of backstage film, rehearsing again and again the consequences for the public woman in American life.

Mothers

As recently as 2013, an article titled "I'm Pregnant. Is My Career Over?" appeared in the online trade magazine *Backstage*. Responding to female readers' fears about navigating their work lives while pregnant, the magazine's staff and writer Robert B. Martin offered reassurance, stating that, instead of a hardship, it is "another opportunity for you to not only share your experience, but also add depth to your acting career." With a list of seven action items, the writers convey best practices for pregnant actresses, all the while insisting that the experience will be "fun" and "special." The necessity of such a list, however, implicitly suggests that pregnancy is something that requires careful navigation. Number 1, for example, alerts the actress to announce both the pregnancy and her willingness to pursue work through it—"Make sure your agent knows and that you communicate clearly that you are still marketing yourself and that you are open to projects during your pregnancy"—while number 3 advises them to "blast an email/postcard alert to all casting directors" to "let them know your awesome news and that you will be available through the entire nine months!" An insecurity regarding the pregnant woman's place as a performer undergirds these recommendations, including advice for responding to potentially offensive reactions by casting directors who express "shock" or "surprise" by the woman's "pregnant look." In these situations, the writers suggest, "let them know it's no problem and thank them for their time.... Just be nice. Say thank you, and go." The article conveys how anxieties about adverse reactions to pregnant women and the real possibility that they will be turned down for certain roles will be a part of the process for these actresses. Despite the celebratory tone that the writers take, they nonetheless affirm women's fears that their careers will be affected, and likely limited, by pregnancy.[5]

Since women entered the stage profession in the seventeenth century, they have had to contend with the reality of pregnancy, the appearance of their pregnant body, and decisions about how to mother their children. While the dressing room has long been a site associated with female deception, writers have also used it as a representational location for satisfying curiosity about the role of the actress mother. Prompted by the increasing number of female stars like Sarah Siddons and Fanny Kemble who lived much of their personal lives in the public eye, attitudes about actresses began to shift from disreputable to respectable and even aspirational in the eighteenth century. This moment coincided with the "age of the domestic woman" in England and in Europe, in which the notion of being a mother was portrayed as being "natural, ideal, and joyful." Eighteenth-century stage actresses lived their lives as mothers overtly, bringing their children to work, embracing breastfeeding, and performing while noticeably pregnant. They became "nurturing rather than desiring" bodies.[6]

A corresponding shift occurred in the representation of the dressing room. As the space most associated with actresses' intimate activities, the dressing room was domesticated, becoming a standard feature of middle- and upper-middle-class architecture. And in sentimental novels of the eighteenth century, these spaces transformed from being places of "sexual excess, theatrical dissembling and feminine agency" that necessitated "containment and censure" of the women within to extensions of women's nurturing roles as wives and mothers. The confluence of theatrical domesticity and the dressing room can be seen most directly in the portrait *Queen Charlotte and Her Two Eldest Sons* (1765), by Johan Joseph Zoffany, in which the Queen sits at her dressing table flanked by the two young princes, who are wearing theatrical costumes. Her own reflection in the mirror stresses the constructed nature of the image, in which the monarch simultaneously plays the roles of ruler, woman, and mother. Popular literature of the era also explored this shift; as Tita Chico argues, in the eighteenth century the domestic dressing room went from being an accusatory space to a celebratory one wherein women still enacted a form of agency, but from within the parameters of their maternal identities.[7]

Overriding concerns about the relationship between the stage and female virtue, however, continued to inform popular attitudes about actresses as painted, promiscuous, public women well into the nineteenth and twentieth centuries.[8]

The cultural conversation about their abilities or deficiencies as mothers was always set against the backdrop of the theater itself and the extent to which children belonged in it. The phrase "born in a trunk" emerged during the rise of popular theater in the late nineteenth century, when career entertainers lived their lives on the road, traveling from town to town and theater to theater on the vaudeville and variety circuits. The cycles of life took place in these transient spaces, and children were raised within them. To be born in a trunk suggests being born in the theater, and specifically in the dressing room. The trunk transformed from an item of personal baggage to a bassinet. Performers used the trunk so frequently for this purpose that a superstition arose, according to theater folklorist Ralph Freud, that one "must never close the lid of a trunk in a dressing room," a taboo that "stems from the very practical fact that since so many children of actors spent their early days sleeping in the top tray of a trunk rather than a crib, the closing of lids might have disastrous results."[9]

Despite their potentially dangerous qualities, trunks were domestic objects in dressing rooms, often the only sign of personal possession and home in the backstage world. Children's occupation of trunks, then, was a natural extension of their domestic qualities, as we see in the backstage film *Broadway to Hollywood* when the baby born to a vaudeville team is fed his bottle in the trunk, and again in Miriam Young's memoir *Mother Wore Tights* (1944) when she describes how she used a trunk as her "play-room" while her parents were onstage.[10] And in her 1957 memoir on which the Broadway and Hollywood productions would be based, Gypsy Rose Lee details the many times she and her mother covertly used their dressing room as a bedroom.[11]

But like the superstition implies, dressing rooms could also be dangerous places for children who, left unsupervised, were prone to neglect and abuse. Dressing rooms were both private and easily penetrated, as the numerous accounts of dressing room thefts in *Variety* demonstrate.[12] This porousness also made them potentially unsafe for children. A 1919 article in *Variety* reported that "a little girl, aged 12, daughter of artists on the bill, was rescued from assault by the alleged 'manager' of a headline actor in a vacant dressing room of a local vaudeville theatre." It explained that "the child's parents were on the stage at the time" and that stage hands and artists responded to the girl's screams and gave the manager a "hearty licking" before throwing him out.[13] Similarly, in her 1954 memoir about growing up on the stage, Lillian Roth describes how she was only five years old when she was sexually assaulted backstage while her mother left the theater to buy sandwiches.[14] While backstage films, including the film version of Roth's memoir (1955), do not admit to this level of abuse, they nevertheless represent, if comically, the difficulties of raising children in dressing rooms given what they depict as a loose, often amoral environment. We see children running amok, for example, in a series of backstage musicals about families on the stage, including *Broadway to Hollywood* (1933), *The Merry Monahans* (1944), *There's No Business like Show Business* (1954), *The Seven Little Foys* (1955), and

Gypsy (1962). The vulnerability of children backstage eventually led the Actors' Equity Association to require that an adult be present to supervise children under sixteen years of age, "someone for whom that is their only job." The stipulation created the role of "child guardian" or "child wrangler," to protect children, but also to communicate with the child's parents who were not on the scene.[15]

Our cultural imagination, however, places the blame for children gone awry on the stage mother. Her presence, represented as overbearing and interfering, is critiqued again and again in film, from *Stage Mother* (1933) to *Gypsy*. She is especially unforgiving in *I'll Cry Tomorrow* (1955) when Katie Roth (Jo Van Fleet), mother to Lillian, becomes enraged in response to her daughter's merely asking what a "stage mother" is and shoves the child to the ground. These portrayals of aggressive mothers reference the real presence of mothers backstage; indeed, the superstition that knitting should not be allowed on the stage is due to the presence of mothers knitting in the wings and dressing rooms while keeping an eye on their children (an activity that is made to appear ominous in *The Country Girl*; see chapter 4).[16] But while these cultural texts seek to limit the stage mother's presence, just as many films condemn the mother for being absent from her children, including those by such notable directors as D. W. Griffith (*Behind the Scenes*, 1908), Rouben Mamoulian (*Applause*, 1929), Josef von Sternberg (*Blonde Venus*, 1932), and Douglas Sirk (*All I Desire*, 1953; *Imitation of Life*, 1959). As these examples show, mothers have been caught in a double bind in backstage film, simultaneously critiqued for their mothering backstage and condemned for their neglect.

The "stage mother" arose in public consciousness in the eighteenth century along with the "cult of womanhood," an ideology that stressed women's innate abilities to be good mothers and to enjoy mothering.[17] Society promoted "an unobtainable ideal of the 'good mother,'" Laura Engel and Elaine M. McGirr write, that was not at all reflective of women's lived experiences.[18] The desire to uphold the maternal ideal in part explains the appearance of what Marilyn Francus has called the "spectral mother," the dead, absent, or missing mother who populates Western literary history. The spectral mother has been particularly associated with stage mothers precisely because of the nature of the work, which requires travel away from home, daytime rehearsals and evening performances, and other disruptions to domestic life. But the spectral mother can be idealized because she is absent. As Francus writes, "Spectral narratives reaffirm maternal goodness without the sloppy immediacy of dealing with mothers." Though this is typically the case, as in the idealization of the dead, spectral mother in *The Seven Little Foys*, the backstage film also exploits the trope of the performer-mother who abandons or resents her children (*The Goose Woman*, 1925; *The Merry Monahans*, 1944).[19]

In many films about stage and spectral mothers, the motherly ideal is affirmed at the end. The mothers return or recommit to their children in *Blonde Venus*, *All I Desire*, and *Imitation of Life*. The backstage musical, however, attempts to strike a harmonious, if precarious, balance between home and career. The semantics of the genre reaffirm the place of entertainment in the characters' and audience's lives; a rejection of the stage would quickly undermine the genre's ideological project. And yet the persistent cultural concern regarding women and mothers in public life also found its expression in the genre, shifting somewhat over the course of the twentieth century according to the contemporary political and social climate. We see these shifts across three films in particular, *Applause*, *Mother Wore Tights* (1947), and *Gypsy*. In each, the dressing room is a symbolic space for birth, a place that simultaneously produces the identities of child and mother.

Mamoulian's *Applause*, in particular, makes literal the connections between birth, motherhood, and the domestic orientation of the dressing room space. In the film, Helen Morgan plays Kitty Darling, burlesque queen, who has a child outside of marriage. Kitty tries to protect her daughter by sending her off to a convent, only to be pressured later by her seedy boyfriend to put the girl in show business. As a pre–Production Code feature, the film presents a bleak and squalid view of burlesque. The press heralded the film for its use of a mobile camera along with early sound technology, but also criticized it for its "sordid" storyline, with "character work too disturbing" and "dialog too pungent," as reported by the *Exhibitors Herald-World*.[20] Kitty cohabitates with two different men in the film, neither of whom is her daughter's father. The second, Hitch, makes repeated attempts to seduce the daughter after she returns from the convent. And through the daughter's subjectivity, we learn how precarious and pathetic her mother's existence truly is.

Desiring to keep her young child with her, Kitty begins training April for a life on the stage. Concerned for her welfare, however, Kitty ultimately sends April away for many years, during which time the daughter longs for her mother, building an idealized view of her that shatters once Kitty brings her home. Back in her role as a stage mother, Kitty is affectionate toward April, but she is also revealed as promiscuous, gullible, and powerless. She performs the ultimate act of the spectral mother by committing suicide at the end of the film, assuming the role of the self-sacrificing mother and freeing April to live the life she chooses.

The dressing room is essential to these identity shifts. Mamoulian frames *Applause* with two scenes in the space. In the first, Kitty gives birth to April, and in the last, Kitty takes own her life. In both sequences, the dressing room appears as a quiet space apart from the hurly-burly of the backstage. It is in this quasi-domestic realm of the theater that the actress meets motherhood and the public self collides with the private one. Mamoulian achieves this narrative integration formally through the location of the dressing room as an in-between space that bridges the world outside and the stage within, but also through symbolic imagery of birth and performance.

Take the first dressing room scene, which occurs after Kitty has finished her performance and faints in the wings. Fellow performers carry her to the

An audience inside the dressing room witnesses the birth of a mother. *Applause*, copyright 1929 by Paramount Pictures.

dressing room and summon a doctor, who sheepishly emerges from one of the theater boxes where he has been rendezvousing with a woman. He alone enters Kitty's dressing room while the performers wait anxiously outside. When he delivers the news that Kitty has had a baby, the motley crew of burlesque dancers, minstrels, and clowns file in to view the spectacle. They surround her chaise longue, where she rests next to baby April, who has been made a makeshift bed in a suitcase. This remarkable sequence begins with an overhead shot in which the audience sees Kitty and April encircled by the admirers and then a reverse, extreme low-angle shot in which we see the astonished faces of the performers looking downward at mother and daughter. The scene ends with a medium close-up of Kitty, who appears bathed in light with drops of sweat and mascara-tinged tears on her face.

The sequence is both a performance of birth and a performance of motherhood. Author Beth Brown, who wrote the novel on which the film is based, conceived of the dressing room in these terms, drawing metaphorical connections between the dressing room's furnishings and the experience of being in labor: "Pain was her make-up now, agony her costume, the couch her stage."[21] Mamoulian reinforces the notion of performance by providing Kitty with an audience, the performers who anxiously wait outside the dressing room door for the "show" to start and then solemnly enter to watch it unfold. The light that bathes Kitty suggests that she has assumed an exalted state. Mamoulian foregrounds the shape of a circle with both of these shots, evoking the biology of birth in which the enclosed womb and the birth canal function as secure and life-giving spaces. It is clear, especially in the low-angle shot, that the director intended the birth to be a double one. The point of view, looking up into the circle of faces, could be the baby's, Kitty's, or both. In this scene, both baby and Kitty have been given new life.[22]

Despite Kitty's best efforts, however, she cannot effectively manage the role of stage mother and deems it best to make herself absent so that April can find happiness. Again, this critical scene takes place in Kitty's dressing room, but this time it is for the purpose of giving a different kind of performance, that of the self-sacrificing mother. Mamoulian frames this scene similarly to the earlier one, with Kitty lying on her chaise longue, facing screen right, and with April to her left. It ends with an overhead, medium shot of Kitty's face, again marred by sweat and tears, as she dies. Kitty gives her final show in the dressing room, a place where she can be alone and perform the kind of motherhood that she deems best, a loving, if dead, one. Her new role as a spectral mother frames the final shot, in which April embraces her fiancé while Kitty benevolently looks down on them from a life-size burlesque poster on the wall behind them.

Ideas about what constitutes the motherly ideal, and how women with careers can or cannot achieve it, became more acute in the postwar era. As Elaine Tyler May has argued, Americans embraced a domestic ideology as a bulwark against both internal and external dangers to the status quo, including communism and threats to national security. "In pursuit of the 'good life,'" May writes of men and women in the 1950s, "they adhered to traditional gender roles and prized marital stability; few of them divorced." But the low divorce rate did not necessarily point to happy marriages, May notes. Many couples believed so firmly in nuclear home life that they "stayed together through sheer determination."[23]

The ideal housewife and mother who emerged in this period, and who gave rise to its backlash in the form of Betty Friedan's *The Feminine Mystique* (1963), was largely one-dimensional; she was a woman who sacrificed her own personal fulfillment for that of her husband and children. Yet as Joanne Meyerowitz has argued, a survey of women's magazines from 1948–1958 reveals a "postwar cultural puzzle" in which the literature applauded both domestic and nondomestic activities for women. In these magazines, she writes, "domestic ideals coexisted in ongoing tension with an ethos of individual achievement that celebrated nondomestic activity, individual striving, public service, and public success." So while a powerful domestic ideology held sway in the postwar period, in the realm of popular culture, the messages about women's place were marked by ambiguity rather than consensus.[24]

What Meyerowitz found to be true in women's magazines is also quite pertinent to the backstage musicals of this era. In many ways, films like *Mother Wore Tights*, *When My Baby Smiles at Me* (1948), *My Blue Heaven* (1950), and *Everything I Have Is Yours* (1952) are part of that "postwar cultural puzzle" that she identifies. These films are in keeping with the family melodramas of the period in which heterosexual marriages and nuclear families are ultimately upheld, but as Jackie Byars has argued, "the narrative contortions necessary to produce the deus-ex-machina endings expose contradictions rather than resolve them."[25] Like the family melodrama, postwar backstage musicals are deeply contradictory, exposing the fissures in social norms and expectations even while affirming them. Remarkably, they treat the symptoms of social upheaval—separation, divorce, adultery—overtly, suggesting that there is conflict in the ways that women and men view their roles as wives and husbands, mothers and fathers. With few exceptions, these films fulfill the narrative conventions of the genre to produce the simultaneity of a happy couple and a happy ending, but in the process they acknowledge the fears and insecurities underneath the 1950s ideal of home and family.[26]

The contradictions of the backstage musical are best expressed in the dressing room sequences. A paradoxical space that is both public and private, the dressing room is a signifier of women's work outside the home and their most intimate space within the theater. There are signs of women's career success, bouquets of flowers and congratulatory telegrams, along with the tools of their trade (makeup, costumes), but the visual evidence of temporary habitation, most notably the open trunks covered with stickers from a life of perpetual travel, make this space representative of home and work at once. By placing the woman in the dressing room, the genre allows for ideas about women's domesticity and women's ambition to coexist and collide.

In the postwar era, the dressing room is where women become mothers, effectively forcing the actress and the mother into one body. Like it is in *Applause*, the dressing room is both a pregnant space and a space for pregnancy. It is where the narrative goes to discover and announce impending motherhood. And it is a place where, in its sequestered interiority, the contemplation of a new life can occur. This new life is, of course, the baby to be born. But it is also, and perhaps more importantly, the woman's new role as mother that the film foregrounds.

Mother Wore Tights initiated a cycle of backstage musicals starring Betty Grable and Dan Dailey as a show business couple. Based on the best-selling memoir by Miriam Young, the film tells the story of a chorus girl turned wife and mother at the turn of the century. In the film, Myrtle (Betty Grable) informs her husband and performing partner, Frank (Dan Dailey), of her "act of God" while he sits at the dressing table removing his makeup. The duo has been successful and is headed to Broadway when Myrtle declares that she wants to live with her grandmother in order to raise the child. Frank objects, desiring her to stay with him, but she insists, arguing, "I'm going to quit for good. I want my baby to have a home and a mother to take care of him." She implores him, "From now on, please just let me be the mama." The couple's intimacy is pronounced by the enclosed dressing room, which allows them to express their emotions surrounding the birth of a child and what it will mean for the act. Myrtle insists that the backstage, with its trunks, hanging undergarments, and peeling wallpaper, is no place to raise a baby. In agreement, the husband and wife embrace as a superimposition of the newborn baby's face enters the shot, temporally holding Myrtle's two identities, performer and mother, as a single image.

Yet Myrtle quickly learns that she cannot remain with her children (eventually two daughters) and still be a good wife to her husband, who needs her on the road. "A wife's place is with her husband, first, last, and always," her grandmother tells her. Myrtle leaves the two children to be raised by the elderly woman and goes back on the stage, becoming a spectral mother who only sees her children on holiday breaks. As one reviewer of the film put it, Myrtle soon realizes "the problems created by a mother who wears tights."[27] Here the film departs from Young's memoir on which the film is based. In the book, Young details how, feeling "lonely" for her baby, her mother decided to bring the five-year-old "Mikie" on the road with her. As a "backstage baby," "born in a trunk and raised in a dressing room," Mikie was nevertheless enthusiastically mothered, by her own mother in between acts and by the other female performers when her mother was on the stage. Young describes in detail how Mikie admired her mother's process of getting ready for the stage, presented by Young as a scene that could take place between daughters and mothers in bedrooms anywhere: "I would stand back of her chair in the dressing room and follow her movements as she made up, as fascinated the thousandth time I watched as the first."[28]

The film version, however, necessitates the separation of mother and children, a function of the wife fulfilling her duty to support her husband's career. Nevertheless, Myrtle is an image of maternal and female perfection; she commits to a life on the stage not for her own career but for the sake of her husband's. And from afar, she remains devoted to her children. In the memoir, she brings her child with her, and in the film, Myrtle thinks about, cares for, and serves her children while on the road. The film is careful to show how both children and mother miss one another, but it also assuages any moments of personal regret with efforts at family reunification (such as the Christmas scene) and motherly devotion. When Myrtle decides to send her children to boarding school, the film shows Myrtle in a backstage dressing room, preparing a dress pattern for one of her daughters; Young recalls that her mother made twenty-one dresses for her, more than any other girl at school had, "by hand in the dressing room between shows."[29] Therefore, the film offers multiple moments of familial reunion, in which Myrtle has successfully performed her duties as wife, mother, and performer. The ease with which she enters into and out of these respective roles appears farfetched, but the film nevertheless insists on its viability with a final scene in which the graduating daughter sings devotedly to her parents.

Both the film and the memoir are invested in presenting the backstage as a site of nurturing families and devoted motherhood. Released in the mid-1940s, amid the social change wrought by the war and the increasing desire for social stability, the texts confirm that even in the most unlikely of spaces, the stage, these ideals can be upheld. In this way, the film appears to fulfill the wish expressed by Mikie's hoofer father in the memoir: "Wouldn't the audience get a big surprise," he says, "if they could come backstage and peek into the dressing rooms and see what the actors and actresses were doing between shows?" Taking a look around, he notes that his fellow performers are each engaged in domestic pursuits—Mikie's mother is "at the sewing machine"; Hilda, wife of another entertainer, is "making lampshades for their new home"; and a "man-and-wife team [are] busy at making hooked rugs."[30] Reassuring its 1950s audience that ideal wives and mothers can exist in even the most unlikely places, *Mother Wore Tights* gives its audience a privileged view of the backstage. There they find stable families and the women who support them.

Fifteen years later, a very different kind of stage mother emerged with *Gypsy*, the Hollywood adaptation of the 1959 Broadway show starring Ethel Merman. The character of Rose bears the markers of earlier stage mothers; she is pushy, loud, and overly present in her daughters' lives. Both the stage and film versions were successful, but Rose's excessive control of her daughter also elicited condemnation and critique from the audience. As Caryl Flinn has documented in her biography of Merman, *Gypsy* tapped into contemporary fears about the influence of mothers. A "smothering-mother," Flinn writes, "Madame Rose was more off-putting and threatening" than previous versions of mothers, an example of popular psychology "putting the blame on mom" for society's ills. Indeed, Rose was conceived as a frightening character. Writer of the play Arthur Laurents told Merman in their first meeting about the role that "Rose is a monster." But as Flinn shows, Merman was always sympathetic toward the character, revealing the inner humanity of this unique stage mother who was judged, as a successful woman in show business, in much the same way she was.[31]

In the film, Rose, played by Rosalind Russell, works to protect and secure her daughters' careers on the stage, going to great lengths to do so. While the memoir details the family's tour through multiple dressing rooms, including those they slept in, the film saves its dressing room scenes for the last third of the film. Their timing coincides not with the mother–daughter act's rise to the top, as with most backstage films, but rather with their decline. Vaudeville is nearing its demise and the act can only get booked in a burlesque house. But like the dressing rooms occupied by mothers in previous films, the space, downtrodden though it is, is pregnant with possibility. In one of the rare musical numbers to take place in a dressing room, the strippers educate daughter Louise (Natalie Wood) in bumping and grinding during the song "Ya Gotta Have a Gimmick." Staged like a performance with Louise sitting on a trunk in the extreme foreground, her back to the camera, each of the three strippers displays her non-talent, the ability to seduce the audience with string lights, a trumpet, and butterfly wings. It is in this moment that Louise first realizes that she too was "born with no talent," a sure sign that she is destined to become one of them. But it is Rose who makes the transformation happen, instructing Louise on the kind of makeup and costumes to wear, the number to perform, and how to execute it.

The birth of Louise as "Gypsy Rose Lee" takes place in the dressing room with a series of thresholds that Louise crosses, each time more fully formed than the last. In the first, she steps through an inner partition that separates the bathroom from the dressing room, wearing a smock over her gown. With hair that is upswept and heavier makeup than usual, Louise has begun her transformation into a star. She removes the smock and is startled by her appearance in the mirror; she stares at the reflection of a grown woman wearing a blue evening gown and long white gloves and exclaims, "Mama, I'm pretty!" The film cuts to a camera position outside the dressing room looking in. Louise is in the background, framed by the dressing room's curtain partition. She walks toward the camera and through the opening, crossing the threshold between the private space of the dressing room and the more public space of the theater. The final step in the birth of the star is when the proscenium curtains part and we see Louise, now Gypsy Rose Lee, walk through them and onto the stage. Each of these moments conveys what Louise was "born" to do; the film visually enacts her transformation with a series of births, starting in the thresholds of the dressing room and culminating with Gypsy's emergence on the stage fully formed.

But the dressing room also marks a moment of renewal for Rose. After succeeding at facilitating her daughter's transformation into a star, Rose must now reckon with her own obsolescence. She sacrificed her chance for marriage by devoting herself to her daughter's career; symbolically, she gives the opera gloves she would have worn for her wedding to Louise as a costume accessory. Standing in Louise's/Gypsy's opulent dressing room at the end of the film, and frustrated by her daughter's newfound independence, she asks her, "What did I do it for?" What follows is a number that is unique for its expression of maternal desire; "Rose's Turn" brings to the foreground the latent desires that Rose has harbored through the production. On an empty burlesque stage, Rose explains to her imaginary audience, "I made you. Wanna know why? Because I was born too soon and started too late.... I could've been better than any of you.... There wouldn't have been signs big enough, or lights bright enough!" Articulating her own dreams for a stage career and implicitly acknowledging the lack of support she had for achieving them, Rose reveals that her stage mothering is a function of her need for self-realization and attention. She asks, "When is it my turn? Don't I get a dream for myself?" Appropriating the lyric heretofore associated with her daughter's career, Rose sings, "Everything's coming up roses," but this time replaces the line "for you" with "for me," the latter two words repeated with increasing urgency seven times.

In *Gypsy* we witness a stage mother who is excessive in her mothering to be sure, but she also reveals herself as a desiring woman, someone who has dreams for herself, not just for her children. It is perhaps this moment of self-indulgence, her refusal to exist only in scrapbooks "in the background," that makes Rose monstrous to audiences. She has sacrificed like stage mothers before, but she refuses to do so in a way that obliterates her own needs. Unlike Myrtle in *Mother Wore Tights* and Kitty Darling in *Applause*, Rose does not quietly recede but rather takes the stage for herself. At the end of *Gypsy*, the stage mother is reborn as a woman.

Wives

Rose is not just a mother in the film, however; she is also a failed wife. Indeed, her inability to settle down and marry (she announces that she has had multiple husbands before) is also part of the dressing room scene. When Rose insists on putting her daughter's career first, her fiancé, Herbie (Karl Malden), finally realizes that she will never be the kind of woman he wants. "All the vows from here to doomsday couldn't make you a wife," he exclaims, yelling, "I want a wife, Rose!" Refusing to be the "worm" who crawls after her, he insists, "I'm going to be a man if it kills me." Herbie leaves Rose in the dressing room, where she tearfully sits waiting for Louise to emerge in costume.

Gypsy is just one example of a backstage film that depicts the career focus of a wife as the reason for her husband's downfall. We see this dual structure emerge in 1908 with *She Would Be an Actress*, a film about a young wife who has aspirations to become a great actress and leaves her hen-pecked, smock-wearing husband behind. Like other, similarly titled films of the era, *She Would Be a Suffragette* (1908) and *She Would Be a Business Man* (1910), *She Would Be an Actress* represents women's efforts and desire to leave home for a role in the traditionally male public sphere. The titles also imply that there are consequences for such errant desires.

The theme of a husband's distress became more prominent in the 1940s and postwar period when man's traditional place as head of household was disrupted by the displacements and new female-oriented labor force of the war years. As David M. Gerber has discussed regarding the popularity of the film *The Best Years of Our Lives* (1946), the reintegration of men returning from war was a source of social concern. In practice, both professional and cultural discourses placed the responsibility for restoring man's place in the home on the shoulders of women.[32] While melodramas like *The Best Years of Our Lives* could depict stable and nurturing female characters who support rather than threaten the men in their lives, the backstage film's focus on career success served the function of delivering cautionary tales. It is no coincidence that the one "bad" wife in *The Best Years of Our Lives*, who refuses to stay at home with her psychologically damaged veteran husband, is a nightclub performer.

In the backstage film, the performing wife is typically a sympathetic character, but she is also a social problem because she devotes herself to the audience rather than to her husband. In *The Hard Way* (1943), Katie (Joan Leslie) aggressively pursues her career as a musical comedy star, with the help of her domineering sister Helen (Ida Lupino). This work takes her on the road away from her performer husband, Albert (Jack Carson). The disparity between their careers increases with time until Albert, alone and dejected in his shabby dressing room, commits suicide. The space is rife with signs of Katie's success; he plays her record while he applies makeup, he reads an entertainment magazine in which she appears, and a framed portrait of her sits on his desk. The camera frames Albert in close-up against a backdrop of these sounds and images. Foreshadowing his ultimate act, a sign on the wall reads, "Please turn out the lights." The film cuts to the hallway, where a friend hears the firing of a gun. The subsequent shot places us back inside Albert's dressing room, where we see his dead body lying on the floor, the images and voice of Katie still hovering around him. While the suicidal husband is an extreme example of man's distress in backstage film, it is nevertheless a persistent occurrence that our society finds compelling, as the four versions of *A Star Is Born*, the most recent being in 2018, prove. Again and again, they rehearse the conflict between performing wives and the husbands who love them but who ultimately cannot bear their success.

It is more typical, however, to see the relationship between wives and husbands become strained and dissolved in backstage film. *Stormy Weather* (1943), *When My Baby Smiles at Me*, *Everything I Have Is Yours*, *With a Song in My Heart* (1952), *Somebody Loves Me* (1952), *Gypsy*, and both *Funny Girl* (1968) and *Funny Lady* (1975) revisit marital strife in the woman's dressing room, the site that conjures her potential beyond wifely duties. In *With a Song in My Heart*, for example, singer Jane Froman (Susan Hayward) tells her husband, Don (David Wayne), while taking off her makeup at the dressing table, "It isn't easy for any man married to a woman in the spotlight." Attempting to appease him, she offers to stop performing "if it's going to spoil our marriage." He angrily refuses. As in *The Hard Way*, dressing room signage conveys his inner feelings; the Keep Out sign on the door hovers over his head as he exits. Don has been shut out of his natural place as head of household, to which he reacts by getting drunk at a nearby bar. While these films are ultimately sympathetic toward the working wife, an implicit critique of her pursuit of a career remains well into the 1960s and 1970s with Barbra Streisand's portrayal of Fanny Brice, in which Nick Arnstein (Omar Sharif) abandons her in the dressing room multiple times.[33]

In a critical number of films, however, the husband remains in his wife's dressing room as a presence to be reckoned with. To be sure, leaving the dressing room by way of censure or suicide is a critique of the wife's choices, but co-occupying the space introduces an element of, potentially menacing, pressure. In these films, the husband occupies not only the physical space of the dressing room but its reflective surfaces as well. These "man in the mirror" shots create a virtual image of the husband and wife in addition to and in dialogue with their physical presence. Like the multireflected image of woman that we see in so many dressing room scenes, the man in the mirror amplifies the sightlines, interpretations, and tensions in the space.

In *Stormy Weather*, a Black-cast musical made by 20th Century-Fox, a loose backstage plot forms the justification for a series of musical numbers by a famed set of Black artists. A celebratory tale of Black cultural achievement, the film highlights the many positive ways that Black Americans have contributed to American society. Its backstage plot, however, in which Bill "Bojangles" Robinson, as aspiring entertainer Bill Williamson, and Lena Horne, as the singer Selina Rogers, struggle to make a success of their careers and romantic relationship, is unique among Black-cast musicals of the classical era. Unlike *Cabin in the Sky* (1943), released the same year, and previous Black-cast films *Hallelujah* (1929) and *Hearts in Dixie* (1929), *Stormy Weather* places Black Americans in the world of the backstage where opportunity and mobility are promised and achieved.

In this way, the Black-cast musical elides the issue of racial prejudice in any overt fashion, but in its absence, the narrative conflict centers on the issue of gender and women's work outside the home, a particular wartime concern. The two entertainers enjoy life together until Bill gets a Hollywood contract. He comes to Selina's dressing room before their show, armed with a large sketch of a house bordered by a white picket fence. As the pressbook describes the scene, "He wants to settle down with the movie money in a little cottage he has all picked out—but Selina wants to stay on the stage."[34] Bill points to where her room and the nursery will be. She admits the house is pretty but asserts that "it's not for us." Selina becomes adamant when he argues with her, telling her that she has "worked long enough" and that it is time she "settled down." "I don't want to quit," she responds emphatically. "I wouldn't be happy unless I went on with my work, just like you."

The film conveys her initial reaction to the house through the dressing room mirror. She sits in front of her dressing table, surrounded by evidence of her success. The table is commodious and outfitted with a feminine, ruffled lamp, while in the background we see framed photographs of her performances. Through the reflection, we notice that her face registers consternation as she looks seriously at the sketch. Meanwhile, Bill stands at her side, bent toward her as she glances downward at the picture. The shot registers the tension between the couple with their doubled bodies in the mirror as well as their inability to communicate by looking at each other. Conveying a difference in opinion, one that is consequential to their relationship, the man-in-the-mirror shot reveals a husband and wife at cross purposes.

In *Everything I Have Is Yours*, the mirror shot is more explicitly about male power. Played by real-life husband and wife dancing stars Gower and Marge Champion, Chuck and Pamela Hubbard are a married dancing team getting their big break on Broadway. Just before the show, Pamela experiences fatigue and wearily sits at her dressing table. Chuck is concerned but, as will become a pattern in the film, he believes that her maladies are his own and expresses that he is feeling unwell too. She gives voice to this tendency of his, saying resentfully, "Everything I have is yours, that's our song alright, because everything I have you get." Her accusation plays out in the plot of the film when, realizing she is pregnant, she must leave the stage for a house in the country while her husband becomes a star.

The mirror shot in the early dressing room sequence, like in *Stormy Weather*, frames the couple with the wife seated and the husband standing in back and to the side of her. Again, neither of the two looks directly at the other, filtering their gaze through the reflective surface of the dressing table mirror. The shot communicates how Pamela's disdainful look does not register with her husband; he is too engrossed in his own physical well-being to notice. While the background of the reflected image surrounds the couple with evidence of Pamela's achievements—her opulent costumes, a large bouquet of roses, and a framed image of her on the stage—it is Chuck's commandeering of the mirror that renders her feelings unimportant.

As musicals, *Stormy Weather* and *Everything I Have Is Yours* ultimately return husband and wife to each other, albeit without addressing the conflicts that the dressing rooms exposed. More recent directors of backstage films have produced far more consequential man-in-the-mirror shots, exposing the latent power dynamics between husbands and wives who work or aspire to. In the scene from *Revolutionary Road* that begins this chapter, April sits at her dressing table, disappointed that her performance in the community theater production did not go as well as she had hoped. Frank moves toward her as he confirms that "it wasn't a triumph." Instead of shooting the scene as it appears in Richard Yates's novel from 1961, in which Frank focuses on his own appearance in the mirror, director Sam Mendes emphasizes April.[35] The shot is a medium close-up of her body from the waist up. Mendes captures her reflection by placing the camera underneath Frank's outstretched arm, his hand resting on April's back. What we see, then, is an image of April, illuminated by the table's light, as she looks up at Frank, his arm extended behind her. Frank's shadowy torso is in the extreme foreground and fills up a third of the frame, threatening to overtake her altogether. Her expression of pain and anguish as she looks at his form adds to the sense of dread in the shot. As in previous man-in-the-mirror shots, the husband and wife are displaced from each other, but unlike in those others, here the man's faceless figure emphasizes the dominance of his physical presence to the detriment of his wife's well-being.

As director Brian Gibson frames him, the man in the mirror is a menacing figure in *What's Love Got to Do with It*. A biopic based on the life of Tina Turner and her abuse at the hands of her husband, Ike, the film contains brutal scenes of domestic violence. But while Ike's abuse does not occur in the dressing rooms of Gibson's film, the possibility and promise of violence are nevertheless present. The sequence in Tina's dressing room is based on an actual interview from 1964 in which the singer discusses an array of topics, including the moment when she first met and hoped to perform with Ike. As in the real interview, Ike is silent while she talks. Gibson draws out the implied threat that Ike presents, however, by manipulating the spatial dynamics of the dressing room, Ike's placement, and the camera's subjectivity.

In the scene, a white interviewer asks Ike (Laurence Fishburne) and Tina (Angela Bassett) a series of questions regarding the rise of British music, a phenomenon that Ike does not desire to comment on. When the interviewer directs a question to him, Ike does not respond and Tina quickly answers for him, changing the subject to the "great new songs" her husband has been writing. Ike is aggressive in his silence, occasionally glancing at Tina's reflection and smiling at the interviewer before he stands up and slowly leaves the room, crossing in front of Tina's seated figure at the table and placing his hand possessively on her back as he does so.

The scene is tense not only because Ike does not speak and Tina does, but also because of its visual form and aesthetics. A continuous shot of fifty-two seconds, the dressing room scene feels unstable and claustrophobic. Gibson places the shaky, handheld camera closest to Ike; in medium to close-up, Ike's figure fills half the frame. By contrast, Tina's face, which we see reflected in the mirror behind Ike, is diminished. Through abrupt camera zooms, we move closer to Tina, but Ike's figure remains in the frame, revealing the nervous glances she occasionally casts his way and how she cannot escape his control. As Ike stands to exit, the camera zooms out to watch him go and then zooms back in to Tina's reflection. This time, she fills the frame, but as her nervous laughter indicates, this interview has not been a candid one. Gibson never allows Tina to speak directly to the interviewer or to Ike; her responses are always mediated by the mirror, emphasizing her ultimate domination by her husband.

Gibson also uses a grainy film stock to convey the documentary source of the material, the real interview the couple gave in Tina's dressing room in 1964. The rough images parallel and are a continuation of the montage that precedes the interview. In that sequence, which approximates the kind of "success montage" that is familiar to backstage film more generally, we see how Tina's stage success has resulted in a new home, children, and joyous family celebrations. The grainy footage of the subsequent interview in the dressing room establishes a continuity between the two sequences, with the false projections of the latter informing the former. After the dressing room scene, the grainy footage disappears for a sequence at the Turners' home, suggesting that we are back in real time. In that moment, we witness one of the most brutal of Ike's beatings. The violence confirms that the previous two sequences, at home and in the dressing room, are illusions rather than reality. They are a comment on the mediated representation we see of a husband and wife, through home video footage or documentary interview, that does not accurately convey the truth behind the facade.

The "man in the mirror" shot. *What's Love Got to Do with It*, copyright 1993 by Paramount Pictures.

The Lonely Stage

While many man-in-the-mirror shots emphasize marital dynamics, others foreground the power differential between men and women generally. In *Opening Night* (1977), theater director Manny Victor (Ben Gazzara) frequently occupies the dressing room of lead actress Myrtle Gordon (Gena Rowlands). They are not husband and wife, but the film makes it clear that they have had a romantic relationship in the past. Frustrated with her inability to speak the lines of the play *The Second Woman* as written, and by her sporadic, unpredictable behavior generally, Manny interrogates Myrtle repeatedly when they are backstage. In a medium to long shot, the camera holds the figures of both actress and director in the frame. As in *What's Love Got to Do with It*, the female performer has her back to the camera as she faces the dressing table mirror while the man sits awkwardly facing her profiled figure; his profile is reflected in her mirror so that we see two versions of the man watching the woman. Because of the positions of the characters, we are not allowed access to Myrtle directly, only indirectly through her reflection. Manny does not register possession as in other man-in-the-mirror shots. But his attempts to manipulate, through flattery and admonishment, are evident in his communication to her: he tells her, "You're the most exciting woman I've ever known and the greatest actress," but immediately qualifies the compliment with, "but you're not funny anymore." The framing of the shot conveys the audience's distance from Myrtle, Manny's frustration at not being able to understand her, and Myrtle's own inability to articulate her feelings. She is physically and emotionally distant and alone.

Loneliness constitutes a common theme in backstage films about the aging female performer. The films contextualize the actress's current isolation as a function of her rejection of domesticity; not content to settle down as a wife and mother, the performer prioritized her career and the audiences who helped her to sustain it. Agents of their own destinies, these women have achieved greatness, but they are left with a sense of loss. They drink too much, they rely on prescription drugs, their bodies are diseased, and they struggle to get through each day. In biopics about female performers, such as *Film Stars Don't Die in Liverpool* and *Judy*, as well as films that are about fictional performers played self-reflexively by performers themselves, such as *Opening Night*, the narratives are linked by an obsession with the aging woman, who is reckoning with her past choices and relies on her audience to sustain her while "lighting up the lonely stage."[36]

The loneliness of the aging star has a visual language that filmmakers have used as symbolic shorthand for her plight. In *Film Stars Don't Die in Liverpool* and *Judy*, the star's physical weakness is on prominent display in her dressing room. The latter film opens with a series of close-ups of Gloria Grahame (Annette Bening) while she prepares for a stage performance. Taken together, they convey the passage of time and decay. Extreme close-ups of her facial features reveal the age lines around her mouth and eyes. Other close-ups of her hands, busy with unpacking her makeup case full of mementos, show her chipped red nail polish. Another close-up of a lit cigarette on the table foreshadows a life that is quickly coming to an end. The sequence communicates how Gloria is past her prime, confirmed by a close-up of a publicity photo of the real Gloria Grahame, which is tucked into the side of the dressing table mirror. Suddenly, in the first long shot of the film, we see Gloria collapse to the ground, writhing in pain. Director Paul McGuigan emphasizes the tragedy of the moment by placing the camera far away from her and on the floor of the dressing room, forcing us to feel her abjectness and isolation.

Isolation is a theme in *Judy* as well. Judy Garland (Renée Zellweger) accepts an invitation to perform in London because she needs the money. Her film career is over and she can no longer take care of her children, whom she has been attempting to integrate into her stage performances in the United States. The film shows Judy in a series of abject positions, sleep deprived, drunk, and lonely in her hotel room, her dressing room, and the streets of London. A very similar shot to the one in *Film Stars Don't Die in Liverpool* occurs in this film; after struggling through her first performance on the London stage, we find Judy in her dressing room, framed in long shot with the camera at a distance from her and positioned near the ground. She sits deeply hunched over her table, facing away from the mirror with her head in her hands. Flowers and telegrams from well-wishers surround her, and yet she is alone and deeply unhappy.

Scenes of female collapse in the dressing room represent the most private moments of public women. They carry symbolic weight for the ways that they repeat the image of a woman lying prostrate, charting, as melodramas often do, "the trajectory of a [female] body in pain."[37] As Dennis Bingham has written, the female biopic is "weighted down by myths of suffering, victimization, and failure," the representation of society's "acute fear of women in the public realm."[38] The aging actress also has a representational history of being associated with "decline" and "abjectness," as though her age was the price to pay for a life led in the spotlight.[39] It is telling that McGuigan inserts the dressing room scene to foreground Gloria's decline at the beginning of the film given that no such corresponding scene appears in the memoir by Peter Turner on which the film is based. And in *Judy*, director Rupert Goold emphasizes Judy Garland's loss of purpose without her children repeatedly, producing the image of the suffering woman despite all the signs of adulation that surround her. These women have collapsed as a result of their demanding careers, but also as a consequence of their choices to leave family and children behind.

Meeting audiences' need to come to terms with the meaning of successful career women in our society, Hollywood backstage films like the biopics just discussed use a visual language of isolation and collapse to narrate the lives of female stars. Looking beyond Hollywood, the trope of the aging actress persists in nuanced but just as limiting ways. In the independently produced drama *Opening Night*, John Cassavetes presents a backstage film that simultaneously engages, questions, and reaffirms more mainstream depictions of the aging woman.

In response to Manny's accusation that she isn't "funny anymore," Myrtle explains, "I'm just so struck by the cruelty in this damn play." The play to which she refers is *The Second Woman*. Given the highly self-referential thematics and aesthetics of *Opening Night*, however, she could be referencing Cassavetes's film as well. As Todd Berliner wrote of the film in 1999, it disintegrates "the distinctions between reality and fiction, actor and role, between script and improvisation."[40] A play within a film, *Opening Night* confuses the traditional boundaries of Hollywood cinema by foregrounding the connections between the three realities that produce it: "play, movie, and the real world."[41] So while Myrtle is referencing the cruelty of *The Second Woman*, in which she plays the aging female character Virginia, the blurring of lines and the improvisation that characterize Cassavetes's film dialogue might also lead one to interpret Myrtle's line as pertaining to *Opening Night*, its "cruel" depiction of an actress obsessed with her own aging, or even, by extension, the society in which *Opening Night* is created, in which aging women are unfairly judged. As Manny tells Myrtle in an earlier scene, "It's tradition—actresses get slapped"—his mode of delivery making it unclear whether he is referring to the actresses in plays or actresses in society. Myrtle/Virginia/Gena expresses extreme discomfort with either prospect; when ultimately faced with the rehearsal of the slap, she collapses to the ground.

A critical darling that emerged in festivals nearly a decade after it was made, *Opening Night*, like much of Cassavetes's work, highlights the immense acting talent of Gena Rowlands. Her prominence in the film cannot be denied, and it is perhaps for that reason that critics and scholars have been generous in their interpretation of the ideological underpinnings of the film's narrative and aesthetics. In 1989, Lisa Katzman wrote, "In exploring the complex relationship between the neurotic obsession women have with ageing, the denial of death, and madness, Cassavetes treads upon territory investigated in literature by feminists, but never in a film (by feminists or anybody else) with his sensitivity, emotional intelligence and humor." Taking women's "neurotic" tendencies as a given, Katzman interprets Cassavetes's film to be an affirmation of the female experience. Referring to Myrtle's eventual triumph on the stage, despite being so drunk that she can barely stand, Katzman argues that the moment represents a "liberation from sexist ideology" that "transcends gender" by foregrounding the importance of living in the moment.[42]

In her essay on *Opening Night*'s relationship to innovative cinematic form, Homay King discusses Cassavetes's kinship with European film directors like Pier Paolo Pasolini. As she maintains, in addition to the "highly decentered manner" in which the dialogue attribution is communicated, Cassavetes's film also "complicates efforts to attribute point of view and to separate out those looks that belong to the enunciation from those assigned to characters within the diegesis." Arguing that the film goes beyond a gendered critique of the actress, King interprets Myrtle's difficulty with the role of the aging woman to stem from a commitment to artistry: she is afraid "of delivering lines in a mechanical fashion, of ceasing to be moved by her material and settling into a static, unchanging role." King concludes that "aging must be interpreted as a metaphor for shutting down or affective mortality."[43]

There is much that is innovative formally about *Opening Night*, but it also retreads, and disturbingly amplifies, the trope of the lonely and aging female star. It is ambiguous to be sure, but Myrtle's anxieties about getting old, about playing an aged woman on the stage, and about no longer being young and attractive permeate the film. So acute are her fears that she conjures the specter of Nancy, a young "autograph hound" who is hit by a car while running after Myrtle, who visits the actress in the dressing room and haunts her to the point of a violent attack. Simultaneously representing her adoring fans and her younger self (Myrtle refers to Nancy as her "first woman" and to her onstage self as "second woman"), Nancy is a persistent, often unwelcome reminder of who Myrtle used to be. But even after Myrtle brutally beats Nancy, effectively ending the harassment, Myrtle is still haunted by getting older, exclaiming, "This age thing has me coming off the wall." Ultimately, she holds up the play's opening night because she gets drunk to the point of collapse.

Scenes of Myrtle's self-absorption and neediness are interspersed with external forms of condescension and disdain. So while Myrtle demands the adoration of all around her, in one instance forcing Manny to express his love for her in front of his own wife, we also witness the harshness with which others pass judgment on her life choices. Interrogating Myrtle in the dressing room, Manny easily reduces her fears to her own personal failings, including rejecting marriage and children ("Did that ever occur to you?"). When she visits Nancy's mourning family, the young girl's father accuses her, "You don't have children. If you did, you wouldn't have come here." And in the final scene, drunk and stumbling to her spot on the stage, she tries to convince herself that she is happy, repeating the line, "I didn't want children," over and over again. So while Cassavetes disrupts our easy interpretation of who is to blame for Myrtle's unhappiness, he nevertheless places the familiar image of the lonely and abject female star on center stage once more.

Cassavetes's unconventional form and the trope of the collapsed female star collide in the final dressing room sequence. Minutes before opening night on Broadway, the cast, crew, and production team wait to find out if the show will go on. Myrtle cannot be found. When she finally arrives, drunker than anyone has ever seen her, Manny and some helpers, including Myrtle's devoted dresser Kelly (Louise Lewis) and assistant Leo (Fred Draper), guide her backstage. Once she gets to the corridor that leads to the dressing room, however, Myrtle collapses. Angrily, Manny instructs those who stand by to leave her alone. He walks to the dressing room, turns around, and glowers at her while she slides, stumbles, and crawls toward the door.

A drunken Myrtle crawls to her dressing room. *Opening Night*, copyright 1977 by Faces Distribution.

Cassavetes highlights Myrtle's abjection with his framing. He places the camera at the start of the narrow hallway so that it captures a series of doorways leading eventually to the bright pink dressing room, aglow from the vanity lights that surround the rectangular mirror. Kelly and Leo stand inside one of the doorways just out of the frame so that Myrtle's prostrate body lies in the center of the shot and Manny's figure stands imperiously in the background. Left alone and without support, Myrtle's abjection is supreme. And Manny subjects her to the humiliation of being unable to walk by herself by refusing to assist her. As though the abjection is too extreme for even us to see, Kelly quickly steps to the dressing room door once Myrtle has crawled her way inside, furtively looks at the camera, and closes it.

The dressing room is a site of madness, self-pity, and punishment in the film. It ultimately reveals Myrtle as yet another woman on the verge of a breakdown because she is getting older and has made choices that have left her alone. When she makes it through opening night, becoming more sober as the play goes on, she delivers a powerful performance and wins the ecstatic applause of the audience. The cast rush to congratulate her and offer their many compliments. Myrtle enjoys this moment, lapping up the adoration. Seemingly, the pain and suffering have all been worth it and Myrtle is at the top of her career once more. But Cassavetes's ending does not provide a resolution or reconciliation of the actress's troubles; indeed, it is very likely that she will suffer the same crisis of identity in her next play. Instead, he gives us an image of another aging actress, like those we find in so many backstage films, who crave audience approval at the expense of sustaining more lasting personal relationships. For that choice, she will always be on the verge of collapse.

As a liminal space, dressing rooms are multivalent for wives and mothers. Symbols of female ambition and domesticity, they can be sites of social approval or censure. For the aging female star, they are certainly the latter. For while fictional characters like Myrtle in *Opening Night* confirm how women's choices to reject domesticity lead to personal unhappiness, even stories about real women are selected for their potential to explore dramatic female tragedy. The sad endings of Judy Garland and Gloria Grahame are well known, but it is the telling of their stories that makes their lives symbolic for public women everywhere. It is in the dressing room that women, real and fictionalized, must reckon with their relationship to the social constructs that are wives and mothers.

But men have had their own experiences in the dressing room, a site where masculine authority is repeatedly challenged by female intrusions and where male objectification on the stage must be checked. Chapter 4 outlines how the figure of the leading man has been a persistent trope for filmmakers to explore the relationship between society's expectation of what a leading man should be and the human failings of the men who occupy that role. Stymied by their own personal weaknesses and pressured by women stronger than themselves, the leading man must fight to reestablish the dressing room as masculine space.

4

Leading Men

• • • • • • • • • • • • • • • • • • • •

> Leading man. The male star-lead, or other leading part.
> —Wilfred Granville, *The Theater Dictionary* (1952)

Halfway through *Once upon a Time in Hollywood* (2019), an angry Rick Dalton (Leonardo DiCaprio) threatens his mirrored reflection, "You don't get these lines right, I'm gonna blow your fuckin' brains out tonight, alright?" He unravels in his dressing room trailer situated on the backlot of a new Western television series. Berating himself for drinking eight whiskey sours the night before and then forgetting his lines on set, the actor admits to being an alcoholic and mocks himself for being a "fuckin' baboon," which he then imitates with a series of monkey sounds. Like a baboon at the zoo, he paces inside the tight space while throwing, kicking, and breaking things. He is unhinged, a far cry from the cool outlaw character he is playing onscreen and the Hollywood star he has carefully constructed for the public.

A backstudio picture about a television star whose career is in decline, Quentin Tarantino's film is concerned with the division between Dalton's onscreen persona and his offscreen private life. Projections of a rugged masculinity characterize the star's performances, while moments of insecurity like those in the dressing room betray Dalton's confidence as a construction of the media. The dressing room scene is a moment of self-reckoning that literally rocks the film; Dalton's histrionics in the trailer force it to rattle, shaking the interior mirrors and curtains with every violent movement the actor makes. Shot with a stationary handheld camera and edited with a series of jump cuts, the film emphasizes Dalton's insecurity by making the audience feel the unsteadiness of the space with a series of abrupt transitions from one shot to the next. Dalton's image is refracted by a mirror on either side of the frame, a visual indication of his split self. And the final shot in which he threatens his reflection produces another form of instability by using direct address. Standing to the side of the mirror, Dalton points a finger at himself. Because of the angle, however, his reflection peers directly at the camera. Caught up in the madness, the film's audience becomes implicated in the actor's rage, adding another layer of discomfort in the dressing room.

Like the dressing room scenes in *Raging Bull*, the scene is crucial for displaying the downward trajectory of the male lead. In an earlier scene, a producer tells Dalton that his time in the spotlight is coming to a close: "Down goes you, down goes your career as a leading man." The stakes go beyond the personal here; they also have consequences for the fate of white male authority. Waiting near the valet stand after meeting with the producer, Dalton becomes emotional. His friend Cliff (Brad Pitt) warns him "not to cry in front of the Mexicans" and quickly gives him a pair of sunglasses to hide the tears. In a later scene, Cliff vindicates white manhood in a battle of strength with Bruce Lee. These moments in which white men must ultimately control the racial and ethnic Other suggest that leading-man films are invested with a social imperative; they must rectify white men's place in relation to those whom society deems to be potentially threatening, including people of color and women. Dressing room scenes like the one in *Once upon a Time in Hollywood* make a spectacle of the leading man's insecurity as a crucial step on the way toward restoring white male confidence and leadership.

While backstage films with male protagonists are produced with less frequency than those with women, they are nevertheless critical in number and originate with the beginnings of cinema at the turn of the twentieth century. They range across genre, including musicals, melodramas, jazz films, backstudio films, biopics, and superhero movies. They take as their subject the figure of the leading man, most typically a white and straight male actor who has the starring role in a performance or production, such as Rick Dalton. The pleasure of performance is certainly a primary reason for these films' long-standing appeal; after his dressing room diatribe, Dalton goes on to deliver a winning performance on the set. But leading-man films endure because they are about the cultural figure of the leading man himself. They shape and mediate what it means to be a man and what happens to the individual, society, and the nation when masculine leadership is absent. Like *Once upon a Time in Hollywood*, leading-man films situate these dynamics in the dressing room, a space of intimate spectacle where male insecurities can be exposed away from the prying eyes of the public. We view the dressing room's furnishings, location, and inhabitants, including dressers and wives, as markers of the relative importance and strength of the male star. And we watch private moments of self-reckoning as the leading man faces his reflection in the vanity mirror. Such scenes cinematically convey the fracturing and fragmentation of the self and its social consequences. The leading man in Hollywood's backstage narratives is a fundamentally troubled figure, besieged by doubt and haunted by inner demons that collectively project an image of weakened and vulnerable (often white) manhood.

Hollywood films have consistently explored the archetype of the leading man in crisis. He is weakened by modern society, and therefore made vulnerable to women and people of color, and threatened with obsolescence. These anxieties appear again and again in films ranging from *The Country Girl* (1954) and *A Star Is Born* (1954) to *Birdman* (2014) and *Joker* (2019). While their social and political contexts shift over time, the spectacle of dressing room crises remains consistent. Films made outside Hollywood offer an exception, including Spike Lee's *Mo' Better Blues* (1990), which treat these dynamics differently by the very act of privileging a Black male lead whose relationship to race, gender, and sexuality departs from the white heterosexual norm.

This chapter explores the performance of masculinity, and masculinity's spectacles, in films about leading men. After examining the origins of leading-man films in the first decade of the twentieth century, and the ways that they reflect the actual experiences of men in popular theater, I closely examine the midcentury, the moment when backstage films present leading men who are weak and pathetic. Ginger Rogers abandons Fred Astaire in *The Barkleys of Broadway* (1949), crooners Bing Crosby and Frank Sinatra become alcoholics in *The Country Girl* (1954) and *The Joker Is Wild* (1957), and even Elvis gets labeled a "phony" when he does not measure up sexually in *Loving You* (1957). Choosing the year 1954 as the setting for a case study of the midcentury leading man enables me to focus on three films that rehearse men's suitability as lovers and husbands set against the backdrop of larger forces like aging, death, and cultural and social change. In *White Christmas* (Michael Curtiz), a backstage musical; *The Country Girl*, a cinematic adaptation of Clifford Odets's play; and *A Star Is Born*, a backstudio film, sustained reflections on what makes a leading man "a man who leads" dominate the narrative and get revealed in the dressing room. Regarding the last film, there is no doubt that it is Judy Garland's virtuosic performance as the main character, Vicki Lester, that lends *A Star Is Born* its primary and lasting appeal. And as I discuss later in the chapter, Garland's own emotionally wrenching dressing room scene garnered her an Oscar nomination (she lost to Grace Kelly). As the secondary character, however, James Mason's Norman Maine provides the conflict and the crisis of the narrative. I refocus our attention to Norman because he is the most broken of leading men in this period who, faced with the concurrent success of his wife and the end of his career, decides to kill himself. In this way, *A Star Is Born* adds something unique to the history of leading-man films; it makes a tragedy out of a man who cannot be restored to a place of supremacy.

Taken together, the leading-man films of 1954 provide a rubric for the representation of male crises going forward. In particular, anxieties about women's proximity to male space become more acute in the later films *Mo' Better Blues* and *Magic Mike* (2012), which foreground instances of male collectivity in the dressing room and offer the possibility for alternate interpretations of male bonding that occurs in private spaces away from female influence. The last section of the chapter examines two films that explore the hypermasculine identity of the superhero set amid fears of ineffectiveness and obsolescence. *Birdman* and *Joker* are, to varying extents, backstage films that discursively overlap with the superhero genre. In *Birdman*, actor Riggan (Michael Keaton) is haunted by his superhero alter ego, and in *Joker*, Arthur Fleck (Joaquin Phoenix) holds a job as a clown that prepares him for his ultimate role as a notorious supervillain. Both films reflect on the leading man's dissolution, which manifests as delusions of identity, and explore that process formally with the mise-en-scène of backstage space.

Backstage Masculinity

Most recent studies of masculinity and genre have focused on those films that engage in traditionally masculine exploits, including the Western and action and detective films.[1] These are genres that primarily take place in exterior locales, externalize conflict in the form of physical violence, and emphasize the prowess of the male body. Audiences' fascination with these genres, as many of these studies explore, has much to do with their ability to channel anxieties about Otherness, national weakness, and economic insecurity after the wars in Vietnam and Afghanistan and the threats posed to heteronormative white masculinity by feminism and the movements for civil rights, immigrants' rights, and queer rights.

What happens to the representation of masculinity when we shift our focus from bodies to space, from exteriority to interiority, and from narrative action to mise-en-scène? This is the question posed by Stella Bruzzi, whose attention to style and mise-en-scène in what she calls "men's cinema" liberates us from an emphasis on the body and on individual "masculine" genres. Tracing an "expressive aesthetic" across genres, for Bruzzi, yields a more expansive understanding of how masculinity is conveyed to the spectator in both interior and exterior spaces.[2] Other studies of transgeneric spaces, most notably Pamela Robertson Wojcik's *The Apartment Plot* (2010) and Merrill Schleier's *Skyscraper Cinema* (2009), find nuanced and long-standing representations of masculinity that rehearse male fears of domestication, obsolescence, and the loss of individuality through the cinematic articulation of interior locales including the bachelor pad and the office, respectively.[3] This chapter furthers those analyses by locating other kinds of men and manhood in the interior space of the dressing room, therefore complicating approaches to masculinity that rely on genre and on more externalized forms of gender expression in film. Peering into dressing rooms across a range of backstage film allows us to see the recurring figure of the leading man grappling with and defining his place as a man, rendering the rehearsal and performance of masculinity a central concern of the genre.

Surprisingly, however, these films have received little attention from film critics and scholars. In addition to their distance from the worlds of films more traditionally defined as "masculine," backstage films occupy spaces and structure their orientation to the spectator in ways that have been theorized as "feminine." The musical, a genre that has played a critical role in shaping the backstage narrative's themes and conventions, as Steven Cohan explains, "takes the performativity of male and female stardom as its very premise."[4] The song-and-dance men for which the musical is so popular, from Fred Astaire to Gene Kelly to Elvis Presley, force the collision of body and spectacle, two qualities traditionally associated with women. This problematic at the core of the genre, then, is that it makes "a blatant spectacle of men."[5] Cohan argues that this process does not necessarily feminize them, but rather alters the relationship between the viewer and the viewed, subject and object, along erotic lines.[6] In their frequent interruptions of narrative, musical numbers involving men participate in the "production of masculinity and femininity out of highly theatricalized performances of gender."[7] With its emphasis on access and display, the dressing room becomes an alternate site of performance in backstage film wherein more private stagings of gender play out.

Since the origins of commercial entertainment in the late nineteenth-century theater, the prominence of feminine spectacle has been a subject of concern. Susan Glenn and Linda Mizejewski have charted the rise of chorus and show girls in musical comedy and variety entertainments, with the latter arguing that feminine spectacle was definitional to these forms.[8] Displacing the figure of the male actor as star, a prominent figure in "legitimate theater" through much of the nineteenth century, female stars like Sarah Bernhardt, Lillian Russell, and Marie Dressler—the last a former chorus girl—rose to prominence in this period and quickly became the symbols of American celebrity. Producers like George M. Cohan and the Schuberts understood that the public would pay to see female performers and, in particular, provocatively dressed groups of women. Parallel to this process was the shift from resident stock companies, which consisted of smaller troupes rooted in a specific town or region, to a producer-directed theater trust known as the Theatrical Syndicate, which dominated the control of Broadway and nationally touring productions. Fraternal and labor organizations, created by and for male performers, responded to their loss of control with threats of agitation and even strikes. The earliest of these, the Actors' Society of America (ASA), formed in response to poor backstage working conditions and sought, among other things, to secure "cleaner dressing rooms."[9]

As the most important space where actors do the work of preparation for performance, dressing rooms were a critical part of the construction of a narrative of hardship with which men of the theater used to craft an image of manly integrity, strength, and resilience; and male actors repeatedly wielded this narrative of suffering in their fight against producers, women, and performers of color. Following the ASA's efforts, the White Rats of America formed their organization, which was both fraternal order and trade union, in 1901. Membership consisted of white men working in vaudeville and variety, realms of the theatrical profession that were considered lowbrow but allowed for a greater degree of agency over one's act. The White Rats took pride in these qualities of their profession and merged, as Alison M. Kibler explains, "the nineteenth-century ideal of the artisan (skillful, independent, and manly) but also incorporated the more modern notion of masculinity based on physical power." The feminization of American entertainment, and of vaudeville, rankled these vaudevillians. Going further than excluding women and Black performers, they "cast dramatic actors," who disdained lowbrow forms of theater, "as effeminate and thus undesirable." They bragged about the rough-and-tumble conditions in the theaters they played across the country, calling attention to the "cold, dismal" dressing rooms that were "a great deal out of order in every respect," the endurance of which turned them into "manly performer[s]."[10]

While most dressing rooms on the musical comedy and vaudeville circuits were stark and indecorous spaces within the theater, as described by the many performers who complained about them in the pages of *Variety*, their popular representation has coded them as feminine since the entry of women onto the seventeenth-century English stage. The voyeuristic delights of the dressing room, in which women undress for male pleasure, proliferated in poetry and novels of the eighteenth century. In the United States, the addition of female choruses to musical comedy, made a theatrical mainstay by *The Black Crook* (1866), the burlesques of Lydia Thompson, and *Floradora* (1900), fueled popular accounts of what women were really like in the dressing rooms where they took off their makeup, wigs, and costumes.[11]

Many of the earliest films took male voyeurism of the female occupation of dressing rooms as a provocative and humorous theme, including American Mutoscope and Biograph's production *From Show Girl to Burlesque Queen* (1903), for example, a sixty-five-second film that actively encourages voyeuristic engagement by positioning the female inhabitant of a dressing room in long shot as she undresses for the camera. A popular series featuring a recurring figure known as "Mr. Jack" shows a jolly and lascivious older man who imposes himself on women's backstage dressing rooms, alternately being welcomed by the female performers (as in *Mr. Jack Visits the Dressing Room*, 1904) and being disciplined by them (*Mr. Jack Is Caught in the Dressing Room*, 1904).

But while the majority of these films emphasize female spectacle in the dressing room, male performers occupied dressing rooms in great numbers and emphasized the space's potential for drama in both vaudeville skits and films. Actors created theater-film hybrids, a dynamic new form of entertainment that incorporated the technology of cinema precisely at the moment when the movies threatened to render live entertainment obsolete.[12] Appropriating the movies' dynamic ability to compress space and time, and foregrounding its appearance of realism, actors incorporated the technology to convey the demands and virtuosity of their profession. A case in point is the 1910 skit starring Anthony, a magician. At the beginning of his act, the motion picture screen announces to the audience that he is running late. Next, a short movie with a shot of Anthony in his backstage dressing room reveals him frantically getting ready for the performance. When he finishes, much out of breath, the movie screen rises and Anthony appears live onstage. His harried movements and breathlessness convey how his act is both skilled and physical, prompting an appreciation of his work.[13] Using the dressing room to call attention to the work behind the performance, male performers like Anthony were able to expose the gap between their private and public identities.

Leading Men at Midcentury

The first half of the twentieth century saw leading men appear persistently, if sporadically, in backstage film, from Charlie Chaplin's *The Masquerader* (1914) to the early sound-era musicals starring Al Jolson (*The Jazz Singer*, 1927; *The Singing Fool*, 1928) and the musicals of the war years (*For Me and My Gal*, 1942; *The Hard Way*, 1943). The 1950s, and in particular the year 1954, saw a proliferation of backstage films that placed men on center stage: Warner Bros. released *A Star Is Born* in September of that year, followed by Paramount's *White Christmas* in October and *The Country Girl* in December.[14] Bing Crosby's starring role in the latter two films indicates how the actor's persona underwent a shift that was parallel and related to changes in the Hollywood industry and its generic codes. The leading man was an especially salient cultural subject at the same time that the Hollywood studios felt the pressure of declining box office receipts and new technologies like television. The two musicals *White Christmas* and *A Star Is Born* register the anxieties of the industry, with the former incorporating televisual appeal as an important plot point and the latter self-reflexively commenting on the weakened state of the studios and offering a sharp critique of the star system the studios created and depended on. *The Country Girl* also evokes changing times; the filmmakers adopted the moody, chiaroscuro lighting schema of European art cinema while the actors, most notably Bing Crosby, known for decades as an "easygoing crooner," affected the new style of method acting.[15]

Leading-man films combine the destabilization of Hollywood genres and the industry with concerns about the health and strength of American men in the 1950s. *The Country Girl* is a case in point. In the film's show-within-a-show, actor Frank Elgin stars in the musical play *The Land around Us*, a folk musical like *Oklahoma!* (1943) before it, that delivers a celebratory tale about the resilience of the American people and their right to the land. And yet, despite Frank's projection of calm authority onstage, *The Country Girl* exposes the actor's profound insecurities and moral failings behind the scenes, calling into question his claim to manliness. One review describes how Crosby's Elgin is "a vain and terrified man living on pity and making excuses to himself for his own slackness of spirit." As the reviewer describes, Elgin "is not a hard-luck victim, but a quaking victim of self-contempt in the grip of alcohol and fear and lies."[16] In such films, the dichotomy between the ideal American male and the reality is thematically and spatially defined.

The crisis of postwar masculinity has its origins in the World War II era, during which men fought the war offshore while women worked in factories and guarded the home front. Social scientists and cultural observers noted the changing gender roles with concern and pointed to a difficult readjustment process at war's end. *The Best Years of Our Lives* depicts this dynamic explicitly by exploring the experiences of three demobilized and differently damaged men, from bilateral amputation, to post-traumatic stress disorder, to feelings of obsolescence.[17] The backstage film *The Hard Way* (1943) captures this dynamic more implicitly, with the career ambitions of a rising musical star resulting in the downward spiral and eventual suicide of her performer husband, a crisis that is echoed by *A Star Is Born* a decade later.

With the advent of the Cold War, fears about weakened American men, susceptible to the stronger feminizing forces of women and the sinister influence of communism, intensified. Reactionary responses to such fears stemmed from a variety of sources, including the Eisenhower administration's investment in physical education programs in schools and the rise of *Playboy* as an influential cultural tract that praised the predatory masculinity of the bachelor.[18] In cinema, as Cohan has detailed, "tough guys" and muscular men abounded in Hollywood's "age of the chest," with stars like Rock Hudson and William Holden becoming symbols of an ideal masculinity. But the 1950s was also the age of the bachelor, as both Cohan and Robertson Wojcik have documented, in which a distinct model of male domesticity that was single and decidedly unfeminized also dominated Hollywood screens.[19]

While they are less concerned with the display of male strength and seduction, leading-man films reveal a profound discomfort with the feminizing influences of assertive, opinionated women and their domesticating effects. Backstage films narrativize gender as a performance, a series of masquerades in which men transition in and out of roles that constitute their professional lives as working entertainers and return them to private realms in which they reflect on these multiple identities. To the extent that all gender is a performance, leading-man films provide audiences with a series of masquerades that expose, but then seek to bridge, the distance between men and their projected selves. With few exceptions, *The Hard Way* and *A Star Is Born* being cases in point, leading-man films from midcentury Hollywood restore leading men to positions of leadership at the end. First and foremost, however, the protagonists must reckon with the feminizing influences of their wives and girlfriends.

In the leading-man films of 1954, the men are surrounded, smothered, and haunted by women. Nowhere is this more apparent than in the backstage dressing rooms. In *The Country Girl*, the leading man's wife dominates his dressing room in the theaters the cast uses for rehearsal, the out-of-town tryout, and eventually on Broadway. In stark contrast to Grace Kelly's glamorous persona, her role as Georgie seemingly eschews makeup, pulls her hair into a bun, and wears glasses. Unhappy in her marriage, she has ceased to put effort into her appearance, dressing in the drab attire of a long woolen skirt, a blouse cinched at the neck, and baggy sweater. She lurks in the dressing room, overpowering her husband, who is weakened by self-doubt and alcoholism brought on by the death of their son. Bernie (William Holden), the director of the show, finds Georgie's control of her husband distasteful, sensing that she secretly enjoys Frank's dependence on her. Over the course of the film, Bernie and Georgie take advantage of Frank's absence from the dressing room to argue about what kind of wife Frank truly needs. Georgie insists that Frank is "weak, he is a leaner," to which Bernie responds abruptly, "I don't like strong women, Mrs. Elgin," and blames Frank's lack of authority on Georgie, who "has too much of it."

The cinematic staging of the dressing room sequences calls attention to its cramped quarters, making Georgie's domination of the space all the more apparent. In one backstage scene, Bernie and his producers stand in the wings discussing Frank's performance in rehearsal. Shot in deep focus, the scene depicts multiple planes of action. The producing team stands in the foreground while, down a long corridor in the background, we see the door frame leading to Frank's dressing room. The shot is a *mise en abyme*; Frank sits with his back to the men, removing his makeup in the rectangular vanity mirror that visually echoes the door frame. Frank's figure is only visible for a moment, however, as Georgie emerges from the dressing room, hovering in the doorway, pitting herself between the producers and her husband and effectively eliminating Frank from the frame altogether.

In a subsequent scene, Georgie is waiting when Frank returns from the stage; she quietly knits and delivers admonishing glances at her husband as he drinks too much cough syrup for a feigned chest sickness. The two sequences depict her presence as menacing, spider-like in wait for her prey and in direct violation of the signs posted just outside the dressing room's door that read, "Important— No Visitors Allowed in Dressing Rooms." Her dour dress and demeanor lend credibility to Bernie's fears that she is manipulating Frank, keeping him weak on purpose. The latter sequence also affirms the feminizing forces of the dressing room with Georgie engaging in the domestic pursuit of knitting, a female-associated activity that is out of place in the spartan, male space. In theater history, managers routinely abolished the knitting mothers of child performers from the backstage out of fears that the women would interfere with the smooth running of the show. To this day, theater practitioners consider knitting in the vicinity of the stage a taboo activity that will bring bad luck to the production.[20] In *The Country Girl*, the film conjures Georgie as the veritable knitting mother whose very presence is threatening; she sows doubt in the leading man by infantilizing him.

With its emphasis on female star power, *A Star Is Born* is also a film that makes women's dominance a source of anxiety for the male lead. A love story set against the backdrop of Hollywood moviemaking, the film charts the rise of Vicki Lester (Judy Garland) and the concurrent demise of her husband, Norman Maine (James Mason), through its dressing room scenes. We first encounter Norman when he drunkenly disturbs the backstage activities during a Hollywood benefit concert. For the scene, director George Cukor and production designer Gene Allen constructed a particularly porous and mobile dressing room setting situated just off the stage. Through the use of long, multiseated dressing tables and vanity mirrors as barriers, the dressing room is given an illusion of privacy that is easily exposed by Norman, who, angered by the attentions of press photographers, smashes one of the mirrors, which reveals and temporarily halts the backstage preparations of the other performers. These performers, however, are all women, show girls in bright red costumes and female onlookers in evening gowns. When Norman shatters the dressing room mirror, he reveals the previously all-male space of journalists to be surrounded by female activity. An arresting shot follows Norman's exit from the dressing room into the larger backstage realm, framed by the broken mirror and the bodies of female performers who cast a mix of amused and horrified glances at him. It is a complex shot that frames Norman with the jagged edges of broken glass, out of place in this vibrant, female-dominated space, while photographers exploit the spectacle.

This introduction to Norman establishes his instability, alerts the audience that he has lost stature in the industry, and sets up the film's central conflict between his fading star status and the skyrocketing appeal of his wife. It also

Leading man Norman Maine breaks out of the dressing room. *A Star Is Born*, copyright 1954 by Transcona Enterprises.

anticipates a later scene when, his contract with the studio ended due to his liability as an alcoholic, the studio's press agent dictates a public statement as workers take down the billboard advertisement for Norman's film and replace it with one for Vicki Lester's. Increasingly, Norman's failure indicates, the studio prefers women to men, a fact conveyed by the décor of his press agent's office, in which massive black-and-white glamour photos of female stars like Vicki Lester, Kathryn Grayson, and Audrey Hepburn adorn the walls. Norman is eclipsed not only by his wife but by women in general.

We see Norman very much at home in the dressing room scene in which he invites Vicki to his backstudio bungalow, a multiroom structure that testifies to Norman's once magnificent star status. He sits Vicki at the dressing table and begins to undo the work done by the makeup and hair department at the studio. In his hands, his romantic interest is restored to her original appearance. Vicki is still an unknown, and while Norman believes in her star potential, he is most comfortable when he is in control of her image. The long sequence in which he smears cold cream on her face and carefully removes her makeup is a touching scene that shows how Norman appreciates Vicki's natural beauty, but according to his standards of what she should look like. In the midst of this sequence, the film dissolves from a medium close-up of Norman in the process of cleaning Vicki's face as she sits in his chair to a medium close-up of their dual images in the vanity mirror; Vicki's makeup appears subdued, and Norman dabs it with powder while he observes his actions in the reflection. In contrast to the prior dressing room sequence, here Norman is self-possessed. The mirror is not in shards but intact as Norman reveals himself to be calm instead of violent. Another instance of a "man in the mirror" shot that visually engenders power relations between men and women, this scene in the film reveals how the man is in command of woman's image rather than provoked by it.[21]

Dressing room spaces in leading-man films can suggest the threat of femininity even without a woman present. In *White Christmas*, a series of dressing room scenes early in the film establish respective male and female spaces. Musical entertainers Bob (Bing Crosby) and Phil (Danny Kaye) share a dressing room just offstage of their hit show, "Playing Around." It is relatively spacious, with two dressing tables sitting opposite each other in the foreground and a sink, closet, and sitting area in the background. The room is masculine and tidy with cool tones of brown, beige, and blue. Even one of the few domestic touches, the upholstery of the dressing table chairs, is a beige plaid and without any feminine pleats or flounces. The tables are cluttered with tonics, powders, and brushes, but they are large and utilitarian. The men have hung their pants across the backs of chairs and use the vanity lights as hooks on which to hang their ties. By contrast, the film introduces us to their eventual romantic partners, Betty (Rosemary Clooney) and Judy (Vera Ellen), in their dressing room at a Miami nightclub. Their space is cramped and filled with voluminous fabric, including tufted chairs, a central dressing table with a flounced and ruffled skirt, and tulle-skirted costumes, while the tables hold flowers, delicate bottles of makeup and nail polish, and silver brushes.

This is the space into which the men enter after Phil helps the women to escape their former landlord. Betty and Judy sneak out the window and into an awaiting cab. Phil persuades Bob to join him in the space, closing the door behind them. The film creates anticipation as it denies the camera entrance to the room and forces the audience to reflect on the closed door, which fills the middle part of the frame. The subsequent shot extends this anticipation, this time filling the frame with a close-up of blue feathered fans, held by two hands at the bottom. As the fans fold toward the right, the film exposes what happened in the dressing room: Bob and Phil have become Betty and Judy; they wear strategically placed accessories from the women's blue sequined costumes, including butterfly headbands, scarves, and bracelets. After lip-syncing to the women's signature number, "Sisters," the men rush back to the women's dressing room to avoid detection from the management.

The sequence reveals how the dressing room has the ability to be overpowered by feminine influence even when women are not there. Similar to the quick-change acts that used dressing rooms to reveal the processes of gender transformation, *White Christmas* manipulates the audience's placement vis-à-vis the camera to at first indicate that a change is about to happen and then, through editing, transport the audience in both time and place to realize the manifestation of that change. The men entered as themselves and came out as someone else entirely, as Bob later laments about the experience, "boy, girl, boy, girl."

Once they have retreated to the dressing room after their "sister" act, the men are blatantly out of place. With the landlord chasing after them, Bob and Phil must quickly change and escape the dressing room in the same way the women did before. Confined in the unfamiliar space, they are attacked by its chaos of furnishings and hat boxes falling from shelves. They manage to put their jackets on, but the men still bear the remnants of their masquerade—Phil wears the sequined butterfly on his head and Bob has the scarf around his waist—as they awkwardly scramble out the window. The narrative justification for this quick-change act, outrunning the sheriff, forces the performer to make quick decisions without much thought, allowing for potentially transgressive and subversive narrative turns. In *White Christmas*, it is out of extreme urgency that the men dress as women, and it is with the same urgency that they return to being men once more. But the sequence is not without its consequences: just as they carry the vestigial markers of femininity on their bodies, the question of what makes a man a man lingers through the film. Bob must defend the dignity of his aging former general in the army and he must defend himself as worthy of Betty's masculine ideal, a knight on a white horse. In this way, the dressing room sequence sets up what will be a central concern in the film's project of male restoration and highlights the instability of gender performance.

The feminine influence is entirely absent in Norman Maine's dressing room. *A Star Is Born* sets several scenes in his bungalow, a small house on the studio backlot reserved as a commodious dressing room for the biggest stars of Hollywood's golden age. A space for dressing as well as resting and entertaining, studio dressing rooms such as these bore the imprint of their inhabitant's personality; as one *Los Angeles Times* reviewer put it in 1927, "Little has thus far been told of the furnishings of these intimate dressing-room 'little homes,'" but "here is where is more truly reflected the star's personality as regards choice of furnishings and objects of utility."[22] We get a glimpse of Norman's bungalow when he remakes Vicki's face at his dressing table, but we do not see its extensive décor until Norman invites Oliver (Charles Bickford), the head of the studio, to visit. Norman uses the excuse that he wants to remodel as a ruse to force Oliver to listen to Vicki's recordings. He tells Oliver that his dressing room gives him "the creeps." Citing that it "hasn't been decorated in centuries," he opines, "Don't you think I deserve a dressing room that's cheerful and modern ... and safe?" While Norman's argument for Oliver's visit is disingenuous, the sequence does nevertheless call attention to the actor's bungalow, which in its hypermasculine décor overcompensates for the actor's fading stardom as a leading man.[23] The space is cold, sterile, and uncomfortable. Norman observes that his sofa "stabs him in the back," and he asks Oliver about an oddly shaped wooden chair, "Isn't that the most uncomfortable chair you ever sat in?" Norman's exaggerations notwithstanding, his references to discomfort and stabbings in the dressing room nevertheless lend the space a morbid atmosphere; one that is emphasized by the décor. Norman and Oliver are surrounded by statuary of knights in armor and mounted firearms on the walls. These relics of a bygone era of manhood shape our understanding of the dressing room inhabitant, suggesting that his identity as a leading man is a relic as well. Just like his dressing room, Norman is quickly becoming a thing of the past.

For a leading-man film, *A Star Is Born* is unique for its lack of mirrors in the male performer's dressing room. More mausoleum than dressing room, Norman's bungalow denies the Hollywood actor the more typical moments of self-introspection in the dressing table mirror. The space suggests, in this way, that Norman has lost his sense of self and that it is beyond recuperation. After he commits suicide, it is his dressing room that outlasts him at the studio, as we see when Oliver and Libby open its doors and glance at the darkened space inside. Oliver insists that the dressing room and Norman's name on it will stay as long as he is head of the studio, preserving it as a veritable grave for the leading man.

Two parallel dressing room scenes in *The Country Girl* and *A Star Is Born* strategically deny mirrored reflection when the wives discuss the health and well-being of their husbands. In each, the employer of the leading man and the leading man's wife have extended, emotional conversations about what can be done to restore the leading man's dignity and sense of self. Both films withhold a visual source of reflection, emphasizing in these scenes how the leading man's absence signals his lack of authority; while they hold these conversations out of concern, the wife and the employer are contributing to the leading man's emasculation, revealing that the leading man cannot make decisions for himself. The power of these scenes, in which actresses Grace Kelly and Judy Garland deliver heartrending performances as concerned and attentive wives, calls attention to the emplacement of strong women in these films to fill the gap left by the weakened husband. Not surprisingly, both Kelly and Garland received Oscar nominations for these virtuoso performances.

As in other backstage films, mirrors have the power to fragment and refract their subjects into multiple images, granting or denying subjectivity, destabilizing, and conjuring alternate identities. Leading-man films reveal much about the dressing room's inhabitant via the projection, denial, and substitution of his reflected image. For his embattled character in *The Country Girl*, Crosby filmed numerous mirror sequences that chart the downward spiral of the alcoholic actor. The mirror, as Stefanie Diekmann argues, projects the dressing room's "hidden feelings and fears," becoming a "symbol of self-recognition and revelation."[24] In one such moment, during the show's out-of-town tryout, Frank returns to his dressing room. Standing at the vanity table, we see Frank in medium long shot, contemplating his reflection. But we also see the image of his knitting wife in the mirror. In an atypical reversal of the "man in the mirror," this time the woman is the ominous figure who dominates her husband with her gaze. Disrupting Frank's moment of self-recognition, Georgie's reflection intrudes to pass judgment on her husband, watching disapprovingly as he takes a swig of cough syrup.

Subsequent scenes echo this one in which we see the concerned wife and director in the mirror's image, as when Frank's mirrored reflection also shows Bernie entering the dressing room in the background of the frame and then transitions to Frank alone, framed again by the mirror's borders. These sequences allow the audience to see the leading man questioning his own identity. His lack of self-possession produces a multiplicity of identities in the film frame. Sometimes he is separated from his true self, as in the "complex mirror shots" in which the reflected image constitutes the entirety of the frame; and sometimes, as in shots where we see the leading man looking at his own image, he is both his true self and a virtual image.[25] These dual-image shots destabilize the real and the reflected, holding them in tension with each other and sowing doubt about identity on the part of the character and the audience.

Lastly, *The Country Girl* offers a cheat cut in which the mirror vanishes and is replaced by the viewpoint of the film's audience itself. In a long take, we see Frank at his dressing table, with Georgie standing behind him and Bernie sitting on the table to the actor's right. In the extreme foreground is Frank's dressing table, populated with tissues, cold cream, makeup, and tonics. The camera has taken the place of the mirror, producing the unsettling effect that the audience has become the reflection. We watch Frank's tense face as Georgie turns and exits out the door in the background of the frame. Bernie turns toward Frank to watch the actor take another drink of the cough syrup. In this scene of deception, Frank is lying about his alcoholism and about his professional reliability. The cheat cut forces the audience into the space between Frank's real and virtual selves, revealing the actor's two faces as a metaphor for his unraveling.[26]

Ultimately, however, leading-man films work to restore the male performer to a position of stability. In keeping with contemporary understandings of women's roles, it is the duty of the wife or girlfriend to change her behavior in order to aid in this process. Georgie appears in the final dressing room scene a changed woman. She has become feminine, wearing makeup, jewelry, and a black velvet cocktail dress as she tidies her husband's dressing room. Thus adorned, she is able to receive the chivalrous attentions of Frank, who defends her honor in the face of his producer's rudeness. In *White Christmas*, Betty mistrusts Bob's intentions to honor the old general. Bob must prove to her that she is wrong so that he can return to the position of the chivalrous knight atop his white steed. And even in *A Star Is Born*, in which Norman's actions prevent the possibility of rehabilitation, his wife must uphold his memory by identifying herself first and foremost as "Mrs. Norman Maine." This male restoration project also happens with the restoration of a racial status quo, as in *The Country Girl*, in which the reestablishment of white racial superiority is essential to Frank's recovery as a leading man. Whereas Frank has been diminished in the eyes of all around him, the final scene reveals how he has become, as his Black dresser calls him, "a big man"; Frank's fitness to lead is established not by what we see him do onstage but by his newfound authority over his wife and Black servant. For all their depiction of unstable men in crisis, these leading-man films provide a cultural script for the kind of man who is ready to lead a nation and its people moving forward.

No Women in the Dressing Room

The leading-man films of 1954 establish how the dressing room can be a site of both spectacle and masculinity, therefore laying the groundwork for more explicit examinations of male sexuality going forward. In the backstage films *Mo' Better Blues* and *Magic Mike*, the sexual identities of the male performers take center stage. But while their earlier counterparts stressed character and self-introspection in the dressing room, Lee's and Soderbergh's films emphasize male bonding.

At the end of the twentieth century, the backstage film was still primarily a genre about women and whiteness. From *Broadway Melody* (1929) to *Rock of Ages* (2012), the trope of a young girl making it in the world of entertainment has constituted a mainstay in American culture. These narratives, even when engaging with issues of race as in *Hairspray* (2007), rehearse the mobility and spectacularization of white women.[27] Backstage narratives about Black Americans are fewer and far between. The films *Lady Sings the Blues* (1972), *What's Love*

Got to Do with It (1993), and *Dreamgirls* (2006) are important correctives in which we see Black women aspire to and achieve success, but these films follow in the tradition of envisioning the path toward stardom as a female journey. It is here that *Mo' Better Blues* and *Magic Mike* are significant; both films construct a world in which male bodies are sites of display while their protagonists seek redemption in the world of performance. Lee's film emplaces Black men in this narrative, forcing audiences to see their bodies as both desirous and desiring, spectacular and laboring, thus delivering a nuanced image of Black masculinity onstage and off.

Like the films from 1954, male spectacle creates a tension in which men must perform masculinity to ward off the threat of feminization. In *Mo' Better Blues* and *Magic Mike*, the stage is a site of spectacle where hypermasculine displays define and reaffirm the heterosexuality of the performers. In the former, jazz trumpeter Bleek Gilliam (Denzel Washington) dominates the stage and his trumpet, a symbol of his sexuality in the film, to the delight of mostly female audiences. In the latter, Mike (Channing Tatum) titillates the women in the audience of a strip club by performing a variety of hypermale types—a construction worker, cop, cowboy, and soldier. Their identities as performers, as objects to be desired and commodities to be consumed, render their masculinity vulnerable to feminization and gender slippage. In *Magic Mike*, strip club owner Dallas (Matthew McConaughey) enforces strict rules about contact with women during the show, drawing the line between male and female roles in that space. But transgressions abound and signal the extent to which Soderbergh's film is as much about men as about the boundaries of gender and sexuality. The strippers infantilize Adam (Alex Pettyfer), the young man whom Mike takes under his wing, and feminize him by referring to his first performance as the moment when he loses his virginity. Adam's transformation into a stripper necessitates that he borrow his sister's razor to shave his legs and buy flashy thongs, the discovery of which leads his sister to assume he is gay ("I don't care what your preferences are"), to which Adam quickly and defensively responds, "Whoa, hey, it is not what it looks like!" And though Mike is hypermale in his onstage persona, his costumed performance of multiple identities renders even his offstage presentation unstable. As his stage name suggests, he effects thrilling transformations, such as when he dresses as Marilyn Monroe in a white halter dress and a blond wig and coaxes Adam to attend a beach party.

The typically female behaviors of primping, applying lotion, and shaving legs become activities of male bonding in *Magic Mike*. The dressing room of the strip club is the space where we are first introduced to the men, and it is the space that defines the world of stripping as a male enclave. *Magic Mike* relies on the communal dressing room to establish and emphasize an all-male culture in the otherwise female world of performance and spectacle. The strippers' dressing room is a makeshift space behind the stage. A repurposed kitchen, it has sterile tile floors, fluorescent lighting, and a large stainless steel shelving

The all-male world of the dressing room. *Magic Mike*, copyright 2012 by Iron Horse Entertainment.

unit that runs through the middle of the room. But as we observe from the first shot inside the space, an extreme close-up of a gold lamé thong running through a sewing machine, this is not your average male space. The sequence imbalances gendered behavior, pairing the male taunting of Adam with a demand that he lotion and shave one of the stripper's legs, an activity that happens while Tito (Adam Rodriguez), standing in the background, discusses the merits of a natural shaving lotion he has discovered. But while the scene introduces us to a group of men who have some feminine behaviors, it emphasizes male camaraderie above all. After the close-up of the thong, the film cuts to a long shot of the dressing room space that holds all of the men in the frame as they engage in banter and cross-conversations that initiate Adam into this world. These long shots repeat frequently in the film, foregrounding their group identity as they share stories, lift weights, and drink beer together in the dressing room.

It is there that Mike educates Adam on stripper life, serving as a mentor for a younger generation, a common dynamic in backstage film usually reserved for relationships between women. But in this world of male performance, the display of male sexuality is a form of male homosociality. Adam sits next to Mike as the latter applies a hair product while looking into a small vanity mirror on the center table. The empty space between the tiers of the shelving unit allows Adam to peer to the other side, where another stripper, Big Dick Ritchie (Joe Manganiello), works a handheld pump to elongate his penis. The film cuts to a low side angle on the opposite side of the table with Adam's face framed by the shelving, an extreme close-up of the penis on the left side of the frame and Mike's naked chest on the right. The frame captures Adam's face sandwiched between two male body parts, arresting and entrapping him in the world of male spectacle. The shot also establishes how male sexuality is in service to homosocial bonding before it is offered for female consumption.

Mo' Better Blues does not feature naked male bodies, but it does foreground the (hetero)sexuality of its protagonist, Bleek Gilliam, and uses the dressing room as a male bastion that wards off female intruders. An accomplished musician, Bleek prioritizes his craft above all else. The trumpet, which we first glimpse in the opening credits, is a symbol of his mastery of jazz and of women. The credit sequence is a series of shots that slowly pan up, down, and across the instrument in a montage that juxtaposes the sensuousness of the trumpet with the sensuousness of Bleek's lips, shown in close-up, and the hands of the two female characters, Indigo (Joie Lee) and Clark (Cynda Williams), caressing Bleek's skin as he plays the instrument. The trumpet's phallic imagery, introduced at the beginning of the film, unites Bleek's two desires, his music and women.[28] For much of *Mo' Better Blues*, he dominates both. A euphemism for sex, the title of the film emphasizes Bleek's prowess as a male idol, a quality that first attracted Spike Lee. "I went to see him in Checkmates on Broadway, and when he came on stage, all the women started screaming. So I started writing this movie for Denzel, the matinee idol, the sex symbol."[29] Translating his charisma to Bleek's character, Washington plays the role of a self-obsessed, supremely confident leader, able to command his fellow musicians and the women who adore him. He must repeatedly defend his position, however, given that bandmate Shadow (Wesley Snipes) tries to steal the spotlight and Indigo and Clark threaten to domesticate him or, worse, cause him physical harm, as when the latter bites his lip during sex.

While Lee wrote the character as flawed and in need of redemption at the end, the overt male sexuality of the film reigns supreme for the majority of its running time. As Cynda Williams later reflected, the masculine culture pervaded the atmosphere off camera as well. "It was a man's film ...," she explained. "Many of the men were method actors.... So being method, they were kind of chauvinistic all the time on set." As one of two female characters in the film, Williams, who was new to acting, was on the one hand touted by Lee as a "great discovery" and on the other excluded from the male camaraderie that permeated the film. "They were guys' guys, they hung out with guys, they talked to guys, and women were just there for whatever they were needed for," she observed. In the same interview, Joie Lee, who played Indigo, corroborated Williams's experiences, saying, "It was a boys [sic] club.... There were things that were said and done that you can't get away with today." Williams also noted the unequal treatment of nudity on the set. For their love scenes, Washington used his clout as an actor to refuse to take off his shirt, while Williams had no such option.[30]

The boys' club atmosphere is nowhere more apparent than in the dressing room sequences in the film. Similar to the dressing room in *Magic Mike*, the backstage space at the jazz club is dingy, with little adornment, and decidedly male. Allusions to other male, homosocial spaces abound in the script and in the film. An early treatment follows the bandmates to their dressing room, with evocations of the sweaty male bodies produced by playing sports: "WE FOLLOW Giant as he hands towels to the guys as they go to their dressing room. All of them are soaking wet."[31] More akin to actions taken in proximity to a locker room, the action betrays how Lee conceives of jazz performance as a male sport that takes physicality and skill.[32] Once inside the dressing room, the bandmates spar with one another over whose solo should dominate onstage. But their argument turns into a good-natured "'dozens' free-for-all," a form of verbal combat waged by Black men in the homosocial spaces of barbershops and street corners.[33] Intending to make a film about "relationships," Lee foregrounds the connection between the bandmates, holding the group of them in the frame with long shots in the dressing room and allowing their banter to play out within the shot as opposed to fragmenting the space and the characters within it.[34]

The one time that harmony breaks down and fragmentation occurs is in the scene in which piano player Left Hand Lacey (Giancarlo Esposito) brings his white, French girlfriend into the dressing room space. He is late to the club and the bandmates are already nervous. When he finally enters with Jeanne (Linda Hawkins), the band confronts him. They repeatedly tell her to leave, a process that quickly escalates to profanity. Giant, the band's manager, played by Spike Lee, eventually yells at her, "If you ain't in this group, get the fuck outta here. That means you!"[35] After she leaves, the men argue about why she cannot share their space, to which Left Hand Lacey responds accusingly, "It's because she's white." For this sequence, Lee uses the mirrors of the dressing room for the first and only time in the film. While the film's dressing room scenes emphasize the relations between the bandmates over any individual, self-introspective moment, Jeanne's identity as white and female prompts reflective and fractured framings. Casting his disapproval in musical terms, Bleek says, "Wrong key bringing your lady in here," as Left Hand Lacey sits down at his vanity table. Lee films over Left's shoulder, holding his reflection in the center of the frame flanked by a photograph of Jeanne taped to his mirror on the left and the reflection of his bandmates on the right. Left proceeds to discuss Jeanne's whiteness with the band through his reflection in the mirror, maintaining this framing; the men deny whiteness is a problem while Lee distances Left and his girlfriend from the group. Left asks them to show some respect for Jeanne, to which a bandmate replies, "Respect the dressing room!" and another echoes, "Respect yourself," implying that Left is doing his band and himself a disservice by allowing her to enter. They tease him by placing a cut-out image of a naked Black woman on Left's mirror, revising the framing so that Left's reflection now sits between pictures of the two women; the Black woman's picture, the men argue, is more appealing. Lee's use of mirrors isolates Left and exposes his contradictions as they appear to his bandmates; while the film does not imply that Left aspires to whiteness, his desire for a white, French woman suggests that he is veering too much from the values of the Black male communion that the space engenders. Bleek has the final word, reminding Left that the group of men operate by a code that excludes women from their backstage realm: "Everyone knows what the rules are. Remember what the rules are."

Guarding the dressing room space from female influence is a project that both films pursue in service of defining what is a leading man. Male camaraderie in

The men tease Left Hand Lacey (Giancarlo Esposito) about his desire for white women. *Mo' Better Blues*, copyright 1990 by Universal Pictures.

the dressing room is an essential experience for pitting masculinity against female spectacle in *Magic Mike* and female intrusion in *Mo' Better Blues*. But both Soderbergh and Lee remove their leading men from the dressing room, and the world of performance, in order for them to find redemption. In both instances, the leading men separate from the group and pursue their own path away from their hedonistic lifestyles, which the stage represents, and toward domesticated, monogamous relationships. Bleek goes from being the self-absorbed, womanizing artist to being a family man. The action in the film script describes this turn. He can no longer play trumpet after a brutal fight in a back alley, so he turns to Indigo, a schoolteacher and, the film suggests, a natural wife and mother. "Bleek is a desperate man, and he does what desperate men do: Beg and plead," the script's action reads. Indigo takes him back and they marry and have a baby in quick succession at the end of the film. The narrative turn also allows Bleek to find personal fulfillment without being exploited by the white managers of the club. As Lee told the *New York Times*, "Musicians are low-priced slaves, whereas athletes and entertainers are high-priced slaves. . . . It's their music, but it's not their nightclub, it's not their record company. . . . A lot of money can be made off black artists, and a lot of what racism is about is financial gain."[36] Liberating Bleek from these racist structures in American culture, Lee allows his protagonist to play music on his own terms and in the interest of fostering a love of jazz in his son. This redemptive turn for a leading man in crisis also provides audiences with a rare character in backstage films, a Black male performer with a complex personal life in which sexuality and emotional maturity get developed through a series of familial, fraternal, and romantic relationships off the stage. Unlike numerous jazz films in which Black men feature, *Mo' Better Blues* demonstrates how Black musicians are not merely performing bodies but are the product of the larger social and cultural forces of Black life. For Lee, this is the true "genius" of the Black jazz musician.[37]

In a dramatic sequence toward the end of *Magic Mike*, the lead dancer also makes a choice to leave the performing life. Mike is tired of his partying lifestyle and is disgusted by Dallas's exploitation of the strippers. Like Bleek, Mike does not own his body's labor. While he gets tips thrust into his thong by the adoring female audience members, the earnings of the night ultimately go to Dallas. As Martha Shearer argues, these strippers are the precarious figures of economic recession. Sitting in the dressing room at the end of the film, Mike silently decides to leave his job as a stripper and follow his dream of designing artisanal furniture, as Shearer describes, his "fantasy of entrepreneurial mastery," which can only be found away from the commodification of his body.[38] Soderbergh films him in close-up, cutting between the dancer's wary expression and his fellow strippers as they commune with one another in their backstage space. The noise is cacophonous as the music blasting from the stage and the gregarious voices of the strippers combine. Mike sits silently while his framing apart from the group signals his growing distance from them. Soderbergh uses crosscutting for the first time in this dressing room sequence, alternating between the dressing room and the stage. Dallas strips to his thong for an adoring audience as the film cuts to Mike exiting the dressing room, passing by a full-length mirror as he does so that temporarily holds him, ingenue Adam, and stripper Tito in its reflection. Adam's reflection watches Mike pass under the room's exit sign, a spatial marker of the dressing room's limits and a symbol of the dancer's relinquishing of his "Magic Mike" persona. Similar to the way Lee uses mirrors sparingly in *Mo' Better Blues*, Soderberg introduces a mirror in this moment to visually register two thematic developments: the breakdown of communal male bonding and a character's experience of self-doubt. In this way, Soderbergh redefines masculinity at the end of the film, showing his leading man in crisis and allowing him to find redemption outside the dressing room with a woman who represents stability and domesticity. Holding both visions of masculinity in precarious balance, however, Soderbergh shows how Mike's exit leads to Adam's entry into the role of the leading man. Dallas embraces Adam in the dressing room with the question, "You ready to be the man?" to which Adam says, "I've been waiting for this time." Thus anointed, Adam takes the lead onstage as Mike seeks a more meaningful relationship. The film performs various forms of masculinity on the stripper's stage, but it also demonstrates how certain types of masculinity are defined behind the scenes as well.

Inside Out

Anxieties about aging and obsolescence are at the core of more recent leading-man films. Whereas *Mo' Better Blues* and *Magic Mike* feature strapping, handsome, and self-assured male protagonists who occupy a world of men, the films

Birdman and *Joker* depict leading men as isolated, forgotten, and frail. In this way, these latter films are more in dialogue with 1954's leading-man films, especially *The Country Girl* and *A Star Is Born*, in which the protagonists are self-immolating and pathetic, unable to meet the challenges of everyday life. The characters Frank Elgin and Norman Maine both drink themselves to the point of incapacity, and the void they leave as leading men is filled by their steadfast and loyal wives. Twenty-first-century leading men Riggan (Michael Keaton) and Arthur Fleck (Joaquin Phoenix) appear on the scene as already physically vulnerable, not from drinking necessarily but from the processes of aging (*Birdman*) and malformation (*Joker*), respectively. And it is not only the women who threaten them but a larger society that cares too little for their existence. Finding oneself and one's place in the world has always been a concern of dressing room scenes, but in these leading-man films, the need for love, attention, and validation is paramount. As the Susan Sontag quote that sits on Riggan's dressing room mirror serves to remind him, "A thing is a thing, not what is said of that thing." But locating the truth of one's place in the world is not as simple as looking in the dressing room mirror. The films demonstrate that, in the battle between the self and the representation of that self, the latter wins. Directors Alejandro González Iñárritu and Todd Phillips place their protagonists in a world in which self-affirmation is achieved by making oneself the subject of spectacle.

Despite being weak and vulnerable, Riggan and Fleck have twinned versions of themselves, the superhero and supervillain, respectively; in their imagined lives, they are "superior" men, exceptional in their abilities to command attention and authority, to lead men, and to impress with their "super" abilities to become media sensations.[39] Riggan was, and still is harassed by, his superhero character Birdman, a winged creature at the center of a series of blockbuster movies for which the actor was known before turning to Broadway. And in *Joker*, Phillips reimagines his supervillain character as a populist hero who finally achieves the admiration that he has been seeking through the meting out of vengeful justice. Whether superhero or supervillain (there is a question in both films whether Birdman and Joker are truly good guys or bad guys), the contrast between the leading man's real identity, as a powerless and weak individual, and his superior self is a glaring one that ultimately constitutes the difference between death and survival. These leading men reject obsolescence as their fate, but their only recourse is a fictionalized form of masculinity created and circulated by modern media.

Both films open in the dressing room. Positioned behind the leading man in long shot, the camera slowly moves toward him, gradually bringing the audience closer to his body. Riggan sits suspended in the air with his legs crossed and wearing only his underwear. Fleck sits at his dressing table wearing a white undershirt. The mise-en-scènes of the dressing room scenes firmly establish these men as performers. They are in the process of becoming their professional selves, going from a state of undress to dress. The tools of the dressing room, makeup and mirrors, surround them. And the windows that frame the men in this space establish the interiority of the location but also indicate the wider world against which the men are positioned.

The films quickly establish the porousness of the barrier between inside and outside. Inside the dressing room, the men's insecurities display themselves on their bodies. González Iñárritu ends the moving shot in a medium close-up of Riggan's back, revealing the age marks and wrinkles on his skin. Later in the film, we hear Riggan despair about his body, pulling at his skin and grumbling, "I'm fucking disappearing!" The voice of Birdman constantly harasses Riggan, reminding him of his movie star past, calling him "lame" and "a joke," and telling him, "Without me, all that's left is you, a sad, selfish, mediocre actor grasping at the last vestiges of his career." As Birdman, a celebrity and public figure, he was recognized, admired, and relevant. As Riggan the actor, he is insecure, out of his depth, and small. Birdman's voice is seemingly in Riggan's head, a "mental formation" as the actor refers to it, but Birdman is also a superhero, a global figure who circulates worldwide in various mediated formations. He exists both inside and outside Riggan.

We first encounter Birdman as a voice in Riggan's dressing room. As Riggan sits cross-legged, we hear the superhero talking to him: "How did we end up here? This place is horrible. Smells like balls. We don't belong in this shit hole." Indeed, the dressing room is dank and grimy with old paint on the walls, a rusty radiator, and cheap furniture. The camera stays in medium close-up of Riggan's chest as he walks to answer a video call from his daughter. Riggan lowers the screen of his laptop and we face his reflection in the mirror. The presence of a Birdman movie poster inside the reflection, however, creates a *mise en abyme* effect. The poster sits just over Riggan's right shoulder and serves as a second reflective object in the shot, registering who Riggan once was and who he might still become. Establishing the symmetry between the two figures, Riggan's mirrored reflection and the Birdman poster reflect the actor at similar scales, a medium close-up of his figure with eyes that look directly outward. While the dressing room mirrors serve as a reflective site where Riggan questions his self-worth, the Birdman poster is the real object of reckoning. It takes on a life of its own as Birdman's voice gets stronger and more abusive. At one point, Riggan tries to hide the poster, first in the bathroom and then in the closet. Later, he smashes it completely.

Joker's Arthur Fleck begins his performative career as a clown. We first encounter him in the dressing room of the clown agency Ha Has; he is in the process of making up. He shares the dressing room with other men, but they are unaware of his presence. Similar to the dressing room in *Birdman*, this dressing room is grungy, an extension of the garbage-cluttered streets outside. As his favorite set in the film, production designer Mark Friedberg wanted the dressing room to feel "weird," "haunted," and "rough." He constructed it with "a lot of glass, wood, and painted metal. Urban. Tough."[40] Flanked by metal windows on either side, Fleck sits alone with his reflection in the mirror, a small figure framed against the larger, cold city.

The clown is the gestational costume for Fleck's later supervillain identity. Phillips shows us an extreme close-up of his face in this first scene in which Fleck watches himself in the dressing table mirror. As we later learn, he cannot control his emotions and finds it difficult to function in society. We get a glimpse of his attempts to perform emotion in the first dressing room scene when, in extreme close-up, he grotesquely stretches the sides of his mouth into excessive "happy" and "sad" positions. Like Riggan's, Fleck's body is also weak, not from aging but from abuses he sustained as a child. In a subsequent dressing room scene, after he has been beaten by a gang of Latino and Black kids in an alley, he sits hunched over on a bench, his bones protruding underneath his skin and bruises all over his back. A fellow performer, Randall (Glenn Fleshler), sympathizes with him, calling them "fucking savages" and "animals," telling Fleck that "they'll take everything" from him if he lets them. The white resentment felt toward peoples of color is acute throughout the film; Randall surreptitiously gives Fleck a gun, telling him to "protect himself," a gesture of solidarity between white men. The scene communicates how the world outside the dressing room is a dangerous place and Fleck, a vulnerable and disenfranchised white man, is ill-equipped to care for himself.[41]

Ha Has therefore provides Fleck with two weapons, his clown persona and the gun, that ultimately lead him out of the dressing room and into a position of strength. What was only a costume generated by the interior world of the backstage becomes Fleck's identity that ultimately gives him confidence and strength to engage in acts of violence that settle old scores. He suffocates his mother as punishment for her negligence, murders Randall for being an insincere friend, and shoots television personality Murray Franklin (Robert De Niro) for mocking him. As proof that the Joker is no longer merely a costume, Fleck arrives for his appearance on TV's *The Murray Franklin Show* already dressed. In the studio dressing room, he leisurely reclines in the chair while smoking a cigarette. The dressing room mirror, unnecessary because there is no additional makeup or costume to put on, becomes a surface for making a statement instead. With red lipstick, Joker writes, "Put on a happy face," a directive lifted from Ha Has that had forced him to smile through tears. In this dressing room, Joker intends the phrase to draw attention to the hypocrisies of society. The pain he has endured as a function of his outsider status leads him to weaponize his clown costume, turning himself into a supervillain who, in the wake of society's negligence, forces everyone to notice and reckon with him. Like Riggan's Birdman, Fleck's Joker starts as an imaginary character and, through delusion and violence, becomes a larger-than-life leader of the society that shunned him.

Riggan's interior world in the dressing room also gets turned inside out. Failing to achieve the admiration he desires in his new play, Riggan finds fame

Arthur Fleck arrives to his dressing room already transformed. *Joker*, copyright 2019 by Warner Bros.

unintentionally. During a performance, he steps outside the theater for a cigarette and gets locked out. The robe he is wearing gets caught in the stage door, so the actor must walk through Times Square in his underwear. The tourists take photos and videos of him as he finds his way back to the lobby. While he manages to make his entrance for the next scene in the play, the real entertainment is the one he has just delivered in Times Square.

When he meets his daughter Sam (Emma Stone) in the dressing room, she shows him the viral video on her smartphone, telling him, "Believe it or not, this is power." The sequence echoes Riggan's first appearance in the dressing room when, wearing only his underwear, he grapples with his inner demons. Associated with the intimate spectacle of the dressing room, his underwear and otherwise naked body reflect vulnerability, the leading man stripped to his very essence. Showing Riggan in his underwear again, but this time in the very public space of Times Square, González Iñárritu brings the intimacy of the dressing room to the outside world. But he also shows how intimacy becomes mediated with the use of handheld devices. As Celestino Deleyto has phrased this transformation, Riggan learns that "the rules of the game have changed and traditional validation must coexist with visibility, virality and constant upgrading."[42] The dressing room scene makes Riggan's dependence on media most apparent, confirming what the Birdman poster has been communicating all along. Making a spectacle of himself, naked in Times Square or as the Birdman superhero, translates into personal fulfillment and cultural value. Symbolically, this dressing room scene witnesses Riggan take stock of himself not in the vanity mirror but on his daughter's smartphone.

Foreshadowing Riggan's ultimate capitulation to a globalized, popular persona, one that has power and esteem, the Times Square video anticipates Birdman's escape from the dressing room. Riggan allows his "mental formation" to overtake him. He drunkenly imagines himself to be Birdman, jumping off a building and transforming into the winged, superhero creature of the poster. He soars as pyrotechnics explode around him. But ultimately, the freedom he experiences outside the dressing room makes his failures inside the theater more obvious.

In another attempt to make a spectacle of himself, Riggan plans to take his life onstage. Like Joker, Riggan keeps a gun in the dressing room that he intends to use as a public display of capitulation. Lying in a hospital bed after he has failed the suicide attempt, Riggan is wounded, but perhaps closer to Birdman than ever before. His facial bandages simulate the superhero's iconic mask as he gazes at the birds flying outside his window. When he disappears, Sam frantically looks out and up to the sky. Something she sees makes her smile contentedly; Birdman and her father have become one. Like Fleck, Riggan is ill-equipped to find happiness as an ordinary man, but as a superhero created by mass, globalized media, he achieves immortality and transcendence. In both instances, the dressing room is the staging ground for the leading man to expose and reckon with his weaknesses, but also to liberate their superior, more masculine, if delusional selves.

Throughout the long history of leading-man films, it is the dressing room's quality of instability, its porousness and its tools of transformation, that allows for the destabilization of masculine identities, prompting questions about leading men's aptitude and authority. The cause of their vulnerability changes over time, from the threat of femininity and domestication to aging and obsolescence. But in the end, leading-man films and the dressing room in particular allow for society to admit that masculinity is not a fixed concept, that "leading" is not a natural male pursuit. Leading-man films have also explored broader social issues, including the ill effects of substance abuse, the reconciliation of hypermasculinity with meaningful relationships, and the struggle to define oneself against the ubiquitous forces of celebrity and globalized media. The dressing room shows us that the tools of self-destruction and repair are one and the same, giving the leading man the power to redefine the terms by which he identifies as a man and his ability to lead. While not as numerous as films about female performance, leading-man films have been a persistent and recurring site for dialogue on masculine precarity and its implications for society.

Thus far, we have seen how dressing rooms have shaped and reflected the insecurities of its inhabitants, but most backstage films also position these sisters, wives, mothers, and leading men so that they can ultimately overcome society's pressures and challenges. For those dressing room inhabitants who occupy a more circumscribed social position, including peoples of color and queer performers, the space becomes the means by which society's limitations can be exposed. These masqueraders call attention to and question their marginalized position in the wake of not being able to change it.

5

Masqueraders

●●●●●●●●●●●●●●●●●●●●

> It is a superstition in dressing rooms that make-up boxes should never be "cleaned out" as this is said to bring bad luck.
> —Wilfred Granville, *The Theater Dictionary* (1952)

During an evening's vaudeville performance at the Brooklyn Theatre, Al Jolson sat before his dressing room mirror, "glum and dispirited." He had achieved success as a performer and proved that he could "win applause," but he wanted to produce laughter as well. He complained to his "old darky" dresser who inhabited the dressing room with him and who was busy laying out the performer's clothes.[1] "Why don't you black up, Mr. Al?" the dresser asked him. "We folks are thought to be funny," he explained. "Sure enough they'll think you am funny." Taking the dresser's suggestion, Jolson applied burnt cork before he went onstage. As the account goes, the subsequent performance "went like the proverbial house afire" and proved to be a "turning point" for Jolson's career.[2]

This origin story for Jolson's birth as a Blackface comedian appeared in the promotional materials for *The Jazz Singer* (1927) and in numerous other articles and newspapers, culminating in Joe Laurie Jr.'s nostalgic account of Blackface in vaudeville published in *Variety* in 1954.[3] With one exception, the stories foreground the role of the Black dresser, alternately referred to as an "old darky," a "southern darky," and an "old negro," whose idea it was for Jolson to blacken his skin. Eric Lott has documented how Blackface minstrelsy's origins are often told as moments of racial encounter in which "issues of ownership, cultural capital, and economics arise" and serve to assuage anxieties regarding "cultural 'borrowing.'"[4] The dressing room setting for this encounter, however, also brings to the fore the hidden dynamics of backstage labor, in which Black servants often performed the dual roles of personal valet and professional dresser. Casting the dresser as an "old Southern darky," the narrative naturalizes the man's servile role by emphasizing his helpful disposition all the while admitting that he would not be paid (as Jolson admitted, "I was unable to employ a regular dresser").[5] Understood in this way, the dresser's suggestion that Jolson "black up" might ultimately have been self-serving; with the ironic awareness that white men in Blackface are always successful on the stage, the dresser might have hoped to finally receive wages for his labor.

While this dressing room story breaches the boundary between servant and dresser, the space also prompts other identity shifts as well. A place for trying on the Blackface mask, the dressing room transforms from a site of preparation to one of simulated performance. As the *Radio Digest* account documents, Jolson "blackened up and rehearsed before the old darky." When he finished, his dresser "chuckled and said, 'Mistah Jolson, you's jus' as funny as me."[6] Jolson assumed an alternate identity in the dressing room, that of a Blackface comedian, while the dresser transformed into an audience member charged with assessing the authenticity of Blackface performance. The approval of the dresser, a Black man himself, lends legitimacy to Jolson's new persona, but it also foregrounds the racial "counterfeit" as performance, a spectacle of the birth of a masquerader.[7]

It is unclear whether Jolson's dressing room encounter is true. By 1954, *Variety* spun a very different tale about Jolson's Blackface origins, attributing the suggestion of Blackface to the white vaudevillian J. Francis Dooley.[8] But the story of the Black dresser in the dressing room nevertheless haunts Jolson's Blackface screen performances, at once inserting and erasing his Black co-occupant of the space. The films *The Jazz Singer* and *The Singing Fool* (1928) engage the history of representing Black men in backstage realms; they are suspiciously hovering in and around dressing rooms and having their legitimacy, as backstage workers and onstage entertainers, called into question. These backstage specters receive visual representation in the Blackface acts of white performers like Jolson, for whom the cork is a form of ghostly masquerade.

This chapter spotlights the masqueraders of the dressing room, the minstrels, cross-dressers, and drag performers whose acts of transformation are essential to accessing the space and hence ensuring social survival. Beyond white minstrels in Blackface, social outsiders, including Black Americans, Latinos, and queer performers have used the cinematic dressing room to stage masquerades of racial and gendered cross-dressing.[9] In keeping with the tradition and cultural practice of masquerade, these performers showcase the "breach [of] divisions of bodies and ideological divisions."[10] Not surprisingly, the boldest statements on racial and gendered masquerade emanate from outside Hollywood's major studios, ranging from race films (*Paradise in Harlem*, 1939) to "B" movies (*Copacabana*, 1947), documentaries (*Ethnic Notions*, 1986; *Paris Is Burning*, 1990), play-to-screen adaptations (*The Ritz*, 1976), and independent films like Spike Lee's *Bamboozled* (2000). The masquerades by these marginalized characters are both necessary and consequential, personally meaningful and culturally significant. The dressing room threshold is a boundary to be crossed and exposed as a form of limitation in these films; the space promises access to opportunity, but at the cost of personal transformation. Standing at the threshold, the masquerader must ask, "Can I enter?" "Can I leave?" and "On what terms?" Acts of racial and gendered masquerade accentuate the capacity of the dressing room as a site for transformation; and in turn, dressing rooms maximize masquerade's potential for negotiating the boundaries between the self and society.

Ghosts

The dressing room has long been associated with a certain amount of fear. Real-life performers and their cinematic counterparts experience a "nervous atmosphere" in the dressing room, a consequence of performance anxiety, financial insecurity, and temporal pressure.[11] As Ralph Freud, chronicler of theatrical folklore, has explained, "It was natural then, that these workers would establish for themselves gremlins, both good and bad, to help them face these hazards."[12] Superstitions in the dressing room gave performers a measure of control over the space that would protect them from the instability of theatrical life. For example, dressing room 13 is always bad luck. Whistling in the dressing room can lead to being fired from the show (and fray the tense nerves of the other occupants in the process). Placing shoes and hats on shelves above the performers' heads is taboo (presumably because those items could fall and cause injuries). And if you forget something in the dressing room, you must not retrieve it, but rather have someone else bring it to you.[13]

Beyond thwarting the forces of bad luck, however, a number of dressing room superstitions function to bridge the divide from one show to the next. They help to determine who had access to the dressing room in the past and to identify the remnants from the past that still haunt the present. For example, performers must destroy an item in the dressing room at the end of one show's run in order to prevent "any evil spirit or residue of failure from following to the next play."[14] One should never clean out the makeup boxes in dressing rooms but rather use the old makeup, housed preferably in an old cigar box. These practices also extended to clothing; it is said, for example, that Al Jolson "never wore new clothes on opening night."[15] Performers' privileging of previously used materials foregrounds the importance of repetition and memory in the theater and emphasizes the significance of ritual as a response to the ghosts, both good and bad, who haunt the backstage.[16] As Marvin Carlson has argued, "All theatrical cultures have recognized, in some form or another, this ghostly quality, this sense of something coming back in the theatre, and so the relationships between theatre and cultural memory are complex."[17] But whereas Carlson is interested in exploring the haunted materials that constitute performance itself, including the dramatic text and the actor, this chapter looks to the backstage realm, and specifically representations of dressing room masquerades, which have the ability to conjure the ghostly apparitions of Others.

As a place of anxiety and fear, the backstage realm is a vulnerable location within the theater. Dressing rooms represent the most private of spaces for performers. It is where they leave their most personal possessions while onstage, prompting anxiety about who is entering and exiting the dressing room when the inhabitant is not there. Not responsible for items left in dressing rooms (a sentiment expressed by the signage in later dressing room films), managers refused to be held accountable when valuables went missing while performers were doing their turn.[18] These conflicts took on a particularly racialized meaning, however, in the number of accounts in which "colored" men were accused of theft. In 1906, Rice and Elmer, a white vaudeville duo, complained to *Variety* that while doing their act on the stage, "someone unlocked our trunk and took our two vests with contents," including a gold watch, a diamond stud, an Elk's Lodge charm, and some cash. The writers offer a warning to other readers, explaining that "so many artists carry dressers and helpers that the stage manager on the opening day is not acquainted with them." They more explicitly specify the racialized meaning behind the term "dresser" when they continue, "They say there was a colored fellow on the stage who claimed to be Lew Hawkins' dresser and he was noted looking around the dressing rooms, but he was not seen after the show started on Monday."[19] In Philadelphia that same year, the accusation was even more direct. As *Variety* reported, the police sent out an alarm to "arrest on sight a colored man" with "brown skin and clean-shaven face; also neat dresser." Blamed for a series of thefts in actors' dressing rooms, the man allegedly went to theaters and "asked for some one on the bill, and after his departure jewelry has been missed." Stating that he was "well informed on theatricals," the report insinuated that the man was familiar with backstage spaces.[20]

These and other reports seeking a "colored thief" who had been seen backstage and then eluded capture expose the ways that the vulnerability of dressing rooms, exploitative labor practices, and racial ideologies converge. The mere sighting of a Black man backstage conjured an element of fear and distrust, despite their employ as dressers and their purported loyalty (as in the Jolson story), to say nothing of their identity as performers in their own right. To the latter point, a group of Black performers banded together in 1920 to form the Dressing Room Club in New York, an organization that promoted the visibility and welfare of Black vaudevillians and dramatic artists. By calling themselves the Dressing Room Club, they conjured the backstage space most associated with Black backstage labor and criminality and emphasized artistic accomplishment instead.

Their public activities included staging shows and parades, handing out awards, and extending financial support to their members. They supported Black-produced shows like *Shuffle Along* by buying box seats on their opening nights. They ceremoniously gave a diamond-studded medal to *Shuffle Along* cast member Florence Mills. They used their club rooms at 140 W. Thirtieth Street to give white journalists a glimpse of the club's "backstage" workings. And perhaps most significantly, they staged an elaborate pageant during which they re-created Black acts from the past to prove "the progress of their race in theatricals." "Old timers, long since gone to their reward, were impersonated by members of the club in an evening's entertainment" that included the "lone banjoist of reconstruction days, Sam Lucas," and made it appear that others, like Ernest Hogan, the comedian and singer, "were there." The casts of contemporary shows *Running Wild* and *Shuffle Along* participated in the pageant. With the event, the Dressing Room Club conjured the past as a means of informing the present, demonstrating Black achievement as a continuum in the theater. Invoking the private but not inviolate realm of the dressing room, the club's members emplaced artists, not valets and thieves, in the backstage space.[21]

Journalistic reporting on the ghostly moves of backstage thieves and the Dressing Room Club's conjuring of past performances rendered the early twentieth-century dressing room a space of racial haunting. Pregnant with the vestiges of past performances, that "sense of something coming back," the dressing room is a site of cultural memory. On film, it functions as an archive of racialized performance. Early sound cinema, including Jolson's *The Jazz Singer* and *The Singing Fool*, narrativizes this archive by foregrounding Blackface minstrelsy, a form of "racial cross-dressing" that at once conjures and disappears the Black laboring body on which it is based.[22] But just like the earliest minstrel posters in which a row of Blackface minstrels are mirrored by their whiteface counterparts to convey the feat of racial transformation, racial cross-dressing in the dressing room is a spectacle in its own right, boosting the cultural position of the masquerader who has the power to put on and take off the mask while naturalizing the "cultural robbery" that has been performed.[23]

As Jolson's origin story attests, dressing rooms are sites of racial exchange and masquerade in which the presence of a racialized body, the Black dresser, at once haunts the backstage space and gives birth to an alternate identity, the Blackface comedian. As he demonstrated in *The Jazz Singer*, and subsequently in the follow-up feature *The Singing Fool*, Jolson could emit pathos as an actor, especially when wearing Blackface. Despite his dresser's prediction, however, Blackface does not make Jolson funny in these films. Instead, donning Blackface is an emotionally wrenching experience of rupture. Jolson cries for his mother and his son through and because of the mask. The audiences respond not with laughter in these sequences but with an emotional outpouring of support.

The association of Blackface with tragedy runs counter to Jolson's account in the dressing room. If Black "folks are thought to be funny," then why does the donning of the mask render Jolson sad? The narratives of both films hinge on loss, the manifestation of which appears through the otherwise "funny" Blackface mask. Jolson's masked characters are embodiments of, as *Hollywood Filmograph* put it, "carefree carnival moods and deep shaken moments of tragedy, song and sorrow."[24] He assumes the identity of two bodies in one, conflating the identities of the jovial Black dresser and the mournful white entertainer. According to Michael Rogin, the Blackface sequences in *The Jazz Singer* function to convey the "split self" of Jewish immigrant and American jazz singer, a binary opposition along which the entire film is structured.[25]

But it matters that these scenes of racial masquerade take place in the dressing room, a representational site of racial haunting and cultural memory. Filmmakers manipulate the surfaces of the space, its reflective and frame-within-frame possibilities, in order to accentuate and narrativize processes of transition. In *The Jazz Singer*, Jakie's dressing table is adorned with framed images of his mother and his costar Mary Dale. The film positions Jakie next to both in separate shots, using their hovering images to frame the interpersonal relationship the performer has with each one and suggesting his inner struggle to make both happy. His Blackface persona is consequential to the breaking of ties with one and the strengthening of ties with the other. Similar intraframe dynamics exist in *The Singing Fool*. This time, the frame that sits on his table is of his young son, referencing the experience of paternal separation demanded by his career as a Blackface comedian.

Spectrality also serves the function of cultural memory in both films. In the first, it appears in the mirror of the vanity cupboard. While Jakie observes himself in Blackface makeup, the reflection dissolves to an image of Jakie's rabbi father in synagogue. The image pains Jakie, who cannot bring himself to sacrifice his career on Broadway in order to attend to the demands of filial devotion. In *The Singing Fool*, by contrast, the apparition is not a superimposition, enclosed in a cabinet case, but a physical presence in the room with him. It is his Black dresser whom the film frames, with blurry focus, and who haunts Jolson, standing behind the fully realized Blackface performer.

These apparitions appear as a result of Blacking up, giving visual expression to the split self within. They are both tragic occurrences, contradicting Jolson's origin story about Blackface as enabling of laughter. And they call forth the cultural memories that Jolson's character seeks to distance himself from. In the former, Jolson's distance from his Jewish upbringing is a point of tension in the narrative. In the latter, the intertextual reference to a Black dresser, and the film's juxtaposition of the actual Black man and the simulated one, forces an acknowledgment of the mask as a construction, separate from, if nevertheless based on, the original.

Operating in a tragic rather than the comic mode, these two Blackface scenes also build on the cultural memories of Blacking up, drawing both on Jolson's origin story and on each other. In both films, Jolson applies his makeup in the same way, with two strokes of the finger on either side of his face first, and then filling in the gaps. Revealing it in a continuous shot, the films portray the ritual of Blacking up as a process that has "come back again," providing continuity from the origin of the Black body to the body of the white Blackface performer. *The Singing Fool* brings this process full circle by emplacing a Black dresser in the room with Jolson's character, suggesting in the framing of the two men a discursive link that visually transfers the ownership of Blackness to the white performer. But the dresser also invokes the two dominant scripts that make Black men's presence backstage culturally legible. In the first, and in keeping with Jolson's origin story, the dresser is a loyal servant, there to attend to the physical and emotional needs of his master backstage. The film also engages the second script, however, with its specter of Black criminality. After being caught sleeping on the job, the dresser explains, "When a man sleeping, he ain't getting' into no trouble." Nodding in agreement while reminding him of whose dressing room it is, Jolson responds, "But be careful where you sleep." The insinuation that were it not for laziness, the dresser would be in "trouble" indicates the film's ambivalence about the Black presence backstage, acknowledging it to be both necessary for backstage work to be performed and challenging to control.

Finally, it is the overwhelming presence of time as a structuring device in the dressing room that makes these racial hauntings consequential. Jolson's characters must ready themselves for the stage if the show is to go on. *The Jazz Singer*

The Black man in the dressing room. *The Singing Fool*, copyright 1928 by Warner Bros.

creates this tension with numerous visitors to the dressing room urging Jakie to hurry up. *The Singing Fool* achieves it by crosscutting between the dressing room and the stage. In both films, however, Blackface is the visible evidence of a personal tragedy, the loss of a loved one. To be sure, Blackface allows Jolson to give voice to his pain; as Lott explains, Blackface is a form of "racial feeling" for the white body.[26] But with the added element of time that the dressing room introduces, Blackface also ensures the collective good. At stake is both Jolson's performance and the success of the show. Jolson must exit the dressing room in Blackface in order for the show to go on. As a representation of popular entertainment, the show within the film hinges on these racial masquerades. The dressing room sequences are critical to both films in this way for they archive popular entertainment's dependence on racialized performance.

American culture's insistence on Blackface comedy is the tragic premise on which *Paradise in Harlem* is built. Made only six years after *The Singing Fool*, the race film is one of the rare instances in which Black performers, and a Black production team, treat the subject of Blackface minstrelsy explicitly. *Paradise in Harlem* is also part of a larger cycle of "Harlem" films that featured "black America's best-known urban space" in order to "capitalize on Harlem's vogue" as well as conjure "the area's transformative potential and risk."[27] Both the elements of transformation and risk are present in the narrative of the film, which follows comic actor Lem Anderson (Frank Wilson), who must leave the stage and go into hiding when he is falsely accused of murder. Lem's transformation from comic to outlaw, however, is framed via the more quotidian transformation of the Black performer into a Blackface minstrel. The real tragedy for Lem is that he has an ambition to be a dramatic actor and play Othello on the stage, but the "public" will not allow it. As he tells his nephew in the dressing room, "They keep saying, 'Go on back to your cork and your comedy,'" continuing sadly, "The public's not ready for that dramatic stuff." What is understood between the men, and by extension the film's Black audience, is that society demands comedy from Black performers while it reserves Shakespeare for white ones.

The film wields the space of the dressing room, especially its frame-within-frame mise-en-scène, to convey both the power and the limitations of the mask. It creates a series of restrictive boundaries within the film frame, using the interior boundaries of the vanity mirror to visually constrict Lem. We witness him entrapped in such a way when we first meet him, sitting at his dressing table and looking at his reflection in the mirror as he finishes the application of burnt cork to his face. He is laughing and joking with his nephew as he does so. The mirror provides the audience with what they expect to see in a Blackface minstrel, a good-natured comedian who joyfully applies his craft. But the camera soon tracks backward and pans to the interior of the room, reframing Lem and his nephew in medium shot away from the mirror. Denying the audience the reflection of the minstrel, the film offers a depiction of the "real" space of the dressing room, adorned with rectangular photographic portraits of Black artists and occupied by his nephew, an upwardly mobile law student. It is in the real space, away from the mirror's construction, that Lem confesses his hopes and dreams for a career without the cork.

Significantly, *Paradise in Harlem* never offers the audience a glimpse of Lem's Blackface comic turn. The film showcases other Black artists on the nightclub stage where he works, including Lucky Millinder and his orchestra, Mamie Smith, and the Juanita Hall Singers. Lem's performance is absent by contrast. Perhaps the choice was a concession to an audience who was already very familiar with Blackface comedy, or a decision to showcase newer, more positive styles of contemporary performance. But ultimately, by denying screen time to Blackface comedy in a narrative that otherwise privileges entertainment, the film devalues the masquerade, relegating it to a fiction, a constructed image much like the mirror's framing of Lem's mask.

Constrained to the dressing room in this way, Blackface makes itself strange. In an opposite process from that seen in Jolson's films, Blackface calls on the past of racialized entertainment in order to destabilize and constrict rather than liberate its wearer. The application of the mask, which we see in the opening sequence, is a persistent ritual that entraps Lem in the mirror, in the dressing room, and by extension, in the wider world of show business. He cannot escape it and is doomed to repeat the past again and again. After Lem has performed offscreen, the film returns us to his dressing room, where he sits before the mirror once more. His mask is removed and he is wearing his street clothes. But this time the mirror fragments his reflection, providing an image of only the lower half of his face and his upper body. He cannot see his whole self without the Blackface mask; without it, he only exists in fragments. These dressing room sequences, framing a spectral performance that we do not have access to, set the stage for Lem's larger personal drama of being trapped. Framed for a murder, Lem is ostracized from society, but that form of social marginalization began with his endless application of the Blackface mask.

The haunting of Blackface entertainment is also the subject of Spike Lee's *Bamboozled*, a backstage film about the production of a *New Millennium Minstrel Show* for network television. Producer Pierre Delacroix (Damon Wayans) devises a plan to reform Black representation on the screen by making a spectacle of its most extreme example, Blackface minstrelsy. The plan backfires, however, when audiences applaud rather than decry the entertainment. Performers Manray (Savion Glover) and Womack (Tommy Davidson) are wooed by the money and the chance to showcase their dancing and comedic skills. But they move from a position of willingness to dejection with each successive application of Blackface makeup. Like Lem, Manray and Womack become entrapped by the mask and haunted by its racial delimitations.

Hauntings take many forms in the film. The most obvious occurs near the end when, pained by the effect of his minstrel show on society and the performers, Delacroix begins to hallucinate. The Black ephemera he has collected, which include clocks, figurines, teapots, and a "jolly n----- bank," hark back to a time, as his assistant Sloan (Jada Pinkett Smith) describes, in which Black Americans were considered "inferior, subhuman." Suddenly, the bank, which feeds coins into its exaggerated mouth, begins to move by itself, rapidly consuming money as Delacroix looks on in disbelief. Surrounded by the collectibles, which depict grotesque versions of Black stereotypes, such as mammies, Uncle Toms, and pickaninnies, Delacroix begins to feel paranoid that these disturbing inanimate objects are coming alive.

Bamboozled draws formal parallels between these collectibles and the creation of stereotypes that occur in the dressing rooms of the television station. It is in the dressing rooms that the ghosts of Blackface past first haunt the present. Lee presents the first scene in which we witness Manray and Womack Black up in pseudo-documentary fashion, a mode Lee engages at alternate points in the film. As we watch the performers meticulously create the makeup from burnt cork, Sloan provides voiceover narration. "As usual, I did my research," she explains. "We should blacken up like they did back in the day, keep the ritual the same." The cyclical and circular qualities of Blackface, its formulation and application of burnt cork, are atavistic dressing room activities that call on the experience of the hundreds of Blackface minstrels who have sat at dressing tables like this one before. Attending to Blackface as "ritual," *Bamboozled* links the present to the past. As Womack angrily describes it, "New millennium, huh? It's the same bullshit, just done over." Like other rituals, Blackface is an invariable performance that never really goes away.

Lee also uses the dressing room in order to convey the effect of Blackface on the performers themselves. Similar to the frame-within-frame mise-en-scène of earlier backstage films, *Bamboozled* uses the borders of mirrors and photographs in order to capture and constrict dressing room occupants. Manray's and Womack's mirrors are adorned with multiple images of Blackface performers; as visual referents, the photographs instruct the performers on the authentic application of the cork. But tucked into the borders of their dressing table mirrors as they are, they also serve as a reflection of the self. Lee's camera alternates between close-ups of the men applying Blackface and medium shots that hold the performers' reflection, as their Blackface personas, and the images of prior Blackface performers in the same discursive space. Such shots convey how the past has entered the present once more.

Other dressing room sequences, such as the first one, in which Sloan provides voiceover narration, draw the connection between the Blackface performer and the replication of racial caricature. The sequence begins with Sloan's instruction on proper application of the cork and medium shots of the performers as they attend to each step. As the sequence progresses, however, the camera gets closer and closer to the men, until the screen fills with a single facial feature such as the eyes or the lips. Throughout this process, the mirror's reflection becomes more and more fragmented, constricting and dividing the body of the performer until he is unrecognizable as a human being. The camera changes position throughout, from low canted angles to high-angle close-ups that inject a sense of disorientation into the space. Like the grotesque collectibles that come alive later in the film, the dressing room sequence demonstrates how bodies are reduced to a series of parts, robbing the individual of their humanity and presenting a disturbing and grotesque creature in its wake.

Tellingly, the one alternative that Lee provides to Blackface, Delacroix's father, Junebug, is also ensnared by the legacy of Black representation. Talking to his son in another backstage dressing room, Junebug recounts how he rejected a career in movies because he could not "say that stuff they want me to say." But while he rebuffed Hollywood and he does not perform in Blackface, he still wears a mask of sorts. He tells his son, "Remember what I always taught you ... every n----- is an entertainer," a testament to the reduction of Black Americans' value to a servile position in white society. Wearing a bright orange suit and bowler hat reminiscent of the days of Black vaudeville, Junebug feels the need to "always keep them laughin'" in order to ensure his survival. He is just as entrapped by the past, unable to escape decades of Black spectacle in the popular imagination. Lee conveys Junebug's precarious position and his emotional distress through a series of canted angles that foreground his reflection while displacing his real self to offscreen space. Junebug drinks his sorrows away in his dressing room, longing for the career that might have been.

While *Bamboozled* places importance on the perpetual act of Blacking up, some Black productions have emphasized the significance of removing the makeup after a performance has ended. In *Ethnic Notions* (1987), a film that likely inspired Lee's haunting images of caricatured figurines and its documentary approach to the history of Black stereotype, Marlon Riggs ruminates on what it must have been like for Black performers to take off Blackface. This shift in emphasis is telling for the ways that it calls attention to the internal struggles of the performers themselves as they reckon with what they must do to exit the dressing room and reenter society. Through the use of staged performance sequences, interspersed with archival footage and talking head interviews, Riggs conveys what it felt like to have one's body be regulated by the time it takes to put on and take off the mask. Featuring choreographer Leni Sloan's "eulogy" to Bert Williams as a moment of dramatic re-creation, the film introduces a recuperative dimension to understanding performances of the past. Whereas Lee uses clips from Hollywood films of the 1930s in order to expose the derogatory roles suffered by Black actors, Riggs pushes our interpretation of such images further to imagine the lived and temporal dimensions of the mask.

Sloan's eulogy takes place in a re-created dressing room set on a spare black stage. Dressed as Williams in a gray suit, Sloan sits at a wooden dressing table with his body slightly turned toward the camera. He brags about his ability to drink copious amounts of alcohol, something he is "becoming famous for" in addition to his "blackface makeup," "white gloves," and "comic gait." But it is not just drinking that he does in the dressing room. In a subsequent moment in the film, we see Sloan as Williams again, this time facing the mirror with his back to the camera as he applies Blackface. In medium close-up, Sloan's reflection occupies the center of the shot with a partial view of his back on the left side of the frame and total darkness on the right. A frame within a frame, Williams's reflection is set apart from the real space of the stage; it is in this moment that the performer tells a story about how he surprised a bartender who did not want to serve him a drink by revealing how much money he had in his pocket, the result of being one of the most popular entertainers on Broadway at the time. He laughs like the jolly minstrel he appears to be, not unlike in the opening sequence in *Paradise in Harlem*, where Lem performs his Blackface role in similar fashion in the dressing room mirror.

Also like that earlier film, *Ethnic Notions* creates a visual break between the performer and the real man underneath. Laughing at his stunt at the bar, Williams lowers his head. Riggs cuts to a tighter frame of the reflection so that when Williams rises again, we see his image in medium close-up. He has stopped laughing and, with tears in his eyes, he observes, "You know, it ain't really that funny." Switching from the comic to the tragic mode, Williams describes how all of his professional success never translates into equal treatment in life. Bringing the audience even closer, the camera zooms into Williams's face so that it fills the screen as he describes the indignity of needing to rely on a white escort in order to enter a club. "Ain't I a responsible human being?" he asks the audience. Williams goes on to describe how he receives numerous offers to visit the club from white admirers, but he must always remind them, "This ain't exactly my regular skin tone and it takes considerably longer to remove blackface than you can imagine." Inevitably, those white admirers do not wait for him to extract himself from the mask. Sloan ends the performance by lamenting, "It's no disgrace to be a black man, but it's terribly inconvenient."

The inconvenience of Blackface removal has repercussions for Williams's mobility offstage just as the application of Blackface enables his onstage success. In this way, the tragedy of the mask extends to real life as well. The performance sequence, set apart as it is from the rest of the film by Sloan's monologue, gives the audience the rare view of a Black performer grappling with the experience of taking the mask off as a labored process. And it references Williams's dogged efforts to embody racial performativity onstage and off. As Camilla F. Forbes has documented, after a show Williams would invite the white press to his dressing room, where he would not only reveal himself to be contemplative and composed, in contrast to his comic "darky" role onstage, but also stage the removal of the mask and the revelation of the skin underneath.[28]

Ethnic Notions also counters and corrects previous cultural depictions of Blackface removal. While Eddie Cantor's character realizes that Blackface is "tough to put on and take off" in *Kid Millions* (1934), he naïvely assumes that his Black dresser does not have that problem. "You know you're lucky?" he asks

132 • The Dressing Room

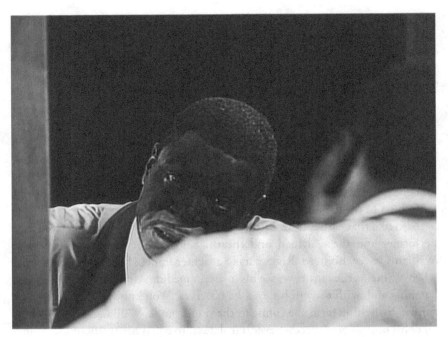

Leni Sloan impersonates Bert Williams in an imaginary dressing room scene. *Ethnic Notions*, copyright 1986 by Signifyin' Works.

the uncredited Sam McDaniel, who merely responds with a knowing smile. In an even earlier era, Blackface removal was also a popular vaudeville skit. The Blackface comedians Cameron and Flanagan staged a welcome hit with the skit "On and Off," which consisted of fourteen minutes of the two men in a dressing room. They quarrel with each other "during the process of washing up and dressing for the street." Aside from the novelty of seeing the performers restore their whiteness once more, the comedic appeal of the skit relies on the passage of time through which their lengthy quarrel continues, a testament to the many minutes needed to wash off the mask.[29]

By featuring the labor required by a Black performer to put on and take off the mask, *Ethnic Notions* explores the underlying humanity of the counterfeit. While the film is considered, along with Riggs's *Color Adjustment* (1992), to be a more "straightforward" documentary (as opposed to the more personal and reflexive *Tongues Untied*, 1989), it nevertheless remains unique for its juxtaposition of primary source material and live performance.[30] Riggs uses the archive dynamically; he suspends, choreographs, and closely frames Black collectibles to emphasize their grotesque qualities. And he uses them, along with film clips, to frame the live performance sequences in order to put the present and the past into conversation. The dressing room scene conveys how the present is haunted by the past of cultural memory, including performance acts that were left "unfinished," as Sloan describes Williams's show. Riggs and Sloan reincarnate Williams in the dressing room, insisting on his humanity with the mask and without.

Realness

As with racial masquerades in the dressing room, the fracturing of the self, achieved through personal transformation and its mirrored reflection, imbues the space with figurative power. Historically, masquerades have staged the "metamorphosing before one's eyes, caught in the very moment of transformation" to produce the "double body."[31] Exposed, the double body prompts the "insistent question of the really" in the dressing room. Who are these masqueraders really? Are they the person behind the mask or the mask itself? Or are they a combination of both? If "appearances are a kind of reality," as Richard Dyer asserts, then the double body of masquerade, in which the real and the imagined are presented as one, has the power to create a new reality.[32]

The dressing room's production of the double body renders it a queer space. Bridget Sundin has argued that queer hauntings overwhelm dressing rooms in films like *Morocco* (1930), in which we can see glimpses of Marlene Dietrich's "multiple embodiments" of gay/straight, man/woman, star/actress.[33] The masquerader's body subverts and critiques normative identities, flaunting the destabilizing dynamics of transition and transgression in the process. Like the act of applying Blackface, this form of masquerade provides an attraction, a performance of identity transformation. When members of marginalized groups occupy the dressing room, these backstage masquerades can be liberatory, especially when they symbolize a form of social mobility previously not available to them. Along with these performances, however, comes concurrent and embedded critique of the limitations of identity. As such, dressing room masquerades draw attention to who has access and the terms of entry and exit; in the process, they allow for the transcendence of the self, and for society, by acknowledging and exposing very real social inequalities. Masqueraders, including cross-dressers (*Adolph Zink*, 1903; *The Masquerader*, 1914), drag performers (*Paris Is Burning*), and Latina immigrants (*Copacabana*, *The Ritz*), use the dressing room for this purpose; they are invested in creating a new kind of "realness" for themselves and for the world that they live in.

Adolph Zink and *The Masquerader* are two early films that feature the queer double body of masquerade. The first, an untitled theater-film hybrid for vaudeville, *Adolph Zink* features the quick-change artist of the same name. A master of the theater-film hybrid, Zink interspersed live impersonations in front of an audience with filmed scenes of him in the dressing room. For the act, Zink would call attention to his short stature (he was a little person) by telling his live audience, "Remember that goods come in little packages. I trust you will like this little package," after which he would invite them to his dressing room to watch his quick changes. The filmed performance of the dressing room shows Zink engaging in various "antics with his dresser," such as "gags about his size, boyish appearance, pugnacity (reported in newspapers), a 'No Smoking' sign, and cross-dressing material in his act," which included impersonations of actress Edna May as a Salvation Army girl, the music hall singer Lottie Collins, and Chicago politician "Bathhouse John" Coughlin, for which he dons baggy pants, a short jacket, and mustache.[34] The film ends with a series of medium closeup shots of Zink's face while he puts on makeup and wigs.

This dressing room film, which lasts a remarkable eight minutes in duration, exposes the labor and wonder behind performative masquerade.[35] Allowing the audience to see his quick changes in action, Zink not only demonstrates the subversion of seemingly fixed attributes like physical size and gender but also reveals the method by which those attributes are subverted. Such masquerades of identity were attractive to audiences for whom the unsettling effects of modern life also displaced notions of the self.[36] Zink's demonstration of how such dislocations are achieved, shaped, and controlled allows him to emphasize his skill as an entertainer, something that could not be accomplished by the impersonation act onstage alone. The imperative of a quick change in the dressing room produces an affective experience for the viewer, who feels the rush to outrace time as one person transforms into another. Zink conveys the harried nature of his work by performing the transitions between impersonations in rapid succession, repeatedly running in and out through the door, which sits prominently in the center of the shot. With the help of his tall, lanky dresser, he quickly casts off one costume and puts on the elements of another. Sometimes, these rapid shifts cause accidents, such as when Zink trips over his floor-length skirts or falls off his chair while the dresser removes his heeled boots. But the dressing room space produces such anarchic antics. Its glut of costumes, makeup, and wigs that accumulate in a small, enclosed space prompt both transformation and mishap. Zink and his dresser do much to emphasize both. They hold up Zink's bloomers to the camera, present his costumed face and body in direct address to the audience, and boldly defy the prominent "No Smoking in the Dressing Room" sign that hangs above the door by smoking cigars. Bucking forms of authority, they disregard the theater attendant who pleads with Zink to rush to the stage, and beat up the policeman who charges in to enforce the smoking ban. The cross-dressing impersonations and Zink's diminutive stature also lead to transgressive forms of intimacy and discipline, as when, aroused by Zink's transformation into a young girl, the dresser attempts to steal a kiss, and later the policeman gets erotic pleasure from placing Zink over his knee and spanking him. The final shots of the film, medium close-ups of Zink at his dressing table, demonstrate his transformations more intimately with only Zink in the frame, emphasizing his expert ability to apply powder, liner, mustaches, and wigs. In contrast to the harried but comical antics of the dressing room we have seen, the action in these final shots is calm and steady, showing a professional performer at work.

At this early moment in backstage films, we see how temporal duration is a central feature of the dressing room's material and figurative power. But time has always mattered in the theater. Being late for one's act could result in dismissal and subsequent economic hardship. And if the show does not go on, not only does the offending performer lose their professional identity, but before the 1919 Actors' Equity Association strike, payment was withheld from the entire cast and crew.[37] The ubiquitous phrase "The show must go on" has its origins not in a commitment to one's art but in the dire need to avoid material suffering. Time therefore has a desperate quality in the theater that Zink and many others have exploited for dramatic ends.

But time also matters to our understanding of identity. Displacing notions of the self, the dressing room forces the collision of private and public identity formations, which male performers like Zink explicitly display as anarchic entertainment. At the dawn of cinema, urbanization, industrialization, and migration had set people free from stable markers of identity. The cinematic dressing room provides a space for performers to narrativize and reckon with these transformations. Zink's crossings of the dressing room threshold are laden with meaning as he materializes new identities under pressure. His backstage film conveys how change, not stasis, is necessary for survival onstage and in life.

Early films about masqueraders take as their theme transformation of the self. Like Zink's act, such masquerades often involve cross-dressing as women for the sheer spectacle of the transformation but also in order to gain access to opportunities otherwise closed to them. Such is the case in the aptly titled *The Masquerader*, in which Charlie Chaplin gets hired and then fired as an actor at Keystone Studios. Upon arriving on set, the director (Charles Murray) leads Chaplin to the dressing room, a dingy space with a wall of closets and a long, dual-sided dressing table at the center. Wigs, towels, and makeup are scattered across the surface. A fellow actor, played by Fatty Arbuckle, and Chaplin sit opposite each other as they prepare for their roles. At first, it would seem that Chaplin is at a disadvantage in this space. He tries to steal a swig of his neighbor's soda and drinks hair tonic instead. When he reaches for the soda around the edge of the table a second time, Arbuckle responds with a rap on the knuckles. Patting his face with powder, Chaplin sneezes into Arbuckle's, prompting an open conflict that Chaplin escapes only because he is needed on set. After missing his cue, Chaplin causes havoc, fighting with the director and technicians, and ultimately getting thrown off the studio.

He returns, however, not as himself but as an Italian actress who wants a job in motion pictures. As a woman, Chaplin attracts the attentions of the director, who clears the dressing room of all men to make way for an intimate moment with his new leading lady. The predatory acts to which women are susceptible in the dressing room, as depicted in this scene, were something Keystone founder and director Mack Sennett warded against at his actual studio. To protect the women on his set, he always had a "lady gendarme" present, and while he prided himself on running an easygoing work environment, he did instill one "strict rule," as he told interviewer Art Friedman in 1964: "No man was allowed to go in a lady's dressing room," a rule that even he had to abide by.[38] It is the flagrant defiance of this rule that earns the fictitious director his humiliation in *The Masquerader*. When the director returns to the dressing room in the hope of rendezvousing with his actress, he finds that she is a man in disguise, thus embarrassing and infuriating the director, who, along with the disgruntled actors he displaced, chase Chaplin through the set, resulting in Chaplin's fall down a well, where the film ends.

Chaplin's masquerade as a woman authorizes his access to the studio lot and his increasing control of the dressing room space. What had been denied him as a man becomes available to him as an attractive female; the director graciously opens the dressing room door for his new leading lady to enter. And whereas the powders and tonics of the dressing room attacked Chaplin as a male actor in the first sequence, he wields these tools as a form of power in the subsequent scene during which Chaplin restores his true identity. In a remarkable shot during the latter sequence, Chaplin sits alone at the dressing table, dressed from the breast down as a woman, revealing the corset underneath his dress and his bare chest above it. While he sits, he applies the makeup to restore his mustache, creating the effect of a double body, with a man's face on a woman's figure. As Zink does in his revelatory quick-change act, Chaplin allows his audience to see gender transformation in action. In doing so, he subverts the authority, and the manhood, of his employer.

Chaplin's *The Masquerader* reveals that access to the dressing room, and the opportunity for social mobility that it represents, takes an element of subterfuge; he must transform himself, into a woman in this case, in order to enter. The cinematic masquerades of later eras, however, present a more explicit examination of social outsiders and their place in the world of popular entertainment. In a limited number of backstage films, including two that will be discussed here, *Copacabana* (1947) and *The Ritz* (1976), Latina im/migrants occupy dressing rooms.[39] Historically reserved for white women, the backstage film has largely denied women of color roles as protagonists except in rare cases.[40] This choice on the part of producers, directors, and writers has systematically excluded such consummate performers as Carmen Miranda and Rita Moreno from accessing the powers of the dressing room in the genre, preventing them from playing multidimensional characters who self-actualize through transformation and performance. Typically positioned as the comedic sidekick to white actresses Betty Grable, Vivian Blaine, and Alice Faye, Miranda's characters entertain and support the white leads on their journey to onstage success and backstage romance. As Sean Griffin has insightfully discussed, the exclusion of performers of color from integration into the narratives of these films underscores and legitimizes their exclusion from social integration as well.[41] And as Moreno has argued again and again, she has been limited in her career by the social expectation that she play the Latin "spitfire" who, in her dress, mannerisms, and speech, represents a permanent outsider to mainstream America.[42]

Copacabana and *The Ritz* present the rare exception to these exclusions. Tangential to the major Hollywood studios (the former was made by Beacon Productions and the latter was a U.K. production filmed at Twickenham Studios), both films feature Latina im/migrants as stars. In the first, Miranda plays Carmen Navarro, a featured Brazilian singer in the Copacabana nightclub in New York, where it was also shot on location. In the second, Moreno is Googie "Rita" Gomez, a Puerto Rican performer in a gay bathhouse in New York. Both portrayals realize the actresses as versions of themselves, the names Carmen and Rita being references to the real-life performers. And both films develop the women's characters in dressing room scenes that reveal the trials and tribulations of making it in America. Taken together, *Copacabana* and *The Ritz* are significant backstage films not only for their inclusion of Latinas in their narratives but also for the ways that they acknowledge and challenge the limitations of being a member of a marginalized group.

As sites of transformation and transgression, dressing rooms play an important role in both films. It is in that space that Carmen and Googie give expression to their real and imagined selves. But like masquerade itself, the transcendence of the body, and its associated limitations, takes on added meaning. Both women effect the "double body" of masquerade to gain entry to the dressing room in these films; they use the space to blur the boundaries between self and other, reality and construction, containment and liberation. In this way, the dressing rooms at the Copacabana and the Ritz are queer spaces that confuse and alter social norms, producing an alternate reality, if only for the duration of the film.

In *Copacabana*, Miranda embodies the dual identity of masquerade in her role as a Brazilian singer who must also pretend to be the French chanteuse Mademoiselle Fifi, a character who distinguishes herself from Carmen with a blond wig, a veil to hide her face, and a more modest, if just as form-fitting, costume. When her agent Lionel (Groucho Marx) rashly promises to deliver two entertainers to the club instead of one, he must invent a second one and convinces Carmen to play both parts. Mayhem ensues as Groucho holds Carmen to a tight schedule of costume changes and performances in which she frantically shifts from Carmen to Fifi and back again.

A sequence early in the film attests to the physical toll that such a doubling entails. After Fifi's first performance, we see her at her dressing table. Lionel yanks at her veil and wig, producing grimaces from Carmen, who eventually kicks him out of the room. The film uses superimposition and dissolves to merge the spaces of onstage and backstage, the dressing room doors and the dressing room interiors, to show how Carmen manages the ruse. In one medium close-up of the performer at her dressing table, she looks with disgust at her reflection as she powders her face, a glance that the film audience experiences directly, as the camera is positioned in place of her mirror. Shots of her performances as Carmen and Fifi visually overlay the different dressing room doors that serve as boundaries between the effortless show onstage and the frantic preparation backstage. The superimposition of performance, dressing room door, and dressing room interior produces a complex merging of space and time that is far from "child's play," as Lionel dismissively calls it. Backstage, we witness Carmen experience her double body as anxiety, pressure, and pain.

In addition to satisfying the pretentions of Lionel, however, Carmen must become Fifi in order to be successful. Upon her first performance as the chanteuse, Fifi is a hit. A montage of *Variety* headlines communicates as much, in effect necessitating that Carmen continue the ruse indefinitely because of its profitability. As Fifi, the blond-wigged Carmen instantly becomes a sensation. The nightclub owner places her in the upstairs lounge of the Copacabana, patronized by a more elegant, select clientele, in contrast to the open and public experience of the ground floor. Carmen's and Fifi's spatial positions symbolize their relative social positions as well. As Carmen says, "up for Fifi, down for Carmen" is a dynamic that manifests in their private and professional lives. Fifi wins a Hollywood contract and the affections of the club owner, thereby upsetting Carmen's own ambitions as a Brazilian singer and the romantic entanglements of the club. Fed up with Fifi, Carmen yells at Lionel, "I hate her! She's not only driving us crazy, but she's ruining everybody's life!" They decide to "kill" her in a staged dressing room battle. Lionel conjures an angry reaction in Carmen when he pretends to deliver Fifi's insults, calling her a "Brazilian ham" and telling her she cannot sing. Carmen screams at Fifi, "I kill you, you Parisian pig!" while she smashes vases, upsets furniture, and throws the contents of her dressing table at the door. The nightclub owners listen to these sounds with horror in the hallway. When they manage to beat down the door, they see a triumphant Carmen standing in the middle of the chaos with Fifi nowhere to be found. "Fifi?" she responds to them. "I fix her good."

Having killed Fifi, Carmen liberates herself from her alter ego's clutches. But eventually she must prove that Fifi was a construction when she and Lionel are accused of murder. The police and the club's owner refuse to believe that Carmen could also be Fifi, the implication being that the two women are so radically different. It is not until she kisses them that they realize that Fifi's passion in fact emanated from Carmen.[43]

The creation of the Carmen/Fifi double body at once disguises and exposes the real. Carmen engages in an effective masquerade that conceals her true self. But the new identity, the Carmen/Fifi hybrid, also reveals society's unequal treatment of the two women; the double body is the mirror by which social hierarchies are recognized and exposed. It is "truth in the shape of deception," as Terry Castle writes of masquerade, that creates an alternate reality for the dressing room inhabitants. The film introduces Fifi as a desired being only to do away with her in the end. Carmen's murder of Fifi restores her true self, but only after she has proved that Fifi's successes are her own. In an instance of life imitating art, Carmen Miranda replicated her role as Fifi on the actual Copacabana stage upon the film's release. The show's reviewers applauded the performer's agility in moving beyond her "Brazilian Bombshell" persona, something she was unable to do for most of her Hollywood career.[44]

Both *Copacabana* and *The Ritz* create models of the Latina protagonists to expose the limited ways in which women of color are allowed to circulate in society. Whereas Carmen/Fifi was conceived by a male production team (not Miranda herself), Googie "Rita" Gomez was the creation of Rita Moreno. A literal construction of the dressing room—Moreno writes about how she invented the character during "a hundred 'idle' hours in dressing rooms" of Broadway theaters—Googie was a chance to vent her frustrations about being pigeonholed as a fiery Latina; her Oscar-winning role in *West Side Story* (1961) only served to amplify her persona as a "spitfire" rather than correct it. Drawing on all the tropes of the spitfire, Moreno describes Googie as "the worst Hispanic cabaret singer of all time." "Her gestures were operatic, her eyelashes were a mile long, and her makeup was applied with a trowel," she writes in her memoir.[45] Googie is also temperamental, a hallmark of the spitfire, swinging rapidly from anger to elation. She is trying to make it in show business, despite her inauspicious act at a gay bathhouse, and does whatever she can to achieve it, including attempting to seduce the man she mistakenly believes is a Hollywood producer.

False identities abound at the Ritz, a queer space where all who enter do so under an assumed identity in order to live the lifestyle they desire. While Googie is one of the lone females, she nevertheless embodies a double body because of the presumption, based on the context and her outlandish dress and makeup, that she is a cross-dresser. Hiding out from the mob, straight man Gaetano Proclo (Jack Weston) encounters a series of challenges to his heterosexuality, including from Googie, who lures him into her dressing room.

A converted boiler room that steams and produces loud noises, Googie's dressing room is makeshift, just like the construction of her persona. Both characters are mistaken about the other. Proclo believes Googie is really a man and, in turn, Googie mistakes Proclo for a Hollywood producer. That neither character is what they appear foregrounds the dressing room's destabilizing atmosphere. Googie has cluttered the space with makeup, sprays, wigs, costumes, photographs of celebrities, and even a hot plate where she makes a grilled cheese sandwich. She flatters Proclo that he too could be an actor given his "guapo" looks, citing the careers of singers Catarina Valente and Vicki Carr. Proclo objects, insisting that they are "real women," to which Googie responds, "Oh, no," calling them "plastic Puerto Ricans!"

Googie gives Proclo a glimpse behind the scenes of how Latinas, as both racialized and female, are made with the tools of the dressing room. He watches in amazement as she applies fake eyelashes and then, unhappy with their placement, yanks them off with an offhanded curse, "Chit!" All the while she is constructing her image, she critiques others like Valente and Carr for being fakes (Valente

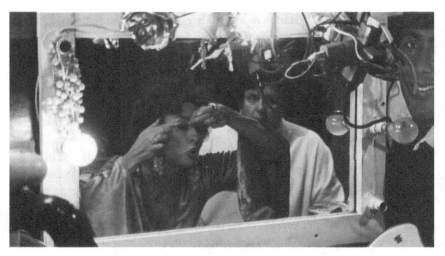

Googie Gomez (Rita Moreno) tries to apply fake eyelashes. *The Ritz*, copyright 1976 by Courtyard Films.

was French but famous for her multilingual singing ability, and Carr was Mexican American). But this level of authenticity is unimportant in this space, where how one appears matters more than who one is. Googie insists that she, unlike those other "plastic Puerto Ricans," is the "real thing." But when she tries to seduce Proclo, she confuses him further by suggesting that realness must be granted. She exclaims while lying on top of him, "Make me feel like a real woman!" He is saved from her advances, and the exposure of her real female body, by one of Googie's backup dancers who knocks at the door and tells her it is time for the show.

Googie's comments about plastic Puerto Ricans are self-reflexive, calling attention to her own overblown stage act in the bathhouse as well as Moreno's persona as a spitfire. The inclusion of Googie Gomez in the queer space of the bathhouse queers her identity, allowing for an exploration of what is real that is simultaneously about gender, sexuality, and race. Moreno's excessive portrayal of Googie, especially her accent and malapropisms, which the actress says were modeled on her mother, also trouble the real. Googie is a product of the cultural imaginary and, to an extent, an authentic simulation by a daughter of her mother. She is at once the product of endless frustrations at being typecast or denied roles and a loving spoof of a family member who never fully assimilated into mainland American society.

As Brian Herrera writes of cultural appropriation in the 1970s, Googie was one of several examples in which Latin American–descended performers, including Luis Valdez, Charo, and Chita Rivera, constructed, maintained, and questioned Latin stereotypes for popular consumption. As with Googie, these stereotypes were polysemic cultural products and therefore had the ability to challenge, but also, depending on the audience, to reinforce and affirm. Googie's performance is entertaining to be sure, and Moreno won the Tony Award for her performance in the original Broadway show, but it is also presented as a critique by Moreno herself. As Herrera writes, it is both "funny... and just a little bit frightening."[46] He posits that Googie is Moreno's effigy, an effort to "entomb the stereotype" by bringing it to life in such grotesque detail.[47] Read as constructions of the dressing room (Googie being quite literally born in a dressing room), both Carmen/Fifi and Googie are effigies of Latina performers who must be given life before they are killed. The murders are figurative in both films; Fifi is a fake, and Googie is a product of our cultural imagination. But the dressing rooms present the Latina body as a double body, constantly shifting and negotiating the necessity of masquerading as Other.

In *Paris Is Burning*, a documentary about drag balls in New York City, masquerades are a critical tool for survival and endurance. Rather than being effigies created only to be destroyed, the gay Black and Latino participants in the drag ball display a different kind of double body, one that exudes what they call "realness," the illusion of a straight man or woman. Marginalized by their race, class, and sexuality, the subjects in director Jennie Livingston's film use drag "realness" as a survival strategy. As Dorian Corey, an older drag performer, explains, "It's not a take off or satire, no, it's actually being able to be this." Strutting and voguing in the performance space of the ballroom, the participants are judged for how perfectly they can embody their straight counterpart, with categories of straightness including "town and country," "school boy / school girl," "executive," "military," and "high fashion evening wear." Like the stereotypical figures that Latinas have conjured, the drag participants re-create a popular image that already circulates in mainstream society. But rather than critiquing it, they aspire to it. As Corey describes, "It's really a case of going back into the closet, they give the society what they want to see, and not be questioned, rather than have to go through prejudices about your life." The film foregrounds the homophobia of the 1980s in this way, using Corey's narration, the testaments of other drag queens like Pepper LaBeija, who documents his ostracization from the family home, and the tragic fate of Venus Xtravaganza to frame the otherwise vibrant and joyous space of the drag ball. As Corey states, "When they're undetectable, when they can walk out of that ballroom into the sunlight and onto the subway, and get home and still have all their clothes and no blood running off their bodies, those are the femme realness queens." Livingston places this narration over images of Venus blow-drying her hair, presumably getting ready to venture outside. As such, the sequence serves as a foreshadowing of the end of the film when we learn from another drag queen that Venus was later strangled, her body stashed under a bed in a hotel room.

This explanation of "realness," its projection of what straight, white society wants to see, reframes our understanding of the performance sequences. The drag competitions are unsettling for the ways they show brown and Black people who "worship at the throne of whiteness," as bell hooks observes, "even when such worship demands that we live in perpetual self-hate, steal, lie, go hungry, and even die in its pursuit."[48] As Caryl Flinn observes, *Paris Is Burning* uses intertitles and the introduction of characters "as objects to get to know, facets of the same exotic show."[49] Flinn argues that the film's performance of spectacle, for a primarily white and straight audience, shows "the problems in attaching a simple progressive or subversive label to Livingston's film." While critics are disturbed by the film's ability to comfortably situate white audiences in the position of the voyeur who is entertained by exotic spectacle, it has, as even hooks admits, both "progressive and reactionary" elements.[50]

Corey's contributions are key here. An older drag queen who identifies as a "professional," someone who has witnessed the shifts in drag culture over several decades, Corey's testimony is another structural device that Livingston uses to explain the world of drag balls to the uninitiated. But Corey's role is more important than that. Except for in Corey's sequences, *Paris Is Burning* rarely ventures into backstage space, a remarkable choice given the film's subject of performance and its emphasis on dressing as transformation. Indeed, Corey's dressing room is the only one to which we gain entry.[51] While Livingston interviews numerous participants in the drag balls, she chooses to speak to them in either domestic spaces or the street. By contrast, the director places us inside Corey's dressing room multiple times, and it is where she leaves us at the end. So while the dressing room is a significant space, it is nevertheless only associated with Corey, and not the "children," as the younger participants are called.

Why this absence in a film that is replete with performance and performing bodies? Livingston distinguishes between the dressing room and the other spaces in the film in order to convey the difference between masquerade as professional performance and masquerade as real life. Whereas the dressing room enables transformation with its visible tools for creating illusion, the street denies that an illusion is in effect. Filming outside the dressing room underscores the ways that drag children try to erase "the mistakes, flaws, giveaways," as Corey says, in order to "make [their] illusion perfect." Dressing rooms, by contrast, expose the illusion, creating the potential for a doubled self who performs and then returns to the real. For the drag children, it is not performance that they are after, but rather a wholesale transformation that will allow them to move, undetected, in a hostile world. While so much of the appeal of *Paris Is Burning* hinges on the spectacular showmanship of the drag ball sequences, the film also works to convey how the boundaries of performance break down when what is at stake is day-to-day survival. These masquerades venture beyond the world of performance and attempt to change the circumstances of real people.

Livingston understands Corey as a performer and therefore associates him with a dressing room in which the tools of performance are made available. He is surrounded by feather boas, sequined costumes, reams of fabric, makeup, wigs, lights, and mirrors. In one framing of the space, the film reveals a neon sign that

Dorian Corey in his dressing room. *Paris Is Burning*, copyright 1990 by Art Matters Inc.

says "Stage Door" in the background of the room, indicating its proximity to the actual site of performance. And yet, Livingston never allows us to see Corey venture through the door, and despite a couple of brief moments in which he appears as a judge or onstage, we do not see Corey perform. Instead, the film uses editing patterns to bring the audience into and out of the dressing room from the drag ball or the street. Indeed, the dressing room leads to and from the street just as much as the stage, conflating performance and realness into a single experience. Sitting apart from the outside, Corey's dressing room is in temporal and spatial limbo; there are no entrances to or exits from the dressing room because he is in a perpetual state of becoming. In each of the dressing room sequences, he applies the same makeup and wears the same dressing gown without ever completing the process of transformation. Nor does Livingston allow us to see his transformation in action with a corresponding shot of his reflection in any of his mirrors. Preparing for a performance that never comes, Corey sits outside time and "realness," thereby better able to comment on it.

It is in Corey's dressing room that we get glimpses of Livingston, her boom mic, and the subjective presence of a very mobile camera. The director frames Corey through an opening in the table, replicating frame-within-frame constructions of other backstage films. But as if to make us aware that this is an authentic portrayal of a dressing room, rather than a constructed one, Livingston abruptly and awkwardly changes the position of the handheld camera, bringing it closer and to the side of the performer. The inelegant motion makes us aware of her presence and, along with a few cuts in the interview, repositions the camera to reveal Livingston sitting in a corner with the boom mic pointed at Corey while he speaks. These shifts in perspective further enhance our access to the space and frame Corey with the plentiful tools of his dressing room. The shifts also emphasize the presence of Corey's cat in the room, who sits contentedly on a pillow behind the performer and, in one cleverly edited sequence, mimics the performer's grooming activities with his paw. This is a quiet and contemplative dressing room; its introspective atmosphere foregrounds its separation from the world outside.

It is clear that Corey's interview was a long one and that Livingston and her cinematographer spent considerable time in the space. Corey's ease as he leisurely applies makeup, and the languid movements of his cat, indicates a departure from the more spectacular visuals of the film. They also diverge from a mode of direct address that characterizes the other interviews that Livingston conducts. Corey never looks at Livingston or the camera in the dressing room, preferring instead to focus on the act of making up. While he presumably responds to questions by the filmmaker, he never acknowledges as much, delivering his comments more as a series of ruminations rather than as an interview. Livingston emphasizes the intimacy and timelessness of the dressing room, allowing both Corey and the film to reflect on what drag is and is not, what it was and what it is today.

It is therefore fitting that the film should end in this space as Corey discusses the dashed dreams he once had to be a star. Like Googie, he laments the opportunities that never came. But his seniority as a performer gives him a unique perspective. Foregrounding the difficulty of survival for his community, he applies eye makeup while observing, "You leave a mark on the world if you just get through it." Coming after the news of Venus's death, his insights are tragic and profound, suggesting how hard it is to live from day to day. As a professional, Corey has the wisdom to understand the significance of what the drag children are trying to do, but without judging them for it. For him, the dressing room symbolizes the boundary between public and private, onstage and backstage. The younger drag participants, however, aim for a transcendence of such boundaries and will do whatever it takes in order to move from one side to the other unscathed.

The association of dressing rooms with magic, hauntings, and queerness suggests the uncanny qualities of the space. Dressing rooms are physical locations, both rooted in the time and space of an evening's performance and set loose, the product of past performances and performers gone by. Their timeless quality can be eerie, leading performers in real life to attempt to control their spectral potential with time-honored superstitions and practices that at once pay homage to and ward off the past.

Cinematic dressing rooms have drawn on the space's spectral dimensions in order to convey and reshape society's relationship to race, gender, and sexuality.

The relationship between Black men and the dressing room has proved vexing for white performers, especially those invested in the racial counterfeit of Blackface minstrelsy. Simultaneously emphasizing Black men's ability to entertain and to engage in criminal activity, Blackface comedians like Al Jolson conjured the memory of racial dynamics as a means of naturalizing them so that they could legitimize their own skills as performers. Black filmmakers, by contrast, emplace the Blackface minstrel in the dressing room to decry its persistent limitations and power as a cultural force.

Making backstage films outside the mainstream has also allowed for the visibility and critique of marginalized experiences, including those of Black men, Latinas, and queer performers. Dressing rooms have been essential here for illuminating the potential for masquerade and its personal significance for the marginalized performer. But perhaps more consequentially, dressing rooms have also pointed the camera back at society, shedding light on the reasons why masquerade has been necessary in the first place. Focusing on the dressing room spaces of the marginalized, in all of their variety across feature films, documentaries, musicals, comedies, and gangster movies, allows us to witness how these masquerades have persistently haunted American life.

Epilogue

●●●●●●●●●●●●●●●●●●●●●

The Drama Is Real

As this book demonstrates, I am drawn to dressing rooms for the ways they articulate concepts of space and genre and reflect on intersections of performance and identity. I am also someone who has on occasion inhabited this space. I have two memories in particular that serve as my own personal dressing room scenes. In the first, I am thirteen years old and sitting in the basement of the Elsinore Theatre. Waiting for my turn to sing, I sit nervously with my fellow performers while listening to the acts taking place on the stage just above us. A trap door in the middle of the stage, created in 1926 when the Elsinore hosted live entertainment for the audiences of Salem, Oregon, allowed the actors' trunks to be dropped into the dressing rooms below. The door meant that we could hear the performances from the basement, but it also meant that the performers could hear us. We had strict orders to remain as quiet as possible. I recall the songs of Cole Porter and George Gershwin filling my ears while I breathed in the distinct scent of Aqua Net hairspray mixed with mothballs.

The second dressing room scene takes place in a very different world from the first. In this one, my ten-year-old self is standing at a portable makeup station in a large tent. I am in Woodburn, Oregon, for the annual Cinco de Mayo celebration and my family's dancing troupe, Baile Folklorico de Salem, is a featured act. I am thrilled to be performing alongside my aunts, who busily help me to put on my Veracruz costume, sewn by my grandmother. My aunts also teach me how to apply false eyelashes, a necessity, they say, if the outdoor stadium full of people is going to be able to see my eyes. First, a thin line of glue along the lash line, and then, oh so carefully, place the eyelash. My eyes feel heavy when I try to blink. This temporary dressing room, unlike the other, is cacophonous. I can hear mariachi music blaring and the crowd cheering outside. Performers frantically run in and out, and the sunlight streams through the breaks in the tent's seams.

In both scenes, I remember experiencing the dressing room as its own world, but one that is always penetrated by the outside. Though I would not have used the word "liminality" at the time, I experienced the dressing room as a space that was both inside and out, that created the conditions for self-transformation and also imposed a distinct relationship between self and other. It was a space for creating a sense of individuality and for strengthening ties to family. It was a historical space full of the vestiges of shows past. And it was a transitory space erected for the purposes of a single performance. While I vaguely remember my stage performances, I clearly recall the atmosphere and experience of these dressing rooms.

I have spent considerable time in cinematic dressing rooms for the purposes of writing this book. As I have outlined here, these dressing rooms have identified, shaped, and dissembled American identities, the types of women and men who struggle to reconcile their personal and public selves with society's expectations for who they should be. Looking out over a century of backstage film, dressing rooms continue to be a critical site for making meaning in stories about the lives of performers. Where they are placed, how they are decorated, and who occupies them are variables that have allowed for a range of interpretations by a diverse group of filmmakers working within the Hollywood studio system and beyond. Dressing rooms are portrayed as their own scenes behind the scenes because the types of people we find there continue to have relevance to our lives.

The salience of dressing rooms extends beyond cinema, of course. The rise of social media has meant that real dressing rooms can be entered and experienced like never before. A YouTube video from 2016 shows Barbra Streisand visiting her original dressing room in the Winter Garden Theatre, which she inhabited during the production of *Funny Girl*.[1] The camera is positioned inside the space as she enters along with a team of people holding cameras. Noticing a wall adorned with her own record albums, Streisand exclaims, "Oh, my God! Whose dressing room is this?" Her guide tells her it belongs to actress Sierra Boggess, star of *School of Rock*. Streisand walks though the room reminiscing about how she decorated it (wallpapered with "black paisley" and a black patent leather couch). A photograph that precedes the video shows the performer in this very dressing room; it is strewn with makeup and personal objects like family photographs. Boggess's space, by contrast, is painted a soft purple and bears references to Streisand everywhere. Beyond the albums, Boggess has a framed letter from her idol that wishes her luck and a candle on the dressing table on which Streisand appears as a saint. Streisand writes a note for Boggess before leaving. The video then cuts to a moment "later that day" when Boggess excitedly enters her dressing room, telling the camera that she does not want any of the "energy disturbed." Feeling Streisand's presence in the space, she carefully retraces the performer's steps, finds the note, and excitedly reads, "Dear Sierra, just stopped by, how lovely to see my old dressing room. You're so gifted. Congrats. PS: Love the candle. Barbra." Laughing, Boggess thanks her idol "for existing" and "for not being creeped out by this dressing room."[2]

The video is an example of how contemporary performers understand the dressing room as inhabited space, by performers in the present and by performers from the past. Its haunting by inhabitants from long ago produces meaning for current practitioners like Boggess. With her albums and candle, the *School of Rock* star materialized the spirit of Barbra Streisand, whom Boggess understood to already occupy the space. This dressing room could certainly be interpreted as a site of star worship—which Boggess acknowledges when she thanks Streisand for "not being creeped out"—but it also foregrounds a distinct feature of dressing room experience in which performers understand that it is only temporarily theirs. Dressing rooms have a history that constantly intrudes on the space. While Streisand is a welcome visitor who touches Boggess's belongings and freely uses her pen and paper, the visit ultimately betrays dressing rooms as a place where privacy is violated. Perhaps unwittingly, the camera frames Streisand writing her note below a sign on the wall that reads No Riff Raff—a sign of Boggess's attempts, albeit humorous, to control the space.

Social media has also enabled us to witness less welcome violations of dressing rooms. A recent video on Twitter reveals fans of Lea Salonga filming the actress in her backstage dressing room as she prepares to leave after the show *Here Lies Love*. Salonga is polite but emphatic that they do not belong there and leads them out of the theater. As a story in *The Broadway Blog* phrased it, her show is called "Here Lies Love, not Here's Lea's Dressing Room," a reference to the fans' sense of entitlement and the way that the dressing room, not the show itself, has become the focus of attention.[3] Salonga responded to the intrusion via Twitter: "Just a reminder . . . I have boundaries. Do not cross them. Thank you."[4] A viral cultural event, this dressing room scene communicates how audiences interpret the space as one to be penetrated, an extension of the evening's entertainment.

While social media documents these encounters—wanted and unwanted—dressing room photography tends to emphasize the interiority of the space, showing performers in quiet contemplation or engaging in a "show and tell" of how they make the space theirs. These photographs attempt to create narratives of artistic process in a controlled environment rather than the more unruly dimensions of dressing rooms. In 2015, *Playbill* released a story that featured interviews of various Broadway performers talking about how they decorate their dressing rooms, including sharing the space with small animals, mounting a hammock, creating a mini bar, and hanging family photos.[5] Similar spreads in the *New York Times* present readers with artistic black-and-white photographs of historic dressing rooms along with colorful stories about the more elaborate ones, such as the one occupied by Elizabeth Taylor that, at her request, had a pink bathtub installed.[6] The public's fascination with dressing room décor extends back to the beginning of the twentieth century when trade magazines like *Variety* reported on the more noteworthy adornments, like Miss Elsie De Wolfe's in which she hung strings of electric lights covered in pink lampshades made to look like roses in what the magazine called her "stage boudoir."[7] Much of this reporting was meant to expose what were perceived as unreasonable demands by spoiled actresses, a dynamic that plays out in filmic portrayals of female stars, but it also reveals an attraction to the process by which people who lead public lives strive to establish a private, personal space.

Depicting people in the dressing room automatically renders them consequential as individuals and as social beings. This function of the space has led photographer Michael Kushner to embark on "The Dressing Room Project" on Instagram, a photographic documentation of Broadway performers in the moments before they take "places" on the stage.[8] Those final minutes are loaded with tension and meaning as the performer must prepare for the performance to be given. When asked how cinematic representations measure up to the lived experiences of the dressing room, Kushner was unequivocal in his response. "The drama is real," he said, recounting how he has witnessed performers break down, break out (with an allergic reaction in one instance), receive news of award nominations or show closings, manage challenging personalities in shared dressing rooms, and negotiate altered physical states like pregnancy in others.[9]

In particular, the spectacle of motherhood continues to be a powerful one in Kushner's photographic archive. One of his most popular images is of actress Kenita Miller standing in her dressing room while nine months pregnant during the run of *For Colored Girls Who Have Considered Suicide / When the Rainbow Is Enuf* (2022) on Broadway. Kushner reveals her in profile, with the warm light of the dressing table shining on her, as she thoughtfully looks down and places her hands on her pregnant belly.[10]

As in cinema, the dressing room is a site for intimate thoughts and actions, but also a space where professional demands intrude. Quotes from Robyn Hurder, who played Nini in *Moulin Rouge* (2019–), accompany Kushner's images of her dressing room shoot. She lays bare the feelings of regret she experiences when her son "begs" her not to go to work.[11] Grateful for the encouragement from friends who believe she has perfectly balanced motherhood and career, she nevertheless opines, "There is guilt." "I will continue to try to keep the scales of motherhood and career even for the rest of my life," she explains, "but there will always be a part of me that feels like I should be doing better."[12]

Behind-the-scenes moments like these convey the stakes of performance and deepen our understanding of the people who provide us with entertainment. But they also foreground the challenges of negotiating family and personal ambition that many continue to face today both on and off the stage. Dressing room scenes, real and imagined, hold the performer in limbo, caught between the freedom of self-definition and the pressure of social expectation. They stage these balancing acts as a persistent and vexing feature of American life; the dressing room has been, and continues to be, a sight to behold.

Acknowledgments

Writing a book is a bit like spending time in a dressing room, preparing for the moment when one's labor is finally brought into the spotlight. But I was not backstage by myself. I was assisted by colleagues, students, archival staff, friends, and family who, in different ways, helped to make this book a reality.

Were it not for a very enjoyable breakfast meeting with Pamela Robertson Wojcik at the Society for Cinema and Media Studies conference some years ago, I would not have had the courage to embark on an entire book about dressing rooms. I am grateful for her vision and her support. And thank you to Pamela, Paula J. Massood, and Angel Daniel Matos, who gave me the chance to test out what would become the book's first chapter in their edited volume, Media Crossroads: Intersections of Space and Identity in Screen Cultures.

I also want to thank my former student Anastasia Perez-Ternent, who accompanied me down many rabbit holes looking for dressing room photos, descriptions, and testimonies. And during the COVID-19 pandemic, Krystal Ledesma was my "legs on the ground" in Los Angeles; she found a way to procure much-needed sources as I continued to make progress on the book.

I want to thank my cohort and the instructors of Middlebury's Scholarship in Sound and Image Workshop. During the summer of 2022, I learned the foundations of video essay making along with an inspiring group of scholars: Nilanjana Bhattacharjya, Joel Burges, Allison Cooper, Lisa DiGiovanni, Will DiGravio, Lucy Fife Donaldson, Andrew Ferguson, Katie Grant, Christian Keathley, Colleen Laird, Dayna McLeod, Jeffrey Romero Middents, Jason Mittell, Viktoria Paranyuk, Alison Peirse, Daniel Pope, Sadia Quraeshi Shepard, and Pablo S. Torres. It was a new and exciting skill that significantly expanded my ability to see, hear, and analyze film.

My American Studies peers at the University of Groningen in the Netherlands and Uppsala University in Sweden gave me a warm and productive reception for the presentation of dressing room chapters in progress. In particular, I wish to thank my hosts, Don Mitchell, Christin Mays, and Anne Martinez.

I spent many hours discussing the writing process with my fellow faculty women of color at Dartmouth, Naaborko Sackeyfio-Lenoch and Kimberly Juanita Brown, in a group supported by Michelle Warren. And I am grateful for the writing group initiated by my friend and colleague Ellen Scott as I navigated the book's revisions.

My colleagues in Latin American, Latino, and Caribbean Studies have been generous with their time and thoughtful with their insights. Thank you to Mary Coffey, Jorge Cuellar, Marcela Di Blasi, Sebastian Diaz, Reighan Gillam, Carlos Minchillo, Israel Reyes, and Analola Santana.

Lastly, my most frequent cohabitants in the dressing room have been my friends and family. This book is dedicated to Sarah, my kindred spirit; Timotea, big sister and a role model for all; Matt, my well of strength and support; and Edith Aliza, the best backstage baby a working mother could have.

Notes

Introduction

1. Rick Lyman, "His Rage Quieted, Jake La Motta Fights for Laughs," *Philadelphia Inquirer*, February 21, 1983, D1.
2. Richard Weiss, *The American Myth of Success: From Horatio Alger to Norman Vincent Peale* (Urbana: University of Illinois Press, 1988).
3. Mark Roth, "Some Warners Musicals and the Spirit of the New Deal," *The Velvet Light Trap*, no. 17 (Winter 1977): 1–7.
4. Armond White, "White on Black," *Film Comment* 20, no. 6 (November–December 1984): 16.
5. Or as Lefebvre phrases it, space is both a "product" and a "means of production." Henri Lefebvre, *The Production of Space*, trans. Donald Nicholson-Smith (Oxford: Blackwell, 1991), 85.
6. See Michael V. Montgomery, *Carnivals and Commonplaces: Bakhtin's Chronotope, Cultural Studies, and Film* (New York: Peter Lang, 1993); Vivian Sobchack, "Lounge Time: Postwar Crises and the Chronotope of Film Noir," in *Refiguring American Film Genres: History and Theory*, ed. Nick Browne (Berkeley: University of California Press, 1998), 129–170; Pamela Robertson Wojcik, *The Apartment Plot: Urban Living in American Film and Popular Culture, 1945–1975* (Durham, NC: Duke University Press, 2010); and Robert A. Davidson, *The Hotel: Occupied Space* (Toronto: University of Toronto Press, 2018).
7. Gale McAuley, *Space in Performance: Making Meaning in the Theatre* (Ann Arbor: University of Michigan Press, 2000), 64.
8. Rick Altman, *The American Film Musical* (Bloomington: Indiana University Press, 1987), 207.
9. Richard Dyer, *Heavenly Bodies: Film Stars and Society*, 2nd ed. (London: Routledge, 2004), 2.
10. Steven Cohan, *Hollywood by Hollywood: The Backstudio Picture and the Mystique of Making Movies* (New York: Oxford University Press, 2019); Karen McNally, *The Stardom Film: Creating the Hollywood Fairy Tale* (New York: Wallflower Press, 2021).

11. Karen Halttunen, *Confidence Men and Painted Women: A Study of Middle-Class Culture in America, 1830–1870* (New Haven, CT: Yale University Press, 1982), xv.
12. Richard Leacroft and Helen Leacroft, *Theatre and Playhouse: An Illustrated Survey of Theatre Building from Ancient Greece to the Present Day* (London: Methuen Drama, 1984), 9.
13. Marvin Carlson, *Places of Performance: The Semiotics of Theatre Architecture* (Ithaca, NY: Cornell University Press, 1989), 130.
14. Carlson, *Places of Performance*, 131.
15. Carlson also translates the word to mean "a place where one observes." Carlson, *Places of Performance*, 128.
16. McAuley, *Space in Performance*, 64.
17. Tita Chico, *Designing Women: The Dressing Room in Eighteenth-Century English Literature and Culture* (Lewisburg, PA: Bucknell University Press, 2005), 50.
18. Chico, *Designing Women*, 51.
19. Chico, *Designing Women*, 49.
20. McAuley, *Space in Performance*, 270.
21. Desirée J. Garcia, "What Happened in the Dressing Room," *inTransition: Journal of Videographic and Moving Image Studies* 11, no. 1 (2024), DOI: https://doi.org/10.16995/intransition.15423.
22. Aoife Monks, *The Actor in Costume* (London: Palgrave Macmillan, 2010), 17.
23. Monks, *The Actor in Costume*, 17.
24. Whitney Bolton, "Actors' Goal: Home Away from Home," *Morning Telegraph*, 195?, "Dressing Room" Clippings File, Billy Rose Theatre Division, New York Public Library, New York, NY.
25. Miriam Young, *Mother Wore Tights* (New York: Penguin, 1944), 110.
26. Lefebvre, *The Production of Space*, 26.
27. McAuley, *Space in Performance*, 67.
28. "An Actress' Fame Is Measured by Stairs She Climbs: Marjorie Wood Has Been Up and Down Often on Dressing Room List," *New York Herald Tribune*, February 25, 1934, D6, "Dressing Rooms" Clippings File, Billy Rose Theatre Division, New York Public Library, New York, NY.
29. Bob Lucas, "Angry McKee Quits Greatest and Goes to Pryor Film," *Jet*, November 11, 1976, 119.
30. McAuley, *Space in Performance*, 67.
31. Penelope Green, "Setting the Stage, Offstage," *New York Times*, March 20, 2008, F1.
32. See Altman, *The American Film Musical*; Martin Rubin, "Busby Berkeley and the Backstage Musical," in *Hollywood Musicals: The Film Reader*, ed. Steven Cohan (London: Routledge, 2002), 53–61; and Sean Griffin, "The Gang's All Here: Generic versus Racial Integration in the 1940s Musical," *Cinema Journal* 42, no. 1 (2002): 21–45.
33. For an analysis of hotels in cinema, see Davidson, *The Hotel*. For spaces of transit like train stations, see Sobchack, "Lounge Time."
34. See Sean P. Holmes, *Weavers of Dreams, Unite! Actor's Unionism in Early Twentieth-Century America* (Urbana: University of Illinois Press, 2013).
35. Wojcik, *The Apartment Plot*; Merrill Schleier, *Skyscraper Cinema: Architecture and Gender in American Film* (Minneapolis: University of Minnesota Press, 2009); Paula J. Massood, *Black City Cinema: African American Urban Experiences in Film* (Philadelphia: Temple University Press, 2013).
36. Wojcik, *The Apartment Plot*, 3, 8.

37 Cohan argues that the backstudio picture should be considered a genre rather than a film cycle because of its longevity, certain moments of cyclical currency notwithstanding. Cohan, *Hollywood by Hollywood*, 3.
38 Wojcik, *The Apartment Plot*, 7.
39 Altman, *The American Film Musical*, 200.
40 Wojcik, *The Apartment Plot*, 8.
41 Lefebvre, *The Production of Space*, 93–94.
42 Carlton Miles, "Those Dressing Room Feuds," *San Francisco Chronicle*, December 23, 1945.
43 Gilles Deleuze, *Cinema 2: The Time-Image* (Minneapolis: University of Minnesota Press, 1989), 83–84.

Chapter 1   Maids

1 Helen Ormsbee, "Cleopatra, and a Playwright, Dress and Scold 'Joey' Stars," *New York Herald Tribune*, June 1, 1941, E2.
2 Helen Ormsbee was a former actress herself and frequent reporter on backstage activities in New York, including in her monograph, *Backstage with Actors: From the Time of Shakespeare to the Present Day* (New York: Thomas Y. Crowell, 1938).
3 Ormbsbee, "Cleopatra," E2.
4 Ormbsbee, "Cleopatra," E2.
5 Gwen Bergner, "Performing Work: Maids, Melodrama, and Imitation of Life as Film Noir," *Signs: Journal of Women in Culture and Society* 47, no. 2 (Winter 2022): 431.
6 "Close Harmony" script (1929), Motion Picture Scripts Collection, Cultural Education Center, New York State Archives, Albany, NY.
7 Peter Erickson, "Invisibility Speaks: Servants and Portraits in Early Modern Visual Culture," *Journal for Early Modern Cultural Studies* 9, no. 1 (Spring–Summer 2009): 24; John Corbett, *Extended Play: Sounding Off from John Cage to Dr. Funkenstein* (Durham, NC: Duke University Press, 1994), 63–64. John David Rhodes offers similar conclusions about the cinematic portrayal of the Black servant in suburban homes, a space that foregrounds their lack of mobility. John David Rhodes, "Passing Through: The Black Maid in the Cinematic Suburbs, 1948–1949," in *Race and the Suburbs in American Film*, ed. Merrill Schleier (Albany: State University of New York Press, 2021), 31–52.
8 "Something about the Perfect Maids Who Serve Stars: For Serenity . . . ," *New York Herald Tribune*, January 15, 1928, G2.
9 "Stage Dressing Rooms: Cause of Disputes between Stars—the Finest in This City," *New York Tribune*, October 11, 1903, B7.
10 "Picture House 'Stars,'" *Variety*, March 27, 1909, 8.
11 "Miss Snowden Gets Contract," *New York Amsterdam News*, August 11, 1926, 11.
12 Linda Mizejewski, *Ziegfeld Girl: Image and Icon in Culture and Cinema* (Durham, NC: Duke University Press, 1999), 3.
13 Tita Chico, *Designing Women: The Dressing Room in Eighteenth-Century English Literature and Culture* (Lewisburg, PA: Bucknell University Press, 2005), 14.
14 "Something about the Perfect Maids," G2.
15 Corbett, *Extended Play*, 63.
16 "Mittie Takes a Long Look at Evening," *New York Amsterdam News*, September 21, 1968, 19.
17 Pamela Robertson Wojcik, "The Streisand Musical," in *The Sound of Musicals*, ed. Steven Cohan (London: British Film Institute, 2010), 128–138.

18 "Beat Maid with Hanger—Maid Sues Sensational Dancer for Damages," *New York Amsterdam News*, January 14, 1925.
19 "Colored Maid Will Most Likely Collect Damages from F. Tinney," *New York Amsterdam News*, December 16, 1925, 5.
20 "Stage Maids Organizing," *Variety*, August 11, 1926, 1, 84.
21 "Bought Dope for Tallulah, Ex-Maid Says," *Chicago Daily Tribune*, December 22, 1951, 12.
22 The Black press reported on cases of domestic abuse, fueled by the recruitment of young women in the South. Citing the case of Bessie Brown, a maid who was "kicked and beaten brutally by a wealthy white couple," writer Marvel Cooke argues the maid is a "symbol of the ill-paid, overworked and mistreated at the hands of their employers." Likening Brown's treatment to that of slaves in the "barbaric and shameful pre-Civil War days when masters whipped their slaves at the post," Cooke conveys how little the condition of Black Americans has changed over the last hundred years. Marvel Cooke, "Help Wanted for the Help," *New York Amsterdam News*, October 7, 1939, 11.
23 Ralph Matthews, "The Truth about Hollywood—and the Race Issue from the Actors' Viewpoint," *Afro-American*, January 9, 1943, 11. For an account of this visit, see Thomas Cripps, *Making Movies Black: The Hollywood Message Movie from World War II to the Civil Rights Era* (Oxford: Oxford University Press, 1993). Ellen C. Scott also discusses the larger efforts of the NAACP in Hollywood in *Cinema Civil Rights: Regulation, Repression, and Race in the Classical Hollywood Era* (New Brunswick, NJ: Rutgers University Press, 2015).
24 Matthews, "The Truth about Hollywood," 11.
25 Matthews, "The Truth about Hollywood," 11.
26 Matthews, "The Truth about Hollywood," 11.
27 Abe Hill, "Broadway Actress Pauline Myers Plays in 'Dear Ruth' 100th Time," *New York Amsterdam News*, March 17, 1945, B7.
28 "Popular Character Artist at Local Theater—Louise Beavers Here Again at Loew Houses," *New York Amsterdam News*, September 21, 1935, 7.
29 Susan Courtney, *Hollywood Fantasies of Miscegenation: Spectacular Narratives of Gender and Race, 1903–1967* (Princeton, NJ: Princeton University Press, 2005), 4.
30 Grant Greschuk, dir., *Jeni LeGon: Living in a Great Big Way* (Montreal: National Film Board of Canada, 1999). In the same on-camera interview, LeGon details how her fellow actors were kind to her on the set but would not acknowledge her around the studio. For the reference to LeGon's cut musical number from *Easter Parade*, see "With Eye on Box Office Hollywood Plans Several Mixed Pictures," *Chicago Defender*, June 5, 1948.
31 Miriam J. Petty, *Stealing the Show: African American Performers and Audiences in 1930s Hollywood* (Berkeley: University of California Press, 2016).
32 Julian Hanich, "Reflecting on Reflections: Cinema's Complex Mirror Shots," in *Indefinite Visions: Cinema and the Attractions of Uncertainty*, ed. Martine Beugnet, Allan Cameron, and Arild Fetveit (Edinburgh: Edinburgh University Press, 2017), 131.
33 The same song returns in *Love Me or Leave Me* (1955) just before its performer, Doris Day, returns to her Ziegfeld dressing room, where her Black maid awaits.
34 Paula J. Massood, *Black City Cinema: African American Urban Experiences in Film* (Philadelphia: Temple University Press, 2003).
35 See Marina Heung, "'What's the Matter with Sara Jane?': Daughters and Mothers in Douglas Sirk's *Imitation of Life*," *Cinema Journal* 26, no. 3 (Spring 1987): 21–43; Jackie

Byars, *All That Hollywood Allows: Re-reading Gender in 1950s Melodrama* (Chapel Hill: University of North Carolina Press, 1991); and Lucy Fischer, ed., *Imitation of Life: Douglas Sirk, Director* (New Brunswick, NJ: Rutgers University Press, 1991).
36 Sandy Flitterman-Lewis, "*Imitation(s) of Life*: The Black Woman's Double Determination as Troubling 'Other,'" in Fischer, *Imitation of Life*, 325.
37 Bergner, "Performing Work," 438.
38 Byars, *All That Hollywood Allows*, 238.
39 Byars, *All That Hollywood Allows*, 245.
40 Lucy Fischer, "'How Do I Love Thee?': Theatricality, Desire and the Family Melodrama," in *A Family Affair: Cinema Calls Home*, ed. Murray Pomerance (London: Wallflower Press, 2008), 108.
41 Michael Stern, "Imitation of Life," in Fischer, *Imitation of Life*, 282.
42 Charles Affron, "Performing Performing: Irony and Affect," in Fischer, *Imitation of Life*, 207.
43 "Colored Maids in Unique Position in Hollywood," *New York Amsterdam News*, May 1, 1929, 13.
44 Judith Rollins discusses the history of the American middle class's employment of Black maids, considering them "symbols of affluence," in *Between Women: Domestics and Their Employers* (Philadelphia: Temple University Press, 1985), 106. Bergner discusses how Annie "increases the value of Lora's whiteness" in "Performing Work," 432.
45 *Imitation of Life* Continuity Script, in Fischer, *Imitation of Life*, 95.
46 Jon Halliday, "Sirk on Sirk," in Fischer, *Imitation of Life*, 228.
47 A. S. "Doc" Young, "Calls 'Rebel Breed' Interestingly Rough: Moore and Kohner Vying in Race for 1959 Honors," *Chicago Defender*, March 26, 1960, 19.
48 I have also had multiple conversations with scholars who remember Annie and Sarah Jane's scenes occurring in a dressing room. See Andrew Asibong, "Discussion of Green's 'Melanie Klein and the Black Mammy: An Exploration of the Influence of the Mammy Stereotype on Klein's Maternal and Its Contribution to the "Whiteness" of Psychoanalysis,'" *Studies in Gender and Sexuality* 19, no. 3 (2018): 183.
49 Flitterman-Lewis, "*Imitation(s) of Life*," 325.
50 Hedda Hopper, "Pick a Part—She'll Play It," *Chicago Daily Tribune*, August 9, 1959, F22.
51 Eric Harrison, "A Hard Lesson from Hollywood's Past," *Los Angeles Times*, July 9, 2000.
52 M.L.A., "Film 'Imitation of Life' New Version of Old Novel," *Daily Boston Globe*, March 30, 1959, 5. Marina Heung discusses the funeral scene as a "public spectacle" that rivals "one of Lora's theatrical triumphs" in "'What's the Matter with Sara Jane?,'" 36.

Chapter 2 Sisters

1 Cover illustration, *New Yorker*, December 9, 1944.
2 These are in the issues from January 25, 1936; December 9, 1944; October 5, 1952; May 1, 1954; and October 4, 1958.
3 See the history of white chorus girls on the stage as told by Susan Glenn, *Female Spectacle: The Theatrical Roots of Modern Feminism* (Cambridge, MA: Harvard University Press, 2000); and Linda Mizejewski, *Ziegfeld Girl: Image and Icon in Culture and Cinema* (Durham, NC: Duke University Press, 1999).

4. Glenn, *Female Spectacle*, 188–215.
5. Lucy Fischer, *Shot/Countershot: Film Tradition and Women's Cinema* (Princeton, NJ: Princeton University Press, 1989), 186.
6. Siegfried Kracauer, "The Mass Ornament," in *The Mass Ornament: Weimar Essays* (Cambridge, MA: Harvard University Press, 1995), 76.
7. Glenn, *Female Spectacle*, 167, 191.
8. See Desirée J. Garcia, "Toil behind the Footlights: The Spectacle of Female Suffering and the Rise of Musical Comedy," *Frontiers* 40, no. 1 (2019): 122–145.
9. Martin Rubin, "Busby Berkeley and the Backstage Musical," in *Hollywood Musicals: The Film Reader*, ed. Steven Cohan (London: Routledge, 2002), 53.
10. Lucy Fischer has analyzed the numbers in Berkeley musicals that present a musical narrative as an expression of urban space. Lucy Fischer, "City of Women: Busby Berkeley, Architecture, and Urban Space," *Cinema Journal* 49, no. 4 (Summer 2010): 111–130.
11. These backstage directives hark back to the beginning of the twentieth century as well, when theater management attempted to regulate the behavior of female performers. See Monica Eugenia Stufft, "Chorus Girl Collective: Early 20th Century American Performance Communities and Urban Networking" (PhD diss., University of California, Berkeley, 2008).
12. Rosamond Gilder, *Enter the Actress: The First Woman in the Theatre* (Boston: Houghton Mifflin, 1931), 149.
13. Tita Chico, *Designing Women: The Dressing Room in Eighteenth-Century English Literature and Culture* (Lewisburg, PA: Bucknell University Press, 2005).
14. "Close Watch in Washington," *Variety*, October 8, 1910.
15. *The Johnie and the Telephone* (1903) and *The Messenger Boy and the Ballet Girl* (1905) are other examples.
16. *The Broadway Melody*, Sequence Synopsis of the Continuity of September 18, 1928, Motion Picture Scripts Collection, New York State Archives, Albany, NY.
17. David M. Lugowski, "Queering the (New) Deal: Lesbian and Gay Representation and the Depression-Era Cultural Politics of Hollywood's Production Code," *Cinema Journal* 38, no. 2 (Winter 1999): 3–35.
18. *Gold Diggers of 1933* (1933), Dialogue Script, Motion Picture Scripts Collection, New York State Archives, Albany, NY.
19. Stufft, "Chorus Girl Collective," 95, 106.
20. John B. Kennedy, "What Chorus Girls Talk About," *Esquire*, February 1934.
21. Mizejewski, *Ziegfeld Girl*, 111.
22. Mizejewski, *Ziegfeld Girl*, 120.
23. Eric Lott, *Love and Theft: Blackface Minstrelsy and the American Working Class* (New York: Oxford University Press, 1993).
24. Scholars have explored the self-reflexive dimensions of this number for both Garland and Lamarr. As Diane Negra has written, the number entrenches perceptions of Lamarr as a foreign actress given that the "Minnie" of the song lyric becomes "Lamarr" when she goes to Hollywood. And Mizejewski argues that Garland's casting in the role of the "dusky belle" is intended to highlight how the star does not conform to Hollywood's standards of female beauty. Diane Negra, *Off-White Hollywood: American Culture and Ethnic Female Stardom* (London: Routledge, 2001), 12; Mizejewski, *Ziegfeld Girl*, 177.
25. Most of these films also elevate white stardom through the presence of a Black maid in the star's dressing room, as I explore in chapter 1.

26 A notable exception from the period of classical Hollywood filmmaking is *Stormy Weather* (1943), the rare backstage film from this era with an all-Black cast, which I discuss in chapter 3.
27 Production Code File, "The Broadway Melody" (1929), Margaret Herrick Library, Academy of Motion Picture Arts and Sciences, Los Angeles, CA.
28 *Fox Movietone Follies of 1929* Script, May 2, 1929, Motion Picture Scripts Collection, New York State Archives, Albany, NY.
29 Freddie Schader, "The Fox Follies—A Merry Melange of Song and Dance," *Motion Picture News*, April–June 1929.
30 For an analysis of the roles migration and urban space play in cinema about Black life, see Paula J. Massood, *Black City Cinema: African American Urban Experiences in Film* (Philadelphia: Temple University Press, 2003).
31 *Hearts in Dixie*, in which Perry also starred, stages a scene in which migrants leave the South at the very end of the film. But *Fox Movietone Follies* is different because it is not an "antebellum idyll" that spatially and socially restricts Black Americans to a time in the antebellum South, as Massood has argued, but rather presents a Black migrant living and working in the North. Massood, *Black City Cinema*, 14.
32 His deception of the creditors reaffirms stereotypes about Black entertainers' potential for "stealing" that existed in Hollywood at the time. See Miriam J. Petty, *Stealing the Show: African American Performers and Audiences in 1930s Hollywood* (Berkeley: University of California Press, 2016).
33 Joseph I. Breen to Mr. Hunt Stromberg, December 3, 1942, Production Code File, "Lady of Burlesque," Margaret Herrick Library, Academy of Motion Picture Arts and Sciences, Los Angeles, CA.
34 Earl H. Leaf to Mr. Gilpin, December 9, 1942, Production Code File, "Lady of Burlesque," Margaret Herrick Library, Academy of Motion Picture Arts and Sciences, Los Angeles, CA.
35 Another film that ventures into backstage space is *Desperately Seeking Susan* (1985), directed by Susan Seidelman.
36 Fischer, *Shot/Countershot*, 222–223.
37 The Gerry Society was also known as the New York Society for the Prevention of Cruelty to Children.
38 Karen Hollinger usefully maps out the scholarly debate about the women's film and the extent to which it reflects a feminist consciousness or a patriarchal appropriation of women's relationships in *In the Company of Women: Contemporary Female Friendship Films* (Minneapolis: University of Minnesota Press, 1998), 4.
39 Jackie Stacey, "Desperately Seeking Difference," in *The Female Gaze: Women as Viewers of Popular Culture*, ed. Lorraine Gamman and Margaret Marshment (Seattle: Real Comet Press, 1989), 54.
40 Desirée J. Garcia, "Intimate Thresholds," Vimeo video, 3:59, posted July 8, 2022, https://vimeo.com/728173086?share=copy.
41 "Dance, Girl, Dance," *Variety*, August 28, 1940.
42 Teresa de Lauretis, "Aesthetic and Feminist Theory: Rethinking Women's Cinema," *New German Critique*, no. 34 (Winter 1985): 167.
43 Donna R. Casella, "What Women Want: The Complex World of Dorothy Arzner and Her Cinematic Women," *Framework* 50, nos. 1–2 (Spring–Fall 2009): 260.
44 Julian Hanich defines the complex mirror shot in his essay "Reflecting on Reflections: Cinema's Complex Mirror Shots," in *Indefinite Visions: Cinema and the Attractions of Uncertainty*, ed. Martine Beugnet, Allan Cameron, and Arild Fetveit (Edinburgh: Edinburgh University Press, 2017), 131–156.

45 The homoerotic dimensions of women sharing space are rarely explored this explicitly in classical Hollywood film, although scholars have applied queer readings to woman-oriented films such as *All about Eve*. See Patricia White, *Uninvited: Classical Hollywood Cinema and Lesbian Representability* (Bloomington: Indiana University Press, 1999).
46 *Sparkle* Pressbook (1979), African Americans in Film Collection, Box 11, Schomburg Center for Research in Black Culture, New York, NY.
47 Armond White, "White on Black," *Film Comment* 20, no. 6 (November–December 1984): 16.
48 White, "White on Black," 15.
49 Stacey, "Desperately Seeking Difference," 115.

Chapter 3 Wives and Mothers

1 "Where All Is Not Gold That Glitters," *Biograph Bulletin*, September 11, 1908.
2 Richard Dyer, *Heavenly Bodies: Film Stars and Society*, 2nd ed. (London: Routledge, 2004), 2.
3 Vivian Sobchack, "Lounge Time: Postwar Crises and the Chronotope of Film Noir," in *Refiguring American Film Genres: History and Theory*, ed Nick Browne (Berkeley: University of California Press, 1998), 144.
4 Robert A. Davidson, *The Hotel: Occupied Space* (Toronto: University of Toronto Press, 2018), 7.
5 Backstage Staff, Robert Martin, "I'm Pregnant. Is My Career Over?," *Backstage*, last updated January 22, 2013, https://www.backstage.com/magazine/article/pregnant-career-50473/.
6 Helen E. M. Brooks, "The Divided Heart of the Actress: Late Eighteenth-Century Actresses and the 'Cult of Maternity,'" in *Stage Mothers: Women, Work, and the Theater, 1660–1830*, ed. Laura Engel and Elaine M. McGirr (Lewisburg, PA: Bucknell University Press, 2014), 20; Marilyn Francus, "The Lady Vanishes: The Rise of the Spectral Mother," in *The Absent Mother in the Cultural Imagination: Missing, Presumed Dead*, ed. Berit Astrom (Cham, Switzerland: Palgrave Macmillan, 2017), 31; Kristina Straub, *Sexual Suspects: Eighteenth-Century Players and Sexual Ideology* (Princeton, NJ: Princeton University Press, 1992), 89–90.
7 Tita Chico, *Designing Women: The Dressing Room in Eighteenth-Century English Literature and Culture* (Lewisburg, PA: Bucknell University Press, 2005), 31.
8 We know from Tracy C. Davis's work, however, that the "actress" was a regular character in Victorian pornography throughout the nineteenth century. The "forbidden zones" of the backstage realm, especially the dressing room, continued to sexually stimulate male viewers while those materials associated with the dressing room (mirrors, flowers, vanity tables, cushions) appearing behind see-through draperies "were common objects carrying exotic weight." Tracy C. Davis, "The Actress in Victorian Pornography," *Theatre Journal* 41, no. 3 (1989): 313.
9 Ralph Freud, "George Spelvin Says the Tag: Folklore of the Theater," *Western Folklore* 13, no. 4 (October 1954): 248.
10 Miriam Young, *Mother Wore Tights* (New York: Penguin, 1944), 110.
11 Gypsy Rose Lee, *Gypsy: A Memoir* (1957; Berkeley, CA: Frog Books, 1999), 209.
12 In chapter 5, I explore how reports about thefts in the dressing room were also a way to express anxieties about black American dressers who worked backstage.
13 "Dressing Room Assault," *Variety*, August 22, 1919, 55, 13.

14 Lillian Roth with Mike Connolly and Gerold Frank, *I'll Cry Tomorrow* (New York: Frederick Fell, 1954), 15.
15 Christin Essin, *Working Backstage: A Cultural History and Ethnography of Technical Theater Labor* (Ann Arbor: University of Michigan Press, 2021), 57.
16 Freud, "George Spelvin," 247.
17 Laura Engel and Ellen M. McGirr, introduction to Engel and McGirr, *Stage Mothers*, 11.
18 Engel and McGirr, introduction, 11.
19 Engel and McGirr, introduction, 11; Francus, "The Lady Vanishes," 27; "PFL 'Applause' Gets Varied Reception; Is Lauded by Lay Press," *Exhibitors Herald-World*, October 12, 1929, 15.
20 "PFL 'Applause,'" 15.
21 Beth Brown, *Applause* (New York: Horace Liveright, 1928), 29.
22 Here I differ from E. Ann Kaplan, who describes the sequence as akin to a funeral procession. It is indeed a solemn sequence, but I would argue that this first dressing room scene is more hopeful than morbid. E. Ann Kaplan, *Motherhood and Representation: The Mother in Popular Culture and Melodrama* (New York: Routledge, 1992), 145.
23 Elaine Tyler May, *Homeward Bound: American Families in the Cold War Era* (New York: Basic Books, 1988), 10, 186.
24 Lisa McGirr, *Suburban Warriors: The Origins of the New American Right* (Princeton, NJ: Princeton University Press, 2002); Joanne Meyerowitz, "Competing Images of Women in Postwar Mass Culture," in *Major Problems in American Women's History*, ed. Mary Beth Norton and Ruth M. Alexander (Lexington, MA: D. C. Heath, 1996), 422.
25 Jackie Byars, *All That Hollywood Allows: Re-reading Gender in 1950s Melodrama* (Chapel Hill: University of North Carolina Press, 1991), 148.
26 I explore these films and their postwar contexts more fully in Desirée J. Garcia, "'What's Happened to Chorus Girls?': Domesticity and the Postwar Backstage Musical," *Journal of Cinema and Media Studies* 61, no. 5 (2020–2021): 31–58.
27 Virginia Wilson, "Mother Wore Tights," *Modern Screen*, October 1947.
28 Miriam Young, *Mother Wore Tights* (New York: Penguin, 1944), 109–111.
29 Young, *Mother Wore Tights*, 121.
30 Young, *Mother Wore Tights*, 158.
31 Caryl Flinn, *Brass Diva: The Life and Legends of Ethel Merman* (Berkeley: University of California Press, 2007), 318, 299, 320.
32 David M. Gerber, "Heroes and Misfits: The Troubled Social Reintegration of Disabled Veterans in *The Best Years of Our Lives*," *American Quarterly* 46, no. 4 (December 1994): 545–574.
33 As I examine in chapter 1, the cost of Fanny Brice's success on the stage is a lifetime of loneliness, which her employment of a Black maid foreshadows and signifies.
34 "Synopsis," *Stormy Weather* Pressbook (1943), African Americans in Film Collection, Box 12, Archives and Manuscripts Division, New York Public Library, New York, NY.
35 Richard Yates, *Revolutionary Road*, 3rd ed. (New York: Random House, 2009), 19.
36 "Lighting up the lonely stage" is the promotional tag line for *I Could Go on Singing* (1963), another backstage film about the lonely life of a singing star, loosely based on Judy Garland's own career.
37 Lucy Fischer, "La Vie en Noir: Woman, Melodrama, and the Biopic," *Quarterly Review of Film and Video* 33, no. 3 (2016): 201.

38 Dennis Bingham, *Whose Lives Are They Anyway? The Biopic as Contemporary Film Genre* (New Brunswick, NJ: Rutgers University Press, 2010), 10.
39 See Josephine Dolan, "Smoothing the Wrinkles: Hollywood, Successful Aging and the New Visibility of Older Female Stars," in *The Routledge Companion to Media and Gender*, ed. Cindy Carter, Linda Steiner, and Lisa McLaughlin (London: Routledge, 2013), 324–351; Elizabeth W. Markson and Carol A. Taylor, "The Mirror Has Two Faces," *Aging and Society* 20, no. 2 (2000): 137–160; and Susan Liddy, "Older Women and Sexuality On-Screen: Euphemism and Evasion?," in *Ageing Women in Literature and Visual Culture: Reflections, Refractions, Reimaginings*, ed. Cathy McGlynn, Margaret O'Neill, and Michaela Schrage-Früh (Cham, Switzerland: Palgrave Macmillan, 2017), 167–180.
40 Todd Berliner, "Hollywood Movie Dialogue and the 'Real Realism' of John Cassavetes," *Film Quarterly* 52, no. 3 (Spring 1999): 10.
41 Berliner, "Hollywood Movie Dialogue," 11.
42 Lisa Katzman, "'Opening Night': Moment by Moment," *Film Comment* 25, no. 3 (May–June 1989): 39.
43 Homay King, "Free Indirect Affect in Cassavetes' *Opening Night* and *Faces*," *Camera Obscura* 19, no. 2 (56) (2004): 108, 110.

Chapter 4 Leading Men

1 See Claire Sisco King, *Washed in Blood: Male Sacrifice, Trauma, and the Cinema* (New Brunswick, NJ: Rutgers University Press, 2012); Barry Keith Grant, *Shadows of Doubt: Negotiations of Masculinity in American Genre Films* (Detroit: Wayne State University Press, 2011); Donna Peberdy, *Masculinity and Film Performance: Male Angst in Contemporary American Cinema* (New York: Palgrave Macmillan, 2011); Philippa Gates, *Detecting Men: Masculinity and the Hollywood Detective Film* (Albany: State University of New York Press, 2006); Brian Baker, *Masculinity in Fiction and Film: Representing Men in Popular Genres 1945–2000* (London: Continuum, 2006); and the majority of the essays in Timothy Shary, ed., *Millennial Masculinity: Men in Contemporary Cinema* (Detroit: Wayne State University Press, 2013).
2 Stella Bruzzi, *Men's Cinema: Masculinity and* Mise en Scène *in Hollywood* (Edinburgh: Edinburgh University Press, 2013), 14.
3 Pamela Robertson Wojcik, *The Apartment Plot: Urban Living in American Film and Popular Culture, 1945–1975* (Durham, NC: Duke University Press, 2010); Merrill Schleier, *Skyscraper Cinema: Architecture and Gender in American Film* (Minneapolis: University of Minnesota Press, 2009).
4 Steven Cohan, *Masked Men: Masculinity in the Movies in the Fifties* (Bloomington: Indiana University Press, 1997), xvi.
5 Steven Cohan, "'Feminizing' the Song-and-Dance Man: Fred Astaire and the Spectacle of Masculinity in the Hollywood Musical," in *Screening the Male: Exploring Masculinities in Hollywood Cinema*, ed. Steven Cohan and Ina Rae Hark (London: Routledge, 1993), 46.
6 Cohan, "'Feminizing' the Song-and-Dance Man," 48. Steven Neale posed the idea that men risk being feminized when occupying cinematic spaces coded as "feminine" in his essay "Masculinity and Spectacle," *Screen* 24, no. 6 (1983): 2–16. The relationship between femininity and spectacle has been influential due to the work of theorist Laura Mulvey but also has origins, as Caryl Flinn has noted, in the work of Jean Baudrillard and Jacques Lacan. Caryl Flinn, "Containing Fire:

Performance in *Paris Is Burning*," in *Documenting the Documentary: Close Readings of Documentary Film and Video*, ed. Barry Keith Grant and Jeannette Sloniowski (Detroit: Wayne State University Press, 2014), 438–455.
7 Cohan studies the dynamics of masculinity, sexuality, and spectacle further in *Incongruous Entertainment: Camp, Cultural Value, and the MGM Musical* (Durham, NC: Duke University Press, 2005); and Steven Cohan, "'Feminizing' the Song-and-Dance Man: Fred Astaire and the Spectacle of Masculinity in the Hollywood Musical," in *Screening the Male: Exploring Masculinities in Hollywood Cinema*, ed. Steven Cohan and Ina Rae Hark (London: Routledge, 1993), 48.
8 Susan Glenn, *Female Spectacle: The Theatrical Roots of Modern Feminism* (Cambridge, MA: Harvard University Press, 2000); Linda Mizejewski, *Ziegfeld Girl: Image and Icon in Culture and Cinema* (Durham, NC: Duke University Press, 1999).
9 Alison M. Kibler, *Rank Ladies: Gender and Cultural Hierarchy in American Vaudeville* (Chapel Hill: University of North Carolina Press, 1999), 177.
10 Kibler, *Rank Ladies*, 172, 173, 180.
11 See Tita Chico, *Designing Women: The Dressing Room in Eighteenth-Century English Literature and Culture* (Lewisburg, PA: Bucknell University Press, 2005).
12 Gwendolyn Waltz, "20 Minutes or Less: Short-Form Film-and-Theatre Hybrids—Skits, Sketches, Playlets, and Acts in Vaudeville, Variety, Revues, &c.," in *Performing New Media, 1890–1915*, ed. Kaveh Askari et al. (Bloomington: Indiana University Press, 2015), 251.
13 "Anthony," *Variety*, August 20, 1910, 12. The exploitation of backstage labor has been a long-standing concern for actors and manifested in the White Rats' list of grievances and the concurrent strikes of the Actor's Equity Union and the Theatrical Wardrobe Attendants Union in 1919. See Christin Essin, *Working Backstage: A Cultural History and Ethnography of Technical Theater Labor* (Ann Arbor: University of Michigan Press, 2021), 179; and Sean P. Holmes, *Weavers of Dreams, Unite! Actor's Unionism in Early Twentieth-Century America* (Urbana: University of Illinois Press, 2013).
14 Anticipating this surge, Charlie Chaplin's *Limelight* was released two years earlier.
15 John Beaufort, "Crosby, Holden, and Grace Kelly Star," *Christian Science Monitor*, February 11, 1955, 11. For an analysis of the interplay between Crosby's persona and his role in *The Country Girl*, see Linda A. Robinson, "Bing on a Binge: Casting-against-Type in *The Country Girl*," in *Going My Way: Bing Crosby and American Culture*, ed. Ruth Prigozy and Walter Raubicheck (Rochester, NY: University of Rochester Press, 2007).
16 Otis L. Guernsey Jr., "The Country Girl," *New York Herald Tribune*, December 16, 1954, 31.
17 David M. Gerber, "Heroes and Misfits: The Troubled Social Reintegration of Disabled Veterans in *The Best Years of Our Lives*," *American Quarterly* 46, no. 4 (December 1994): 545–574.
18 Jeffrey Montez de Oca, "The 'Muscle Gap': Physical Education and US Fears of a Depleted Masculinity, 1954–1963," in *East Plays West: Sport and the Cold War*, ed. Stephen Wagg and David L. Andrews (London: Routledge, 2006), 123–148. On the rise of *Playboy*, see Pamela Robertson Wojcik, *The Apartment Plot: Urban Living in American Film and Popular Culture, 1945–1975* (Durham, NC: Duke University Press, 2010).
19 See Cohan, *Masked Men*; and Wojcik, *The Apartment Plot*.

20 Ralph Freud, "George Spelvin Says the Tag: Folklore of the Theater," *Western Folklore* 13, no. 4 (October 1954): 247.
21 In chapter 3, I discuss the "man in the mirror" as a shot that betrays the power dynamics in dressing rooms shared by husbands and wives.
22 Muriel Babcock, "Dressing Rooms of Stars Reflect Individuality," *Los Angeles Times*, August 28, 1927, D13.
23 As Cohan argues, an awareness of Hollywood's past, and the models of stardom that were associated with it, is a defining feature of the 1954 version of *A Star Is Born*. Steven Cohan, *Hollywood by Hollywood: The Backstudio Picture and the Mystique of Making Movies* (New York: Oxford University Press, 2019), 118.
24 Stefanie Diekmann, "Scenes from the Dressing Room: Theatrical Interiors in Fiction Film," in *Interiors and Interiority*, ed. Ewa Lajer-Burcharth and Beate Sontgen (Berlin: De Gruyter, 2016), 98.
25 Julian Hanich, "Reflecting on Reflections: Cinema's Complex Mirror Shots," in *Indefinite Visions: Cinema and the Attractions of Uncertainty*, ed. Martine Beugnet, Allan Cameron, and Arild Fetveit (Edinburgh: Edinburgh University Press, 2017).
26 Diekmann argues that the mirror in this scene facilitates both his masquerade and his confession. See "Scenes from the Dressing Room," 98.
27 In chapter 2, I examine the relationship between white women's access to opportunity and dressing room spaces.
28 Krin Gabbard has outlined the trumpet's phallic imagery in the film in his essay "Signifyin(g) the Phallus: *Mo' Better Blues* and Representations of the Jazz Trumpet," *Cinema Journal* 32, no. 1 (Autumn 1992): 50.
29 Lynn Norment, "'Mo' Better Blues': Backstage with Spike Lee and the Cast," *Ebony*, September 1, 1990, 76.
30 Tambay Obenson, "'Mo' Better Blues' at 30: Spike Lee's Fourth Joint, as Told by Female Leads Cynda Williams and Joie Lee," *IndieWire*, September 24, 2020, https://www.indiewire.com/2020/09/mo-better-blues-at-30-cynda-williams-joie-lee-1234580482/.
31 Spike Lee, "Love Supreme" Film Script, first draft, April 16, 1989; *Mo' Better Blues* (1990), Film and Television Screenplay, Archives and Special Collections, Loyola Marymount, Coll. 102, Box 36.
32 In interviews, Lee also made comparisons between Black musicians and Black athletes, both of whom are enslaved for their talent and labor to white management. See Samuel G. Freedman, "Spike Lee and the 'Slavery' of the Blues," *New York Times*, July 29, 1990.
33 Lee, "Love Supreme" Film Script.
34 Norment, "'Mo' Better Blues,'" 76.
35 Norment, "'Mo' Better Blues,'" 76.
36 Freedman, "Spike Lee."
37 Freedman, "Spike Lee."
38 Martha Shearer, "E-Q-U-I-T-Y: Generic Boundaries, Gender, and Real Estate in Magic Mike Films," in *Musicals at the Margins: Genre, Boundaries, Canons*, ed. Julie Lobalzo Wright and Martha Shearer (New York: Bloomsbury Academic, 2021), 44.
39 Jason Bainbridge, "'This Land Is Mine!': Understanding the Function of Supervillains," in *The Superhero Symbol: Media, Culture, Politics*, ed. Liam Burke, Ian Gordon, and Angela Ndalianis (New Brunswick, NJ: Rutgers University Press, 2020), 69.

40 Bill Desowitz, "Creating Unstable New York States of Mind for Todd Phillips' 'Joker' and Edward Norton's 'Motherless Brooklyn,'" *IndieWire*, November 14, 2019, https://www.indiewire.com/awards/industry/production-design-recreating-new-york-joker-motherless-brooklyn-1202189588/.
41 Kartik Nair examines how the proliferation of trash in the mise-en-scène is a reference to the 1981 strike by sanitation workers in New York City, which was also the moment when Latinos and Black Americans formed the majority of unionized workers, replacing and causing resentment among white Italian Americans. Kartik Nair, "Striking Out: Visual Space, Production Design, and Labor History in Joker," *Quarterly Review of Film and Video* 39, no. 8, published ahead of print, September 30, 2021, https://doi.org/10.1080/10509208.2021.1981070.
42 Celestino Deleyto, "The Texture of the Age: Digital Construction of Unbounded Space in *Birdman* (Iñárritu 2014)," *Studies in Spanish and Latin American Cinemas* 18, no. 1 (April 2020): 85.

Chapter 5 Masqueraders

1 The term "dresser" refers to either a woman or man whose job it is to deliver and assist with changes of costume. In Hollywood film, however, there is a general distinction between dressers who are valets, and therefore male, and those who are maids and female. Through the 1970s, these roles were often cast as people of color.
2 "Turning Point in Al Jolson's Life," *The Jazz Singer* Pressbook (1927), Warner Bros. Archive, University of Southern California, Los Angeles, CA.
3 The story appears in a *Radio Digest* article in 1929 and, as documented by Charles Musser, in the *Baltimore Afro-American* in 1928 and the *Washington Tribune* the same year. "Microphone Brings Jolson Fame," *Radio Digest*, March 1929, 78; Charles Musser, "Why Did Negroes Love Al Jolson and *The Jazz Singer*? Melodrama, Blackface and Cosmopolitan Theatrical Culture," *Film History* 23 (2011): 207; Joe Laurie Jr., "The Blackface Acts," *Variety*, January 6, 1954, 247.
4 Eric Lott, *Love and Theft: Blackface Minstrelsy and the American Working Class* (New York: Oxford University Press, 1993), 55.
5 "Microphone Brings Jolson Fame," *Radio Digest*, March 1929, 78. These backstage exploitative labor practices extended to Black women as well. See chapter 1.
6 "Microphone Brings Jolson Fame," *Radio Digest*, March 1929, 78.
7 Cedric Robinson, *Forgeries of Memory and Meaning: Blacks and the Regimes of Race in American Theater and Film before World War II* (Chapel Hill: University of North Carolina Press, 2007).
8 Laurie, "The Blackface Acts," 247.
9 I use the term "queer" in order to broadly encompass those whose identity aligns with gender-nonconforming ideas and behaviors, including gay, lesbian, and transgender individuals.
10 Terry Castle, *Masquerade and Civilization: The Carnivalesque in Eighteenth-Century English Culture and Fiction* (Stanford, CA: Stanford University Press, 1986), 77.
11 Ralph Freud, "George Spelvin Says the Tag: Folklore of the Theater," *Western Folklore* 13, no. 4 (October 1954): 247.
12 Freud, "George Spelvin," 247.
13 Freud, "George Spelvin," 247.
14 Lisa Bansavage and L. E. McCullough, *Break a Leg! A Treasury of Theatre Traditions and Superstitions* (Woodbridge, NJ: Silver Spear, 2017), 27.

15 Bansavage and McCullough, *Break a Leg!*, 28.
16 Tales of ghosts who haunt the theater abound in theatrical lore. The "ghost light" that must always be in operation onstage and the practice of referring to payday as the "ghost walk" are two of many examples. Bansavage and McCullough, *Break a Leg!*, 88.
17 Marvin Carlson, *The Haunted Stage: The Theater as Memory Machine* (Ann Arbor: University of Michigan Press, 2001), 2.
18 See, for example, "Dressing Room Robber Starts Right in Again," *Variety*, February 24, 1926, 6.
19 "Artists' Forum-Buffalo, March 7, 1906," *Variety*, March 17, 1906, 7.
20 "After Colored Thief," *Variety*, November 17, 1906, 6.
21 "New Club Formed," *Billboard*, June 26, 1920, 29; "The Dressing Room Club to Parade on Broadway," *Billboard*, July 23, 1921, 10; "Excerpts from the Negro in Drama," *Billboard*, June 10, 1922, 51; "D.R. Club Honors Shuffle Along No. 3," *Pittsburgh Courier*, April 7, 1923, 12; "Actress Honored," *Chicago Defender*, December 29, 1923, 4; "Dressing Room Club Pageant a Hit," *Baltimore Afro-American*, March 7, 1924, 13.
22 Michael Rogin refers to Blackface minstrelsy as "racial cross-dressing" in *Blackface, White Noise: Jewish Immigrants in the Hollywood Melting Pot* (Berkeley: University of California Press, 1996), 103.
23 Lott, *Love and Theft*, 20.
24 "Walking on Thin Ice," *Hollywood Filmograph*, May 3, 1930.
25 Rogin, *Blackface, White Noise*, 80.
26 Lott, *Love and Theft*, 11.
27 Paula J. Massood, *Making a Promised Land: Harlem in Twentieth-Century Photography and Film* (New Brunswick, NJ: Rutgers University Press, 2013), 70.
28 Camilla F. Forbes, "Dancing with 'Racial Feet': Bert Williams and the Performance of Blackness," *Theatre Journal* 56 (2004): 619.
29 "New Acts of the Week: Cameron and Flanagan," *Variety*, December 22, 1906, 5, 10.
30 Roy Grundmann and Marlon Riggs, "New Agendas in Black Filmmaking: An Interview with Marlon Riggs," *Cineaste* 19, no. 2/3 (1992): 52–54.
31 Castle, *Masquerade and Civilization*, 76.
32 Richard Dyer, *Heavenly Bodies: Film Stars and Society*, 2nd ed. (London: Routledge, 2004), 2.
33 Bridget Sundin, "From Tuxedo to Gown: Dietrich's Haunted Dressing Room(s)," *Theatre Symposium* 27 (2019): 112.
34 Gwendolyn Waltz, "20 Minutes or Less: Short-Form Film-and-Theatre Hybrids—Skits, Sketches, Playlets, & Acts in Vaudeville, Variety, Revues, &c," in *Performing New Media, 1890–1915*, ed. Kaveh Askari et al. (Bloomington: Indiana University Press, 2014), 248.
35 The existing print at the Library of Congress comprises a series of shots in the dressing room that have been edited together. In total, the film runs approximately eight minutes, but the entire act as Zink performed it live would have been much longer.
36 See Karen Halttunen, *Confidence Men and Painted Women: A Study of Middle-Class Culture in America, 1830–1870* (New Haven, CT: Yale University Press, 1982); and Ben Singer, *Melodrama and Modernity: Early Sensational Cinema and Its Contexts* (New York: Columbia University Press, 2001).
37 For an account of the strike, see Sean P. Holmes, *Weavers of Dreams, Unite! Actor's Unionism in Early Twentieth-Century America* (Urbana: University of Illinois Press, 2013).

38 Mack Sennett, interview by Art Friedman, April 3, 1964, Arthur B. Friedman Turning Point Interviews, Special Collections, University of California Los Angeles, Box 29.
39 The limited number of other examples include *Redhead from Manhattan* (1943), *Doll Face* (1945), and the much later biopic *Selena* (1997).
40 I discuss examples of women of color in the dressing room in chapters 2 and 3.
41 Sean Griffin, "The Gang's All Here: Generic versus Racial Integration in the 1940s Musical," *Cinema Journal* 42, no. 1 (2002): 21–45.
42 Brian Eugenio Herrera, *Latin Numbers: Playing Latino in Twentieth-Century U.S. Popular Performance* (Ann Arbor: University of Michigan Press, 2015), 128.
43 "Story Summary" (1946), *Copacabana* Production Code File, Special Collections, Margaret Herrick Library, Academy of Motion Picture Arts and Sciences, Los Angeles, CA.
44 For a longer discussion of this film, see Desirée J. Garcia, "Going Places: Musical Latins in Latin Musicals," in *The Oxford Handbook of the Hollywood Musical*, ed. Dominic Broomfield-McHugh (London: Oxford University Press, 2022), 124–141; and Jose, "Vaudeville: Night Club Reviews—Copacabana, N.Y.," *Variety*, May 7, 1948, 166, 9.
45 Rita Moreno, *Rita Moreno: A Memoir* (New York: Celebra, 2013), 240–241.
46 Herrera, *Latin Numbers*, 132.
47 Herrera, *Latin Numbers*, 139.
48 bell hooks, *Reel to Real* (1996; New York: Routledge, 2009), 281.
49 Caryl Flinn, "Containing Fire: Performance in *Paris Is Burning*," in *Documenting the Documentary: Close Readings of Documentary Film and Video*, ed. Barry Keith Grant and Jeannette Sloniowski (Detroit: Wayne State University Press, 2014), 449.
50 hooks, *Reel to Real*, 280.
51 LaBeija's interviews take place in an undefined space that might be a backstage prop room or a living space.

Epilogue

1 *CBS Sunday Morning*, "Barbra Streisand Returns to Her Broadway Dressing Room," YouTube video, 5:57, posted August 28, 2016, https://youtu.be/vPLkKVs GcRc.
2 *CBS Sunday Morning*, "Barbra Streisand Returns."
3 "Uninvited, Audience Members Find Their Way to Lea Salonga's Dressing Room," *The Broadway Blog*, accessed August 7, 2023, https://thebroadwayblog.com/unin vited-audience-members-find-their-way-to-lea-salongas-dressing-room/ (this article is no longer available online).
4 Diep Tran and Logan Culwell-Block, "Lea Salonga Speaks Out after Fans Sneak in Backstage at *Here Lies Love*," *Playbill*, accessed May 28, 2024, https://www.playbill .com/article/lea-salonga-speaks-out-after-fans-sneak-in-backstage-at-here-lies-love.
5 Carey Purcell, "How Do You Decorate Your Dressing Room? Family Photos, Mini Bars, Humidifiers, and Pets for These 18 Stars!," *Playbill*, July 18, 2015, https://play bill.com/article/how-do-you-decorate-your-dressing-room-family-photos-mini-bars -humidifiers-and-pets-for-these-18-stars-com-353328.
6 Penelope Green, "Setting the Stage, Offstage," *New York Times*, March 20, 2008; Jesse Green (text) and Betsy Horan (producer), "Behind the Curtain: The Dressing Rooms of Broadway: 33 Photos over Nearly a Century," *New York Times*, June 7, 2019.

7 "In the Stage Boudoir: Dressing-Rooms of Actresses Models of Luxury," *Variety*, January 12, 1902, 28.
8 Michael Kushner, interview by the author via Zoom, June 20, 2023.
9 Kushner, interview by the author.
10 Michael Kushner (@thedressingroomproject), Instagram, May 9, 2022, https://www.instagram.com/p/CdW8LvJugtM/?utm_source=ig_web_copy_link&igsh=MzRlODBiNWFlZA==.
11 Michael Kushner (@thedressingroomproject), Instagram, February 28, 2020, https://www.instagram.com/p/B9IUy3mpX8F/?igsh=YjJ4NWlzZHooZTVy.
12 Michael Kushner (@thedressingroomproject), Instagram, February 27, 2020, https://www.instagram.com/p/B9F8Q7ApfTE/?igsh=a2pqOXZleHR3dzYy.

Bibliography

Affron, Charles. "Performing Performing: Irony and Affect." In *Imitation of Life: Douglas Sirk, Director*, edited by Lucy Fischer, 207–215. New Brunswick, NJ: Rutgers University Press, 1991.

Altman, Rick. *The American Film Musical*. Bloomington: Indiana University Press, 1987.

Asibong, Andrew. "Discussion of Green's 'Melanie Klein and the Black Mammy: An Exploration of the Influence of the Mammy Stereotype on Klein's Maternal and Its Contribution to the "Whiteness" of Psychoanalysis.'" *Studies in Gender and Sexuality* 19, no. 3 (2018): 183–187.

Bainbridge, Jason. "'This Land Is Mine!': Understanding the Function of Supervillains." In *The Superhero Symbol: Media, Culture, Politics*, edited by Liam Burke, Ian Gordon, and Angela Ndalianis, 63–78. New Brunswick, NJ: Rutgers University Press, 2020.

Baker, Brian. *Masculinity in Fiction and Film: Representing Men in Popular Genres 1945–2000*. London: Continuum, 2006.

Bansavage, Lisa, and L. E. McCullough. *Break a Leg! A Treasury of Theatre Traditions and Superstitions*. Woodbridge, NJ: Silver Spear, 2017.

Bergner, Gwen. "Performing Work: Maids, Melodrama, and Imitation of Life as Film Noir." *Signs: Journal of Women in Culture and Society* 47, no. 2 (Winter 2022): 425–449.

Bingham, Dennis. *Whose Lives Are They Anyway? The Biopic as Contemporary Film Genre*. New Brunswick, NJ: Rutgers University Press, 2010.

Brooks, Helen E. M. "The Divided Heart of the Actress: Late Eighteenth-Century Actresses and the 'Cult of Maternity.'" In *Stage Mothers: Women, Work, and the Theater, 1660–1830*, edited by Laura Engel and Elaine M. McGirr, 19–42. Lewisburg, PA: Bucknell University Press, 2014.

Brown, Beth. *Applause*. New York: Horace Liveright, 1928.

Bruzzi, Stella. *Men's Cinema: Masculinity and* Mise en Scène *in Hollywood*. Edinburgh: Edinburgh University Press, 2013.

Byars, Jackie. *All That Hollywood Allows: Re-reading Gender in 1950s Melodrama*. Chapel Hill: University of North Carolina Press, 1991.

Carlson, Marvin. *The Haunted Stage: The Theater as Memory Machine*. Ann Arbor: University of Michigan Press, 2001.

———. *Places of Performance: The Semiotics of Theatre Architecture*. Ithaca, NY: Cornell University Press, 1989.

Casella, Donna R. "What Women Want: The Complex World of Dorothy Arzner and Her Cinematic Women." *Framework* 50, nos. 1–2 (Spring–Fall 2009): 235–270.

Castle, Terry. *Masquerade and Civilization: The Carnivalesque in Eighteenth-Century English Culture and Fiction*. Stanford, CA: Stanford University Press, 1986.

Chico, Tita. *Designing Women: The Dressing Room in Eighteenth-Century English Literature and Culture*. Lewisburg, PA: Bucknell University Press, 2005.

Cohan, Steven. "'Feminizing' the Song-and-Dance Man: Fred Astaire and the Spectacle of Masculinity in the Hollywood Musical." In *Screening the Male: Exploring Masculinities in Hollywood Cinema*, edited by Steven Cohan and Ina Rae Hark, 46–69. London: Routledge, 1993.

———. *Hollywood by Hollywood: The Backstudio Picture and the Mystique of Making Movies*. New York: Oxford University Press, 2019.

———. *Incongruous Entertainment: Camp, Cultural Value, and the MGM Musical*. Durham, NC: Duke University Press, 2005.

———. *Masked Men: Masculinity in the Movies in the Fifties*. Bloomington: Indiana University Press, 1997.

Corbett, John. *Extended Play: Sounding Off from John Cage to Dr. Funkenstein*. Durham, NC: Duke University Press, 1994.

Courtney, Susan. *Hollywood Fantasies of Miscegenation: Spectacular Narratives of Gender and Race, 1903–1967*. Princeton, NJ: Princeton University Press, 2005.

Cripps, Thomas. *Making Movies Black: The Hollywood Message Movie from World War II to the Civil Rights Era*. Oxford: Oxford University Press, 1993.

Davidson, Robert A. *The Hotel: Occupied Space*. Toronto: University of Toronto Press, 2018.

Davis, Tracy C. "The Actress in Victorian Pornography." *Theatre Journal* 41, no. 3 (1989): 294–315.

de Lauretis, Teresa. "Aesthetic and Feminist Theory: Rethinking Women's Cinema." *New German Critique*, no. 34 (Winter 1985): 154–175.

Deleuze, Gilles. *Cinema 2: The Time-Image*. Minneapolis: University of Minnesota Press, 1989.

Deleyto, Celestino. "The Texture of the Age: Digital Construction of Unbounded Space in *Birdman* (Iñárritu 2014)." *Studies in Spanish and Latin American Cinemas* 18, no. 1 (April 2020): 73–88.

Diekmann, Stefanie. "Scenes from the Dressing Room: Theatrical Interiors in Fiction Film." In *Interiors and Interiority*, edited by Ewa Lajer-Burcharth and Beate Sontgen, 87–100. Berlin: De Gruyter, 2016.

Dolan, Josephine. "Smoothing the Wrinkles: Hollywood, Successful Aging and the New Visibility of Older Female Stars." In *The Routledge Companion to Media and Gender*, edited by Cindy Carter, Linda Steiner, and Lisa McLaughlin, 342–351. London: Routledge, 2013.

Dyer, Richard. *Heavenly Bodies: Film Stars and Society*. 2nd ed. London: Routledge, 2004.

Engel, Laura, and Elaine M. McGirr. "Introduction." In *Stage Mothers: Women, Work, and the Theater, 1660–1830*, edited by Laura Engel and Elaine M. McGirr, 1–16. Lewisburg, PA: Bucknell University Press, 2014.

———, eds. *Stage Mothers: Women, Work, and the Theater, 1660–1830*. Lewisburg, PA: Bucknell University Press, 2014.

Erickson, Peter. "Invisibility Speaks: Servants and Portraits in Early Modern Visual Culture." *Journal for Early Modern Cultural Studies* 9, no. 1 (Spring–Summer 2009): 23–61.
Essin, Christin. *Working Backstage: A Cultural History and Ethnography of Technical Theater Labor.* Ann Arbor: University of Michigan Press, 2021.
Fischer, Lucy. "City of Women: Busby Berkeley, Architecture, and Urban Space." *Cinema Journal* 49, no. 4 (Summer 2010): 111–130.
———. "'How Do I Love Thee?': Theatricality, Desire and the Family Melodrama." In *A Family Affair: Cinema Calls Home*, edited by Murray Pomerance, 107–118. London: Wallflower Press, 2008.
———, ed. *Imitation of Life: Douglas Sirk, Director.* New Brunswick, NJ: Rutgers University Press, 1991.
———. "La Vie en Noir: Woman, Melodrama, and the Biopic." *Quarterly Review of Film and Video* 33, no. 3 (2016): 187–216.
———. *Shot/Countershot: Film Tradition and Women's Cinema.* Princeton, NJ: Princeton University Press, 1989.
Flinn, Caryl. *Brass Diva: The Life and Legends of Ethel Merman.* Berkeley: University of California Press, 2007.
———. "Containing Fire: Performance in *Paris Is Burning.*" In *Documenting the Documentary: Close Readings of Documentary Film and Video*, edited by Barry Keith Grant and Jeannette Sloniowski, 438–455. Detroit: Wayne State University Press, 2014.
Flitterman-Lewis, Sandy. "*Imitation(s) of Life*: The Black Woman's Double Determination as Troubling 'Other.'" In *Imitation of Life: Douglas Sirk, Director*, edited by Lucy Fischer, 325–335. New Brunswick, NJ: Rutgers University Press, 1991.
Forbes, Camilla F. "Dancing with 'Racial Feet': Bert Williams and the Performance of Blackness." *Theatre Journal* 56 (2004): 603–625.
Francus, Marilyn. "The Lady Vanishes: The Rise of the Spectral Mother." In *The Absent Mother in the Cultural Imagination: Missing, Presumed Dead*, edited by Berit Astrom, 25–42 Cham, Switzerland: Palgrave Macmillan, 2017.
Freud, Ralph. "George Spelvin Says the Tag: Folklore of the Theater." *Western Folklore* 13, no. 4 (October 1954): 245–250.
Gabbard, Krin. "Signifyin(g) the Phallus: *Mo' Better Blues* and Representations of the Jazz Trumpet." *Cinema Journal* 32, no. 1 (Autumn 1992): 43–62.
Garcia, Desirée J. "Going Places: Musical Latins in Latin Musicals." In *The Oxford Handbook of the Hollywood Musical*, edited by Dominic Broomfield-McHugh, 124–141. London: Oxford University Press, 2022.
———. "Intimate Thresholds." Vimeo video, 3:59, posted July 8, 2022. https://vimeo.com/728173086?share=copy.
———. "Toil behind the Footlights: The Spectacle of Female Suffering and the Rise of Musical Comedy." *Frontiers* 40, no. 1 (2019): 122–145.
———. "What Happened in the Dressing Room." *inTransition: Journal of Videographic and Moving Image Studies* 11, no. 1 (2024). DOI: https://doi.org/10.16995/intransition.15423.
———. "'What's Happened to Chorus Girls?': Domesticity and the Postwar Backstage Musical." *Journal of Cinema and Media Studies* 61, no. 5 (2020–2021): 31–58.
Gates, Philippa. *Detecting Men: Masculinity and the Hollywood Detective Film.* Albany: State University of New York Press, 2006.
Gerber, David M. "Heroes and Misfits: The Troubled Social Reintegration of Disabled Veterans in *The Best Years of Our Lives.*" *American Quarterly* 46, no. 4 (December 1994): 545–574.

Gilder, Rosamond. *Enter the Actress: The First Woman in the Theatre*. Boston: Houghton Mifflin, 1931.

Glenn, Susan. *Female Spectacle: The Theatrical Roots of Modern Feminism*. Cambridge, MA: Harvard University Press, 2000.

Grant, Barry Keith. *Shadows of Doubt: Negotiations of Masculinity in American Genre Films*. Detroit: Wayne State University Press, 2011.

Granville, Wilfred. *The Theater Dictionary: British and American Terms in the Drama, Opera, and Ballet*. 1952; Westport, CT: Greenwood Press, 1970.

Griffin, Sean. "The Gang's All Here: Generic versus Racial Integration in the 1940s Musical." *Cinema Journal* 42, no. 1 (2002): 21–45.

Grundmann, Roy, and Marlon Riggs. "New Agendas in Black Filmmaking: An Interview with Marlon Riggs." *Cineaste* 19, no. 2/3 (1992): 52–54.

Gunning, Tom. "'Now You See It, Now You Don't': The Temporality of the Cinema of Attractions." *The Velvet Light Trap* 32 (Fall 1993): 3–10.

Halliday, Jon. "Sirk on Sirk." In *Imitation of Life: Douglas Sirk, Director*, edited by Lucy Fischer, 226–231. New Brunswick, NJ: Rutgers University Press, 1991.

Halttunen, Karen. *Confidence Men and Painted Women: A Study of Middle-Class Culture in America, 1830–1870*. New Haven, CT: Yale University Press, 1982.

Hanich, Julian. "Reflecting on Reflections: Cinema's Complex Mirror Shots." In *Indefinite Visions: Cinema and the Attractions of Uncertainty*, edited by Martine Beugnet, Allan Cameron, and Arild Fetveit, 131–156. Edinburgh: Edinburgh University Press, 2017.

Herrera, Brian Eugenio. *Latin Numbers: Playing Latino in Twentieth-Century U.S. Popular Performance*. Ann Arbor: University of Michigan Press, 2015.

Heung, Marina. "'What's the Matter with Sara Jane?': Daughters and Mothers in Douglas Sirk's *Imitation of Life*." *Cinema Journal* 26, no. 3 (Spring 1987): 21–43.

Hollinger, Karen. *In the Company of Women: Contemporary Female Friendship Films*. Minneapolis: University of Minnesota Press, 1998.

Holmes, Sean P. *Weavers of Dreams, Unite! Actor's Unionism in Early Twentieth-Century America*. Urbana: University of Illinois Press, 2013.

hooks, bell. *Reel to Real*. 1996; New York: Routledge, 2009.

Kaplan, E. Ann. *Motherhood and Representation: The Mother in Popular Culture and Melodrama*. New York: Routledge, 1992.

Katzman, Lisa. "'Opening Night': Moment by Moment." *Film Comment* 25, no. 3 (May–June 1989): 34–39.

Kibler, Alison M. *Rank Ladies: Gender and Cultural Hierarchy in American Vaudeville*. Chapel Hill: University of North Carolina Press, 1999.

King, Claire Sisco. *Washed in Blood: Male Sacrifice, Trauma, and the Cinema*. New Brunswick, NJ: Rutgers University Press, 2012.

King, Homay. "Free Indirect Affect in Cassavetes' *Opening Night* and *Faces*." *Camera Obscura* 19, no. 2 (56) (2004): 104–139.

Kracauer, Siegfried. *The Mass Ornament: Weimar Essays*. Cambridge, MA: Harvard University Press, 1995.

Leacroft, Richard, and Helen Leacroft. *Theatre and Playhouse: An Illustrated Survey of Theatre Building from Ancient Greece to the Present Day*. London: Methuen Drama, 1984.

Lee, Gypsy Rose. *Gypsy: A Memoir*. 1957; Berkeley, CA: Frog Books, 1999.

Lefebvre, Henri. *The Production of Space*. Translated by Donald Nicholson-Smith. Oxford: Blackwell, 1991.

Liddy, Susan. "Older Women and Sexuality On-Screen: Euphemism and Evasion?" In *Ageing Women in Literature and Visual Culture: Reflections, Refractions, Reimaginings*, edited by Cathy McGlynn, Margaret O'Neill, and Michaela Schrage-Früh, 167–180. Cham, Switzerland: Palgrave Macmillan, 2017.

Lott, Eric. *Love and Theft: Blackface Minstrelsy and the American Working Class*. New York: Oxford University Press, 1993.

Lugowski, David M. "Queering the (New) Deal: Lesbian and Gay Representation and the Depression-Era Cultural Politics of Hollywood's Production Code." *Cinema Journal* 38, no. 2 (Winter 1999): 3–35.

Markson, Elizabeth W., and Carol A. Taylor. "The Mirror Has Two Faces." *Aging and Society* 20, no. 2 (2000): 137–160.

Massood, Paula J. *Black City Cinema: African American Urban Experiences in Film*. Philadelphia: Temple University Press, 2003.

———. *Making a Promised Land: Harlem in Twentieth-Century Photography and Film*. New Brunswick, NJ: Rutgers University Press, 2013.

May, Elaine Tyler. *Homeward Bound: American Families in the Cold War Era*. New York: Basic Books, 1988.

McAuley, Gale. *Space in Performance: Making Meaning in the Theatre*. Ann Arbor: University of Michigan Press, 2000.

McGirr, Lisa. *Suburban Warriors: The Origins of the New American Right*. Princeton, NJ: Princeton University Press, 2002.

McNally, Karen. *The Stardom Film: Creating the Hollywood Fairy Tale*. New York: Wallflower Press, 2021.

Meyerowitz, Joanne. "Competing Images of Women in Postwar Mass Culture." In *Major Problems in American Women's History*, edited by Mary Beth Norton and Ruth M. Alexander. Lexington, MA: D. C. Heath, 1996.

Mizejewski, Linda. *Ziegfeld Girl: Image and Icon in Culture and Cinema*. Durham, NC: Duke University Press, 1999.

Monks, Aoife. *The Actor in Costume*. London: Palgrave Macmillan, 2010.

Montez de Oca, Jeffrey. "The 'Muscle Gap': Physical Education and US Fears of a Depleted Masculinity, 1954–1963." In *East Plays West: Sport and the Cold War*, edited by Stephen Wagg and David L. Andrews, 123–148. London: Routledge, 2006.

Montgomery, Michael V. *Carnivals and Commonplaces: Bakhtin's Chronotope, Cultural Studies, and Film*. New York: Peter Lang, 1993.

Moreno, Rita. *Rita Moreno: A Memoir*. New York: Celebra, 2013.

Musser, Charles. "Why Did Negroes Love Al Jolson and *The Jazz Singer*? Melodrama, Blackface, and Cosmopolitan Theatrical Culture." *Film History* 23 (2011): 196–222.

Nair, Kartik. "Striking Out: Visual Space, Production Design, and Labor History in Joker." *Quarterly Review of Film and Video* 39, no. 8. Published ahead of print, September 30, 2021. https://doi.org/10.1080/10509208.2021.1981070.

Neale, Steven. "Masculinity and Spectacle." *Screen* 24, no. 6 (1983): 2–16.

Negra, Diane. *Off-White Hollywood: American Culture and Ethnic Female Stardom*. London: Routledge, 2001.

Ormsbee, Helen. *Backstage with Actors: From the Time of Shakespeare to the Present Day*. New York: Thomas Y. Crowell, 1938.

Peberdy, Donna. *Masculinity and Film Performance: Male Angst in Contemporary American Cinema*. New York: Palgrave Macmillan, 2011.

Petty, Miriam J. *Stealing the Show: African American Performers and Audiences in 1930s Hollywood*. Berkeley: University of California Press, 2016.

Rhodes, John David. "Passing Through: The Black Maid in the Cinematic Suburbs, 1948–1949." In *Race and the Suburbs in American Film*, edited by Merrill Schleier, 31–52. Albany: State University of New York Press, 2021.

Robinson, Cedric. *Forgeries of Memory and Meaning: Blacks and the Regimes of Race in American Theater and Film before World War II*. Chapel Hill: University of North Carolina Press, 2007.

Robinson, Linda A. "Bing on a Binge: Casting-against-Type in *The Country Girl*." In *Going My Way: Bing Crosby and American Culture*, edited by Ruth Prigozy and Walter Raubicheck, 47–64. Rochester, NY: University of Rochester Press, 2007.

Rogin, Michael. *Blackface, White Noise: Jewish Immigrants in the Hollywood Melting Pot*. Berkeley: University of California Press, 1996.

Rollins, Judith. *Between Women: Domestics and Their Employers*. Philadelphia: Temple University Press, 1985.

Roth, Lillian, with Mike Connolly and Gerold Frank. *I'll Cry Tomorrow*. New York: Frederick Fell, 1954.

Roth, Mark. "Some Warners Musicals and the Spirit of the New Deal." *The Velvet Light Trap*, no. 17 (Winter 1977): 1–7.

Rubin, Martin. "Busby Berkeley and the Backstage Musical." In *Hollywood Musicals: The Film Reader*, edited by Steven Cohan, 53–61. London: Routledge, 2002.

Schary, Timothy, ed. *Millennial Masculinity: Men in Contemporary Cinema*. Detroit: Wayne State University Press, 2013.

Schleier, Merrill. *Skyscraper Cinema: Architecture and Gender in American Film*. Minneapolis: University of Minnesota Press, 2009.

Scott, Ellen C. *Cinema Civil Rights: Regulation, Repression, and Race in the Classical Hollywood Era*. New Brunswick, NJ: Rutgers University Press, 2015.

Shearer, Martha. "E-Q-U-I-T-Y: Generic Boundaries, Gender, and Real Estate in Magic Mike Films." In *Musicals at the Margins: Genre, Boundaries, Canons*, edited by Julie Lobalzo Wright and Martha Shearer, 41–54. New York: Bloomsbury Academic, 2021.

Singer, Ben. *Melodrama and Modernity: Early Sensational Cinema and Its Contexts*. New York: Columbia University Press, 2001.

Sobchack, Vivian. "Lounge Time: Postwar Crises and the Chronotope of Film Noir." In *Refiguring American Film Genres: History and Theory*, edited by Nick Browne, 129–170. Berkeley: University of California Press, 1998.

Stacey, Jackie. "Desperately Seeking Difference." In *The Female Gaze: Women as Viewers of Popular Culture*, edited by Lorraine Gamman and Margaret Marshment. Seattle: Real Comet Press, 1989.

Stern, Michael. "Imitation of Life." In *Imitation of Life: Douglas Sirk, Director*, edited by Lucy Fischer, 279–288. New Brunswick, NJ: Rutgers University Press, 1991.

Straub, Kristina. *Sexual Suspects: Eighteenth-Century Players and Sexual Ideology*. Princeton, NJ: Princeton University Press, 1992.

Stufft, Monica Eugenia. "Chorus Girl Collective: Early 20th Century American Performance Communities and Urban Networking." PhD diss., University of California, Berkeley, 2008.

Sundin, Bridget. "From Tuxedo to Gown: Dietrich's Haunted Dressing Room(s)." *Theatre Symposium* 27 (2019): 109–117.

Waltz, Gwendolyn. "20 Minutes or Less: Short-Form Film-and-Theatre Hybrids—Skits, Sketches, Playlets, & Acts in Vaudeville, Variety, Revues, &c." In *Performing New Media, 1890–1915*, edited by Kaveh Askari, Scott Curtis, Frank Gray, Louis Pelletier,

Tami Williams, and Joshua Yumibe, 245–253. Bloomington: Indiana University Press, 2015.
Weiss, Richard. *The American Myth of Success: From Horatio Alger to Norman Vincent Peale*. Urbana: University of Illinois Press, 1988.
White, Armond. "White on Black." *Film Comment* 20, no. 6 (November–December 1984): 7–12, 14–16.
White, Patricia. *Uninvited: Classical Hollywood Cinema and Lesbian Representability*. Bloomington: Indiana University Press, 1999.
Wojcik, Pamela Robertson. *The Apartment Plot: Urban Living in American Film and Popular Culture, 1945–1975*. Durham, NC: Duke University Press, 2010.
———. "The Streisand Musical." In *The Sound of Musicals*, edited by Steven Cohan, 128–138. London: BFI, 2010.
Yates, Richard. *Revolutionary Road*. 3rd ed. New York: Random House, 2009.
Young, Miriam. *Mother Wore Tights*. New York: Penguin, 1944.

Index

Note: page numbers in *italics* indicate figures.

Actors' Equity Association, 74, 135, 163n13
Actors' Society of America (ASA), 97, 98
Adolph Zink (1903), 10, 133–134, 166n35
Aeschylus, 6
Affron, Charles, 36
agency, feminine, 22, 72
Alger, Horatio, 3
Ali, Muhammad, 10
All about Eve (Mankiewicz, 1950), 1, 3, 13, 160n45; female desire and competition in, 4, 15, 57–58; identity discovery and transformation in, 57, 58; *Sparkle* compared with, 66–67
Allen, Gene, 102
All I Desire (Sirk, 1953), 35, 74
Altman, Rick, 4, 12–13
American Mutoscope and Biograph, 56, 98
Apartment Plot, The (Wojcik, 2010), 96
Applause (Mamoulian, 1929), 3, 13, 74, 75–77, *76*, 82
Arnold, Eve, 70
Aronofsky, Darren, 61–62, 63
Arzner, Dorothy, 59–61, 63
Asians, 13, 53–55, *54*
Astaire, Fred, 29, 95, 97
audiences, 4, 20, 92; actresses' relationship with, 69; audience space, 3; film audience's access to dressing rooms, 7, 8; identity and, 14; popularity of *Sparkle*, 66; privileged position of, 67; transported between spaces through editing, 69, 104

Babes in Arms (1939), 5, 50
Backstage (online trade magazine), 71
backstage films, 8, 39, 147; audience teased by, 46–47; Black performers denied opportunities, 50; in early cinema (1897–1910), 7, 16; frame-within-frame mise-en-scène of, 129; as genre, 107, 155n37; Latina immigrants in, 136–141, *140*; masquerade and, 15; mobility through transformation in, 13; racial hierarchies of, 14; women directors of, 21–22, 55, 58
backstage musicals, 12, 28, 43, 58, 95; balance of home and career in, 74–75; Black-cast, 84, 159n26; children in, 73–74; female collectives as deviant and subversive, 46; "girl clusters" in, 44; postwar motherly ideal and, 77–78; unresolved tension between spectacle and narrative, 44
back-studio pictures, 12, 94, 155n37
Baile Folklorico de Salem, 146
Ball, Lucille, 59
ballet films, 12, 61–63, *62*
Bamboozled (Lee, 2000), 2, 4–5, 13, 122, 128–130
Bankhead, Tallulah, 27

Barkleys of Broadway, The (1949), 95
Bassett, Angela, 86
Baudrillard, Jean, 162n6
Beavers, Louise, 28
Behind the Scenes (Griffith, 1908), 69, 74
belonging, theme of, 35
Bening, Annette, 88
Bergner, Gwen, 19, 35
Berkeley, Busby, 44, 47, 158n10
Berlin, Irving, 31
Berliner, Todd, 89
Bernhardt, Sarah, 97
Best of Everything, The (1959), 70
Best Years of Our Lives, The (1946), 82, 100
Bickford, Charles, 105
Bingham, Dennis, 89
biopics, 12, 70, 85, 88, 94
Birdman (2014), 9, 13, 95, 96, 116–117; dressing room scenes, 114–115, 117–118; superhero and supervillain twinned in, 114, 118
Black Crook, The (musical comedy, 1866), 98
Blackface minstrelsy, 2, 4, 26, 145; in *Bamboozled* (2000), 128–130; in *Easter Parade* (1948), 121; in *Ethnic Notions* (1986), 130–133, *132*; as form of "racial feeling" for white body, 127; in *The Jazz Singer* (1927), 121–122, 124–127; origins of, 120–121; in *Paradise in Harlem* (1939), 127–128; as racial cross-dressing, 124, 166n22; removal of Blackface, 131–132; in *The Singing Fool* (1928), 121, 124–127; in *Somebody Loves Me* (1952), 34; tragedy associated with, 124–125
Black maid archetype, 3, 6, 12, 13, 161n33; Black actresses' perspectives, 17–18, 19, 28, 40; Black maids as middle-class status symbol, 36, 157n44; challenge to narrative of maids' docility, 26–34; in *Close Harmony* (1929), 19–20; in *Easter Parade* (1948), 22, 23, 28–31, *30*, 36; in *Funny Girl* (1968), 22, 23–25, *26*; in *Funny Lady* (1975), 22, 23–26; in *Glorifying the American Girl* (1929), 22, 23; in *The Goose Woman* (1925), 21; in *Imitation of Life* (1959), 34–40, *37*; in *Love Me or Leave Me* (1955), 22, 23; maids as victims of abuse, 27, 156n22; maids in the background, 19–26; maids in the foreground, 34–41, *37*; in *The Marriage Clause* (1926), 21–22;

public's fascination with, 19; race-gender intersection and, 19; short-lived appearance of, 15; social dynamics of space and, 14; in *Somebody Loves Me* (1952), 22, 23; uncredited roles, 19; white female stars upstaged or eclipsed by maids, 29, 34, 37, *37*, 40
Black performers, 3, 31, 66; Black men and dressing rooms, 145; comedy demanded from, 127; denied opportunities for, 50; "Harlem" film cycle and, 127; Hollywood racial politics and, 29; narrative consequence given to, 63; removal of Blackface and, 130, 131, 132, *132*; in vaudeville, 98, 123
Black servants, 20, 155n7
Black Swan (Aronofsky, 2010), 15, 58, 61–63, *62*
Blaine, Vivian, 136
Blaxploitation genre, 63–64, 65
Blonde Venus (1932), 74
"B" movies, 122
Boggess, Sierra, 147–148
Bolton, Whitney, 9
Bombshell (1933), 36
Breen, Joseph I., 54
Brice, Fanny, 23–26, 83, 161n33
Broadway Blog, The, 148
Broadway Melody, The (1929), 28, 46, 50–51, 56, 107
Broadway Melody of 1936 (1935), 29
Broadway shows, 12, 51, 63, 80, 141
Broadway to Hollywood (1933), 73
Brown, Bessie, 156n22
Brown, Beth, 76
Bruzzi, Stella, 96
bungalows, 12
burlesque, 7, 12, 75
Burlesque (2010), 48
Bushman, Francis X., 22
Byars, Jackie, 35, 78

Caan, James, 24
Cabin in the Sky (1943), 84
camera: handheld, 86, 94, 143; mirrors and, 60, 62, 85, 87, 106, 129–130, 131, 137; mobile, 8, 75, 143; power to transport audiences, 7; privilege of spectator and, 47; as voyeur/peeping tom, 47, 98
Cameron and Flanagan (Blackface comedians), 132

Cantor, Eddie, 131–132
Cara, Irene, 64
Carlson, Marvin, 6, 122–123
Carr, Vicki, 139, 140
Carroll, Nancy, 19
Carson, Jack, 83
Casella, Donna R., 60
Cassavetes, John, 89–92
Cassel, Vincent, 62
Castle, Terry, 138
censorship, 50–51, 61
Champion, Gower and Marge, 84
Chaplin, Charlie, 99, 135, 136
Charo, 140
Chico, Tita, 7, 22, 45, 72
Chong, Peter, 54
choreography, science of, 44
chorus girls, 3, 21, 46, 47, 69; African American, 49; dressing rooms as female domain and, 14; female mentorship and, 48–49; regulations on behavior of, 45, 48, 49, 158n11; white womanhood and, 42–43. *See also* sister acts, as dressing room trope
cinema: backstage films in early cinema, 7; early sound era, 51, 75, 124; European art cinema, 99; fascination with dressing rooms in early cinema, 45; female collectivity in early cinema, 48; identity and, 135; men's cinema, 96; mobility of camera, 9; theater-film hybrids, 98–99; women's cinema, 60. *See also* Hollywood; *specific genres*
circuses, 12
civil rights movement, 15, 18, 23, 96
Claire, Ina, 17, 19
class, intersectional dynamics and, 66
classical orchestras, 12
Clooney, Rosemary, 103
Close Harmony (1929), 19
Cohan, George M., 97
Cohan, Steven, 12, 97, 100, 155n37
Cold War, 28, 100
Collins, Lottie, 134
Color Adjustment (Riggs, 1992), 132
Colored Ladies' Dressing Association, 26–27
comedies, 12, 43, 145
communism, 77, 100
Compson, Betty, 36
concert halls, 12

"confidence man" archetype, 5
Cooke, Marvel, 156n22
Copacabana (1947), 122, 133, 136, 137–139
Corbett, John, 20, 23
Corey, Dorian, 141–144, *143*
Coughlin, "Bathhouse John," 134
Country Girl, The (1954), 74, 95, 99–102, 114; audience's viewpoint in, 106–107; as cinematic adaptation of Odets play, 95; mirror sequences, 106; parallel dressing room scenes, 105
Courtney, Susan, 28
Crandall, Edward, 19
Crawford, Joan, 69–71
Cronin, Evelyn, 27
Crosby, Bing, 95, 99, 100, 103
Crosland, Alan, 47
cross-dressing, racial and gendered, 121, 124, 134
Cukor, George, 102
cultural appropriation, 50, 140
Curtiz, Michael, 95

Dailey, Dan, 78
Dance, Girl, Dance (1940), 8–9, 13, 56; *Black Swan* compared with, 61, 62, 63; crosscutting between stage and dressing room, 59–61; female competition placed at forefront in, 58, 61; precarity of female dancers, 59
Davidson, Tommy, 128
Davis, Tracy C., 160n8
Day, Doris, 13, 156n33
Deleuze, Gilles, 14
Deleyto, Celestino, 117
De Niro, Robert, 1, *2*, 116
Desperately Seeking Susan (Seidelman, 1985), 159n35
De Wolfe, Elsie, 149
DiCaprio, Leonardo, 68, 93
Diekmann, Stefanie, 106, 164n26
Dietrich, Marlene, 133
documentary films, 12, 16, 130, 132, 145, 146; interviews in, 86; about lives of celebrities, 4; pseudo-documentary, 129; race and gendered masquerade in, 121–122, 141
Doll Face (1945), 167n39
Dolly Sisters, The (1945), 56
Dooley, J. Francis, 121
Dove, Billie, 22

drag performers, 121, 133, 141–144, *143*
Draper, Fred, 91
Dreamgirls (Broadway show, 1982), *66*
Dreamgirls (2006), 108
Dressing Room Club, 123
"Dressing Room Project, The" (Instagram) (Kushner), 149
dressing rooms: children in, 73–74; cinematic potential of, 1–2; claimed by Black maid as space of potential, 33; color line and, 67; connection with performance, 3; construction of female star narratives and, 71; décor of, 148–149; denied to interracial woman, 2, 38, 39; as domestic and work spaces, 67, 72, 78; of drag performers, 142–144, *143*; expectations for narrative action and, 11; female competition and, 21; hidden from sight, 4; history of, 6–7; homosexuality associated with, 46; intrusions into, 8–9; as liminal spaces, 8, 51, 92, 147; as manifestation of success or failure, 13; masquerade and, 5; on *New Yorker* cover (December 9, 1944), 42–43; porousness of, 8, 55, 118; privacy and, 8, 9, 53, 59, 102, 148, 149; racial haunting of, 124–133; satisfaction of male pleasure and, 45; as site of female character development, 40; as site of female power, 22; superstitions associated with, 122–124, 144; temporary, 146–147; thefts in, 73, 160n12; transformational qualities of, 22, 43; upward mobility and, 3, 38, 41, 50
Dressing Room Scene, A (1897), 7
Dressler, Marie, 97
Dyer, Richard, 4, 70, 133

Easter Parade (1948), 54; Black maid archetype in, 22, 23, 28–31, *30*, 36; racial appropriation in, 50
Eaton, Mary, 19
Ellen, Vera, 103
Elsinore Theatre (Salem, Oregon), 146
Engel, Laura, 74
Erickson, Peter, 20
Esposito, Giancarlo, 111, *112*
Ethnic Notions (Riggs, 1986), 122, 130–133, *132*
Etting, Ruth, 13
Everything I Have Is Yours (1952), 77, 83, 84–85

Faye, Alice, 136
female friendship films, 67
Feminine Mystique, The (Friedan, 1963), 77
femininity, 45, 67
feminism, 60, 96, 159n38
Fiddler on the Roof (play, 1964), 10
Fierstein, Harvey, 1, 10
film noir, 71
Film Stars Don't Die in Liverpool (2017), 70, 88
Fischer, Lucy, 35, 43, 158n10
Fishburne, Laurence, 86
Fleshler, Glenn, 116
Flinn, Caryl, 80, 142, 162n6
Flitterman-Lewis, Sandy, 39
Floradora (musical comedy, 1900), 98
Floradora Girl (1930), 48
Fontaine, Evan Burrows, 26
Forbes, Camilla F., 131
For Colored Girls Who Have Considered Suicide / When the Rainbow Is Enuf (Broadway show, 2022), 149
For Me and My Gal (1942), 99
42nd Street (1933), 44
Fox Movietone Follies (1929), 51–52, 159n31
Francus, Marilyn, 74
Franklin, Aretha, 64
Freud, Ralph, 73, 122
Friedan, Betty, 77
Friedberg, Mark, 115
From Showgirl to Burlesque Queen (1903), 45–46, 98
Funny Girl (1968), 22, 23–25, *26*, 83, 147
Funny Lady (1975), 18–19, 22, 23–26, 34

Gabbard, Krin, 164n28
gangster movies, 145
Garland, Judy, 29, 30, 49, 95, 102, 106; biopic about (*Judy*, 2019), 70; "lonely stage" and, 88, 91, 161n36; "Minnie from Trinidad" number and, 50, 158n24
Gazzara, Ben, 87
gender, 40, 46, 108, 140, 144; instability of gender performance, 104; intersectional dynamics and, 15, 66; leading man archetype and, 95, 97; sister acts and, 67
Gerber, David M., 82
Gerry Society's Mistake, The (1903), 48, 56
Gibson, Brian, 85–86
Gilder, Rosamond, 45

Gish, Lillian, 19
Glenn, Susan, 44, 97
Glorifying the American Girl (1929), 8, 19, 22, 23, 51
Glover, Savion, 128
Gold Diggers of 1933 (LeRoy, 1933), 5, 9, 47, 49
González Iñárritu, Alejandro, 114, 115, 117
Goold, Rupert, 89
Goose Woman, The (1925), 18–19, 21, 74
Gordy, Berry, 64
Grable, Betty, 78, 136
Grahame, Gloria, 70, 88, 92
Granville, Wilfred, 93, 120
Grayson, Kathryn, 103
Great Depression, 49
Greatest, The (1977), 10
Griffin, Sean, 136
Griffith, D. W., 69, 74
Gypsy (Broadway show, 1959), 80
Gypsy (LeRoy, 1962), 1–2, 9, 74, 75, 80–82; career focus of wife in, 82; strained marital relations in, 83

Hairspray (2007), 107
Hallelujah (1929), 84
Halttunen, Karen, 5
Hanich, Julian, 29
Hard Way, The (1943), 56, 82–83, 99, 100
Harewood, Dorian, 65
Harrison, Jennie, 26
Hawkins, Linda, 111
Hayward, Susan, 83
Hearts in Dixie (1929), 51, 84, 159n31
Hepburn, Audrey, 103
Here Lies Love (Broadway show), 148
Herrera, Brian, 140–141
Hershey, Barbara, 63
heteronormativity, 28, 96
Hogan, Ernest, 124
Holden, William, 100, 101
Holiday, Billie, 64
Holiday Inn (1942), 50
Hollinger, Karen, 159n38
Hollywood, 9, 26, 89; adaptations of Broadway shows, 12; "age of the chest," 100; Black activism in, 15; homoeroticism of women sharing space, 62, 160n45; masquerade films, 121–122; NAACP and, 27; narrativization of backstage life in, 18; racial politics of, 29; stars and starmaking, 4, 99; studio system, 58, 147
homophobia, 141
homosociality, 14, 48, 109
hooks, bell, 142
Hopper, Hedda, 39
Horne, Lena, 84
Hot Time in the Dressing Room, A (1900), 7
Hudson, Rock, 100
Hurder, Robyn, 149
Hutton, Betty, 28, *33*, 34

I Could Go on Singing (1963), 161n36
identity: female identity formation, 43; intersection with performance, 146; limitations of, 133; performance of, 3, 43, 133; transformation of, 5
I'll Cry Tomorrow (1955), 74
Imitation of Life (Sirk, 1959), 2, 9, 15, 74; as "anti-backstage film," 35–36, 39; Black maid foregrounded in, 34–40; as Hollywood classic, 16; as melodrama-noir hybrid, 35
immigrants' rights, 96
immigration, xenophobic reactions to, 49
I'm No Angel (1933), 36
"I'm Pregnant. Is My Career Over?" (*Backstage* article, 2013), 71
independent films, 122
interiority, 7, 20, 43, 78, 115; dressing room photography and, 148; masculinity and, 96; self-reflection of stars and, 71; spectacle and, 31
In the Dressing Room (1903), 8, 48
"Intimate Thresholds" (Garcia, 2022), 58

jazz films, 12, 94, 112. See also *Mo' Better Blues* (Lee, 1990)
Jazz Singer, The (1927), 99, 120, 121, 126–127; foregrounding of Blackface minstrelsy, 124; spectrality and cultural memory in, 125
Johnie and the Telephone, The (1903), 158n15
Joker (2019), 16, 95, 96; dressing room scenes, 114, 115–116, *117*; superhero and supervillain twinned in, 114, 116
Joker Is Wild, The (1957), 95
Jolson, Al, 99, 120, 145; dressing room superstitions and, 122; origin as Blackface comedian, 120, 121
Judy (Goold, 2019), 13, 88

Kaplan, E. Ann, 161n22
Katzman, Lisa, 90
Kaye, Danny, 103
Keaton, Michael, 96, 114
Kelly, Gene, 97
Kelly, Grace, 95, 101, 106
Kibler, Alison M., 98
Kid Millions (1934), 131–132
King, Homay, 90
King, Tony, 65
kitchens, 12
Kohner, Paul, 39
Kohner, Susan, 38, 39
Kracauer, Siegfried, 44
Kunis, Mila, 61
Kushner, Michael, 149

Lacan, Jacques, 162n6
Lady of Burlesque (1943), 9, 48, 51, 53–55, *54*
Lady Sings the Blues (1972), 64, 107
Lamarr, Hedy, 49, 158n24
LaMotta, Jake, 1, 2
Land around Us, The (musical play), 99
Larks behind the Scene (Edison, 1899), 47–48
Latinos/Latinas, 5, 13, 121; double body of Latina immigrants, 133, 136–140, 141, 145; drag performers, 141
Laurents, Arthur, 80
Laurie, Joe, Jr., 120
Lawford, Peter, 29
Lawrence, Florence, 69
Lawrence, Mittie, 24, *26*
leading man archetype, 12, 15, 92, 93–96; anxieties about women in male spaces, 96, 107–113; destabilization of Hollywood genres and, 99; isolated and frail leading men, 113–119, *117*; at mid-twentieth century, 99–107, *102*; origins of, 95; representations of backstage masculinity, 96–99
Leaf, Earl H., 54–55
Lederer, George, 44
Lee, Gypsy Rose, 4, 53, 55, 73, 81
Lee, Joie, 110
Lee, Spike, 2, 95, 110, 112–113, 122, 128, 164n32
Lefebvre, Henri, 9, 13
LeGon, Jeni, 15, 41; in *Easter Parade* (1948), 28–29, *30*, 156n30; in *Somebody Loves Me* (1952), 28, 31–34, *33*

LeRoy, Mervyn, 1–2, 9, 47
Leslie, Joan, 82
Lewis, Louise, 91
Livingston, Jennie, 141, 142, 143, 144
locker rooms, 12
Lott, Eric, 50, 120, 127
Love and Jealousy behind the Scenes (1904), 48
Love Me or Leave Me (1955), 13, 22, 23, 50, 156n33
Loving You (1957), 95
Lucas, Sam, 124
Lupino, Ida, 83

Magic Mike (Soderbergh, 2012), 96, 107, 108–109, *109*, 110, 112, 113
Malden, Karl, 82
Mamoulian, Rouben, 74, 76–77
Manganiello, Joe, 109
"man in the mirror" shots, 14, 83, 84, 164n21; in *Opening Night* (1977), 87; in *A Star Is Born* (1954), 103; in *What's Love Got to Do with It* (1993), 86, *87*
Mankiewicz, Joseph L., 1, 57
Marriage Clause, The (Weber, 1926), 21–22, 36
Martin, Robert B., 71
Martin, Tony, 50
Marx, Groucho, 137
masculinity, 65, 113; fictionalized form of, 114; hypermasculinity, 96, 108, 118; performance of, 95; shift in focus from exteriority to interiority, 96–99; World War II and crisis of, 100
"Masculinity and Spectacle" (Neale, 1983), 162n6
masks, 6
Mason, James, 95, 102
masquerade, 15, 120–122; dressing room superstitions and ghosts, 122–133, 166n16; identity and "double body," 133–145. *See also* Blackface minstrelsy
Masquerader, The (Chaplin, 1914), 99, 133, 135–136
Matthews, Ralph, 27
May, Edna, 134
May, Elaine Tyler, 77
Mayfield, Curtis, 64
McAuley, Gale, 4, 7, 10
McConaughey, Matthew, 108
McDaniel, Hattie, 27, 28

McDaniel, Sam, 132
McDowall, Roddy, 25
McGirr, Elaine M., 74
McGuffey children's readers, 2–3
McGuigan, Paul, 88, 89
McKee, Lonette, 10, 64, 66
Meeker, Ralph, 34
melodramas, 3, 8, 43; emphasis on mother–daughter relationships, 35; family melodramas, 78; leading man archetype in, 94; wives and mothers in, 70
men: Asian characters as racialized Others, 53–55, *54*; Blaxploitation heroes, 65; homosocial domains of, 48, 109, 110; male pleasure, 45; male voyeurism of camera, 47; public sphere as traditionally male domain, 82; reintegration of war returnees, 82; white male authority, 94. *See also* leading man archetype; "man in the mirror" shots
Mendes, Sam, 68, 69, 85
"men's cinema," 96
mentorship, female, 48
Merman, Ethel, 80
Merry Monahans, The (1944), 73, 74
Messenger Boy and the Ballet Girl, The (1905), 48, 158n15
Meyerowitz, Joanne, 77–78
MGM Studios, 29
Miller, Ann, 29
Miller, Kenita, 149
Miller, Marilyn, 21
Miller, Nadine, 28
Mills, Florence, 124
minstrel shows, 12, 128
Miranda, Carmen, 136, 137, 139
mirrors, 6, 14, 160n8; in *The Best of Everything* (1959), 70; in *Black Swan*, 61, 62, *62*, 63; chaos reflected and amplified by, 46; in *The Country Girl* (1954), 106; in *Dance, Girl, Dance* (1940), 60–61; in *Ethnic Notions* (1986), 131, *132*; in *Imitation of Life* (1959), 37; in *Joker* (2019), 116; in *Magic Mike* (2012), 113; in *Once upon a Time in Hollywood* (2019), 93, 95; in *Paradise in Harlem* (1939), 127; in *Paris Is Burning* (1990), 142–143, *143*; power dynamics of dressing rooms and, 29–30; in *Revolutionary Road* (2008), 68; in *A Scrap in the Dressing Room* (1904), 56; in *A Star Is Born* (1954), 102, 103, 105; in *Stormy Weather* (1943), 84, 85; as symbol of self-recognition and revelation, 106. *See also* "man in the mirror" shots

miscegenation laws, 54
mise-en-scène, 9, 45, 114, 165n41; frame-within-frame, 127, 129; masculinity and, 96
Mizejewski, Linda, 49, 97, 158n24
Mo' Better Blues (Lee, 1990), 15, 95, 107, 109–113, *112*; anxieties about women in male spaces, 96; male bodies as sites of display, 108; pervasive homosociality of, 110–111; phallic imagery of trumpet, 110, 164n28
mobility, social, 14, 40–41, 136
Mommie Dearest (biopic film, 1981), 70–71
Mommie Dearest (Crawford memoir, 1978), 70–71
Monks, Aoife, 8
montage, 36, 53, 86, 110, 138
Moore, Juanita, 34, 36, *37*, 40, 41
Moreno, Rita, 136–137, 139, 140, *140*, 141
Morgan, Helen, 75
Morocco (1930), 133
mothers/motherhood, 13, 14; history of mothers on the stage, 72–74; mother–daughter relationships, 80–82; performance of birth, 75–77, *76*; postwar motherly ideal, 77; pregnancy, 71–72, 78, 149; in *Revolutionary Road* (2008), 68–69, *69*; spectral (absent) mothers, 71, 74, 75, 79; stage mothers, 71, 74–77, 80–82; working mother on the stage, 35
Mother Wore Tights (Young, 1944), 9, 73, 75, 78–80; *Gypsy* compared with, 82; "postwar cultural puzzle" and, 77–78
Moulin Rouge (Broadway show), 149
Mr. Jack in the Dressing Room (1904), 46, 98
Mr. Jack Is Caught in the Dressing Room (1904), 7, 8, 46, 98
Mulvey, Laura, 162n6
musical comedy, 7, 12; Black maid archetype and, 18, 20; female choruses in, 98
musicals, 3, 5, 12, 94, 145; early sound era, 99; performativity of stardom in, 97
music business, 64
music halls, 12
Musser, Charles, 165n3
My Blue Heaven (1950), 77

Myers, Pauline, 28
mystery genre, 3, 43

NAACP, 27
Neale, Steven, 162n6
Negra, Diane, 158n24
nightclubs, 2, 12, 39
nostalgia, racial representation and, 18

Odets, Clifford, 95
O'Hara, Maureen, 59
Oklahoma! (1943), 99
Once upon a Time in Hollywood (Tarantino, 2019), 93–94
On the Waterfront (1954), 1
On with the Show (1929), 47, 51
Opening Night (Cassavetes, 1977), 9, 87, 89–92, *91*
opera, 12
Ormsbee, Helen, 17, 18, 155n2
Others/otherness, 35, 96, 123, 141

Pal Joey (musical, 1940), 17
Paradise in Harlem (1939), 122, 127–128, 131
Paramount, 99
Paris Is Burning (Livingston, 1990), 9, 15, 16, 122, 133, 141–144, *143*; doubled body in, 142; drag and "realness," 141–142
partitions, 8, 81
Pasolini, Pier Paolo, 90
patriarchy, 28, 60
Peeping Tom in the Dressing Room (1905), 8
people of color, 3, 13, 14, 119, 166n1; as dressers and maids, 121, 165n1; leading white men and, 94, 95
Pepper LaBeija, 141
Pepys, Samuel, 7
Perry, Lincoln (aka "Stepin Fetchit"), 51, 52, 159n31
Petty, Miriam J., 29
Pettyfer, Alex, 108
Phillips, Todd, 114
Phoenix, Joaquin, 96, 114
Pidgeon, Walter, 24
Pitt, Brad, 94
Playboy magazine, 100
Portman, Natalie, 61
Powell, Eleanor, 29
Powell, Jane, 68

precarity, 52, 59, 67; Black female, 64, 65; masculine, 118; white female, 51, 55
Presley, Elvis, 95, 97
Pretty Ladies (1925), 10, 45
private sphere, 71
prize fighting, 12
Production Code Administration, 50, 54, 75
public sphere, 40, 70, 82

Queen Charlotte and Her Two Eldest Sons (Zoffany painting, 1765), 72
queer performers, 5, 14, 119
queer rights, 96

race, 40, 140, 144; "colored" men accused of theft from dressing rooms, 123; color line and "girl clusters," 49–55, *54*; correction of racial representation, 54, 55, 65–66; intersectional dynamics and, 15, 66; leading man archetype and, 95; light-skinned Black women, 35, 39; mobility and, 35; racial hierarchies, 14, 41, 50; sexuality and, 39; sister acts and, 67; white resentment, 116
race films, 122
racism, 5, 22, 64, 112
Raging Bull (Scorsese, 1980), 1, 2, 2, 13, 94
rags-to-riches literature, 2–3
Randolph, Lillian, 27
Redhead from Manhattan (1943), 167n39
Renaissance theater, English, 7
Restoration theater, 7, 45
Revolutionary Road (2008), 68, 85
Rhodes, John David, 155n7
Rice and Elmer (vaudeville duo), 123
Riggs, Marlon, 130, 131
Ritz, The (1976), 122, 133, 136, 137, 139–141, *140*
Rivera, Chita, 140
Robinson, Bill "Bojangles," 84
Rock of Ages (2012), 107
Rodriguez, Adam, 108
Rogers, Charles "Buddy," 19
Rogers, Ginger, 95
Rogin, Michael, 125, 166n22
Rollins, Judith, 157n44
Rosenman, Howard, 64
Ross, Diana, 64
Ross, Herbert, 25, 36
Roth, Lillian, 73

Rowlands, Gena, 87, 90
Rubin, Martin, 44
Running Wild (Broadway show), 124
Russell, Lillian, 97
Russell, Rosalind, 80

Salonga, Lea, 148
Schleier, Merrill, 96
School of Rock (musical), 147, 148
Scorsese, Martin, 1, 2
Scrap in the Dressing Room, A (1904), 56
Seeley, Blossom, 28, 31, 32, 34
Segal, Vivienne, 17, 18
Seidelman, Susan, 159n35
Selena (1997), 167n39
Seven Little Foys, The (1955), 73, 74
sexual assault, 73
sexuality, 45, 46, 108, 140, 144; heterosexuality, 108, 109, 139; homosexuality, 46; intersectional dynamics and, 15; leading man archetype and, 95; sexual identities of male performers, 107
Shaft (1971), 65
"Shaking the Blues Away" (Berlin song), 31, 156n33
Sharif, Omar, 24, 83
Shea, Gloria, 19
Shearer, Martha, 113
She Would Be a Business Man (1910), 82
She Would Be an Actress (1908), 82
She Would Be a Suffragette (1908), 82
Show Biz Bugs (Warner Bros. cartoon, 1952), 10
Showboat (musical comedy, 1927), 42–43
Showgirls (1995), 48
Shubert brothers, 97
Shuffle Along (Broadway show), 124
Sinatra, Frank, 95
Singing Fool, The (1928), 99, 121, 124; Black dresser in Jolson's dressing room, 126, *126*; crosscutting between stage and dressing room, 127; spectrality and cultural memory in, 125
Sirk, Douglas, 2, 35–38, 39
sister acts, as dressing room trope, 15, 43; backstage as Black female space, 63–67, *66*; color line and, 49–55, *54*; gender identity and, 55–67; girl clusters, 44–49
skene (tent or hut in ancient Greece), 6, 7
Skyscraper Cinema (Schleier, 2009), 96

Sleepy Soubrette, The (1905), 48
Sloan, Leni, 130–131, *132*
Smith, Dwan, 64
Smith, Jada Pinkett, 129
Sneed, Carrie, 26
Snipes, Wesley, 110
Snowden, Carolynne, 22
social media, 147, 148
Soderbergh, Steven, 107, 113
Somebody Loves Me (1952), 3, 9, 83; Black maid archetype in, 22, 23, 28, 31–34, *33*; racial appropriation in, 50
Sontag, Susan, 114
Sparkle (1976), 3, 10, 15, 63–67, *66*
Stacey, Jackie, 58, 67
Stage Mother (1933), 74
stand-up comedy, 12
Stanwyck, Barbara, 53
Star Is Born, A (1954), 95, 99, 100, *102*, 114; awareness of Hollywood's past in, 164n23; hypermasculine dressing room in, 105; versions of, 83; women's dominance as source of male anxiety, 102–103
Stark, Ray, 24
"star phenomenon," 4, 70
Stone, Emma, 117
Stormy Weather (1943), 83, 84, 85, 159n26
Streisand, Barbra, 23, 83, 147–148
Stufft, Monica, 48
"success montage," 86
Sundin, Bridget, 133
superhero movies, 12, 94
Super Spook (1974), 65

Tarantino, Quentin, 93
Tatum, Channing, 108
Taylor, Elizabeth, 149
Theater Dictionary, The (Granville, 1952), 93, 120
Theatrical Syndicate, 97
Theatrical Wardrobe Attendants Union, 163n13
There's No Business Like Show Business (1954), 73
Thomas, Philip Michael, 65
Thompson, Lydia, 98
thresholds, 8
thrillers, 12, 43
Tiller Girls, 44
Tinney, Frank, 26

"tiring room," 7, 45
Tongues Untied (Riggs, 1989), 132
Torch Song (1953), 69–70
Tovar, Lupita, 39
Turner, Lana, 34, 40, 49
Turner, Peter, 89
Turner, Tina, 70, 85

Valdez, Luis, 140
Valente, Caterina, 139–140
Van Fleet, Jo, 74
Variety magazine, 8, 46, 59, 61, 149; on Blackface in vaudeville, 120; on dressing room thefts, 73; on Jane Powell as mother, 68; performers' complaints about dressing rooms, 98
vaudeville, 7, 12, 19; Blackface in, 120; Blackface removal as popular skit, 132; Black performers in, 130; decline of, 80; feminization of, 98; filmed performances, 12; traveling performers in, 73
Venus Xtravaganza, 141, 144
voyeurism, 45, 98, 142

Walker, Ethel, 36
Wallace, Royce, 24
Warner Bros., 3, 10, 99
Washington, Denzel, 108, 110
Wayans, Damon, 128
Wayburn, Ned, 44
Wayne, David, 83
Weber, Lois, 21, 22
Weston, Jack, 139
West Side Story (1961), 139
What's Love Got to Do with It (1993), 15, 70, 85–86, 87, *87*, 107–108
When My Baby Smiles at Me (1948), 9, 77, 83
White, Armond, 3, 66
White, Walter, 27
White Christmas (Curtiz, 1954), 9, 56, 95, 99, 103–104
whiteness, 39, 43, 49, 107, 142; restored through removal of Blackface, 132;

social mobility and, 63; white femininity, 20, 31
White Rats of America, 98, 163n13
Williams, Bert, 130, 131, *132*, 133
Williams, Cynda, 110
Willkie, Wendell, 27
Wilson, Frank, 127
Winslet, Kate, 68, *69*
Winter Garden Theatre, 147
With a Song in My Heart (1952), 83
Wojcik, Pamela Robertson, 12, 96
women: actresses associated with sexual excess, 35, 72, 160n8; backstage films directed by, 21–22, 55, 58–61; competition among, 15, 56–57; as desired objects and desiring subjects, 43; in English Restoration theater, 7; friendships among, 56; "good" and "bad" girl tropes, 5; lonely lives of aging stage performers, 88–92, 161n36; looking and being looked at, 60; mother–daughter relationships, 35; relations between women, 13; as spectacle, 43; white chorus girls, 42–43; white stars' dependence on Black maids, 32, 37; white women's bodies and racial insecurity, 51; wives, 82–86. *See also* chorus girls; mothers/motherhood; sister acts, as dressing room trope
Wood, Natalie, 80
Wyler, William, 24, 25

Yates, Richard, 85
Young, Cleo, 17–18, 19, 27
Young, Miriam, 9, 73, 78, 79

Zellweger, Renée, 88
Ziegfeld, Florenz, 23, 24, 49
Ziegfeld Follies, 3, 19, 22, 49; "girl clusters" and, 44; white women as Ziegfeld stars, 23
Ziegfeld Girl (1941), 48, 49–50, 64
Zink, Adolph, 7, 133–136, 166n35
Zoffany, Johan Joseph, 72

About the Author

DESIRÉE J. GARCIA is an associate professor in the Latin American, Latino, and Caribbean Studies Department at Dartmouth. She has published two books, *The Movie Musical* and *The Migration of Musical Film: From Ethnic Margins to American Mainstream*. She has a PhD in American studies from Boston University and a BA in history from Wellesley College. Garcia has also worked as an associate producer for PBS's *American Experience* and as an actress in the first feature film by director Damien Chazelle, *Guy and Madeline on a Park Bench* (2009).